The Girls in the Van

The Girls in the Van

A Reporter's Diary of the Campaign Trail

Beth J. Harpaz

ORK

THOMAS DUNNE BOOKS
ST. MARTIN'S PF

TO LINDA—
every writer needs a friend like you

THOMAS DUNNE BOOKS.
An imprint of St. Martin's Press.

www.stmartins.com

Book design by Donna Sinisgalli

ISBN 0-312-28126-9 (hc)
ISBN 0-312-30271-1 (pbk)

First St. Martin's Griffin Edition: November 2002

10 9 8 7 6 5 4 3 2 1

Contents

Acknowledgments

It takes a village to raise two small boys while covering a Senate campaign and writing a book.

I owe my biggest thanks to my husband for covering the home front on the many days and nights that I was out covering Hillary. I also could not have completed this book without his service as personal computer technician, editor, first reader, and cheerleader.

A second thanks is owed to my sister and niece, who also helped out with the kids, and to my mother-in-law, whose interest in my Hillary stories was never-ending (and who had a few Hillary stories of her own to tell by the end of the campaign).

My personal "village" also includes my upstairs neighbors, whose doors were always open to my kids, and who were never too busy to listen to my latest obsession over the election; the staffs of the Park Slope Child Care Collective and Congregation Beth Elohim After-School, where my children were always safe and happy when their parents were working; my agent, Jane Dystel, who turned my dream of writing a book into a reality; and my editors at St. Martin's, whose many suggestions made this a better book.

I'm grateful to the Associated Press for giving me the opportunity to cover this fascinating slice of history.

And last but not least, I owe a huge debt of gratitude to my colleagues in the press corps who generously shared their insights and recollections for this book. The girls in the van and the boys on the bus were hysterically funny, often brilliant, and always hardworking, and I was privileged to work alongside them.

Preface to the Paperback Edition

Readers tell me two things about this book. One is that they laughed out loud while reading it, which is the biggest compliment I can think of. I set out to write a book about politics that wasn't just a dry, analytical tome about yesterday's news. I wanted to give readers an inside view of the process, but in a way that captured the absurdity and comedy of the relationship between the press and the politicians— reporters trying to get as close as they can, campaign staffers giving just enough access to get their message across with the proper spin.

The other thing I often hear from readers is that the book vindicates their view of Hillary. This is true whether they love her or hate her. Hillary supporters walk away from the book telling anecdotes about how smart she is or how tough she was in the face of personal attacks. People who hate her walk away repeating the stories from the book that demonstrate the cynical manipulations that have unfortunately become the hallmark of a modern campaign.

When people ask me if this is a pro- or anti-Hillary book, I reply that it's really a Rorschach test. All I did was chronicle what happened when this very famous first lady ran for Senate in a state where she never lived; sometimes that makes Hillary—and the media—look good and sometimes it makes her and the press corps look bad. The impression readers end up with depends a lot on their original point of view.

Many readers have also asked me for my impression of how Hillary's doing as New York's senator. Prominent Republicans like John McCain and Trent Lott warned that she was so accustomed to being a celebrity that she would have problems assuming the low profile of a typical freshman senator. But she was careful, initially, to stay out of the spotlight—so much so that some of her supporters fretted that she'd dropped off the front page and into obscurity after being elected. I don't believe this was accidental. As senator, Hillary often chooses to appear in the company of New York's senior senator, Chuck Schumer, rather than tackling a high-profile issue alone, and she's always careful to let him speak first at joint press conferences. When the thirteen women in the Senate joined together to press for aid for Afghan women, Hillary did not assert herself as a longtime leader of international women's rights; she merely stood with the pack and let others take the lead. And she frequently visits the upstate communities that helped elect her. This not only reassures them that she has not forgotten them and helps cultivate their future support, but it enables her to have a public presence far from the media maelstrom of Manhattan or Washington, D.C.

In her characteristically overachieving mode, Hillary introduced seventy pieces of legislation in her first year in the Senate, more than any other novice senator and even more than a few of the senior lawmakers. Not all of her proposals made it through the legislative process, of course, but most of the bills were either part of her agenda to better health care and education, which helped elect her, or were related to the September 11 disaster, or both. She's called for funding to study the impact of bioterrorism on pediatric health, increased security for nuclear facilities on the Hudson River, and improvements in benefits for September 11 victims, as well as bills related to the upstate economy and education. She's played a visible role in securing disaster relief money from the White House, yet had to back off from the negotiations at one point, because of concern from some New York lawmakers that her presence was antagonizing Republicans.

Above all, the Senate appears to be a good match for her nerdiness; she shows up at every briefing having done so much homework on the issues that she occasionally engenders the resentment of her colleagues. The smartest girl in the class, after all, is rarely the most popular. On the other hand, many of her Republican colleagues have found her surprisingly charming and easy to get along with. Clearly she's learned a lot in the years since she tried to foist an absurdly complex and secretly hatched health-care reform plan on an unreceptive Congress and an angry public. Yet, despite the embarrassment of her failure in that effort, Americans who have been let down by the health-care system continue to look to her as a savior. In a recent movie, *John Q.*, about a man who snaps and takes hostages in a hospital in order to get his son the medical care he needs, Hillary is featured as a heroine, talking about the millions of people who are uninsured in America. On the other hand, she was roundly booed by firefighters, cops, and others attending a VH1 concert to raise money for the victims of September 11. In the Senate, as in the White House, she continues to be one our nation's most polarizing, and fascinating political figures.

Chapter 1

You Wanna Go Forward, You Put It in D

November 6, 2000. We are somewhere in the air between Rochester and La Guardia, in a twelve-seat turboprop plane, playing a Frank Buckley Travel Game that is slowly restoring my sanity.

"For more than thirty years, I've been working on behalf of children," says one of my colleagues in a tone of voice that strikes the perfect balance between self-righteousness and humility.

"Mr. Lazio *does* go on," says another, a broad smile breaking across her face as the rest of us clap in tribute to such a clever dredging-up of one of Hillary's pronouncements from the candidates' last debate. It's a phrase that nobody but us could instantly place.

"Thank you so-o-o-o-o much!" That one is so familiar to anyone who's hung around Hillary for more than five minutes that it's almost cheating, but we all laugh anyway.

"In one school I visited, there was a textbook that actually said, 'Someday there'll be a man on the moon.' " That's my contribution, and I'm gratified that it elicits a cry of "Good one!" and a smattering of applause.

"Hey," I add, "did anyone here ever *see* that textbook?" Heads shake all around. I've yet to find a reporter who actually laid eyes on this book that Hillary has mentioned, oh, about a thousand times, in her speeches on education.

Frank Buckley is a correspondent for CNN, a wickedly funny man who was constantly coming up with games like this, the kinds of games you played when you were a kid and your parents drove to the Grand Canyon. On this trip, he started with a game naming different types of fruit, then different types of accessories—bracelet, belt, scarf, etc. I didn't play either one of those; my mind was too full of Hillary. Then there was a game in which you had to come up with the names of New York's sixty-two counties: Dutchess, Erie, Putnam, Tompkins, Genesee . . . Most of the reporters on this plane were New York City–based, and we petered out of that game pretty fast, but we all knew that Hillary would have won it in a heartbeat. As she never tired of reminding us (and the voters), she'd *been* to all those counties, every last one.

But the game we were playing as we headed back to New York City consisted of lines from Hillary's speeches, and it was exactly what I needed to try to exorcise her from my brain. I am a reporter for the Associated Press, and I spent more than two years writing and thinking and talking about Hillary. I documented her screwups and her finest moments; I dismissed her as an amateur and pronounced her senatorial; I memorized her speeches and obscure facts about her life (middle name, Diane; birthdate, 10-26-47; favorite color, yellow; number of months she took for maternity leave after Chelsea was born, four; where she met Bill, in the Yale law library); I watched her laugh hysterically and I saw her eyes well up with tears; I sang her "Happy Birthday" and I received a present from her for my children; and I asked her everything from whether she had had plastic surgery to her views on a Palestinian state to why a guy who owns strip clubs in Chicago was on the list of donors who slept over at the White House. When she made news, it was exciting; but more often, it was mundane, and the way I entertained myself was by becoming a Hillary Kremlinologist, the type of person who knows that when she drapes a blue sweater over her shoulders without actually putting her arms through the sleeves, she's trying to appeal to suburban women; when she wears a skirt, she's going to church; when she's happy and making jokes with her press corps, she's up in the polls; when she shuts down every question by answering, "I'll leave that to others to characterize," she's gotten a talking-to from Bill about how to get reporters to change the subject; and when she calls somebody "my good friend," she's pandering to whatever ethnic group the alleged friend belongs to.

In *The Boys on the Bus*, a book about the press corps covering the 1972 presidential campaign, author Timothy Crouse said the reporters "followed the candidate everywhere, heard his standard speech so many dozens of times they could recite it with him, watched his moods go up and down, speculated constantly on his chances, wrote songs about him, told jokes at his expense, traded gossip about him, and were lucky if they did not dream about him into the bargain." Twenty-eight years later, about the only difference I saw was that our candidate was a woman—a woman whose staff and whose press corps was more than half female. We were no longer the boys on the bus; if anything, we were the girls in the van.

One of my colleagues, Tish Durkin of the *New York Observer*, said you knew you'd spent too much time with Hillary when you're in a restaurant and you imitate her way of saying "Thank yeeewww!" and you can't understand why the waitress isn't laughing. Suddenly you realize that not everyone in the universe spends all his or her time making fun of Hillary. In my case, that realization came when a neighbor told me how polite my son was. "Really?" I asked, surprised to hear that Danny, a typically boisterous seven-year-old, had impressed someone with his manners. "Yes," said the woman. "I heard him tell someone, 'Thank you so-o-o-o-o much!'" I assured her that he wasn't being polite, he was just making fun of Hillary.

One evening near the end of the campaign when I got home late, I put my toddler, Nathaniel, on my lap, hoping to score some of that elusive quality time I keep reading about in parenting magazines. I offered to sing one of his favorite songs, "Take Me Out to the Ball Game," only to have him chirp back, "No! I wanna sing the Hillary song!" I tried the baseball song instead, but he kept interrupting me to demand "the Hillary song." Finally I gave in and launched into a takeoff of the Beatles' "Yesterday," now "Hill-a-ry," a collaboration of lyrics by my husband, myself, and an assignment editor who had heard me serenading the newsroom with it one morning.

Hill-a-ry
All your troubles seem so far away!
Now it looks as though you're here to stay
Oh, you believe in Hill-a-ry.

But perhaps the truest sign that I, like many of my colleagues, was suffering from Hillary Traumatic Stress Disorder was the dog episode. As I'd walked to the subway a few days before the election, a man in a dark suit with a German shepherd on a leash had come toward me, and in sheer reflex, I'd started to slide my knapsack off my shoulder and down my arm, ready to open it up for the dog to sniff. Fortunately I realized, before making a total fool of myself, that this individual was not one of Hillary's Secret Service agents, checking me for explosives with the K-9 unit; he was just walking his dog.

As I flew home this night, the night before the day that would deliver me from that beat, that obsession, that story, I tried to imagine Life After Hillary. Very soon, I'd be able to work an eight-hour day, get through a Saturday without checking my e-mail for Hillary's schedule, make dinner for my children, read a novel, and hum a song that was not about Hillary. But aboard that plane, I couldn't get her out of my mind, and given my obsessive state, the Frank Buckley Travel Game was highly cathartic. I could just blurt out any Hillary phrase kicking around in my brain and it counted as my turn.

The game was also a good way to take everybody's mind off the plane ride. If it hadn't been obvious that any attempt by the pilots to kill us all would also have caused their own deaths, I would have been certain that they were trying to do us in. More likely, we suspected they were simply trying to make us late for every one of our stops. First they aborted a takeoff for no apparent reason, slamming on the brakes just as we were about to become airborne en route from La Guardia to Binghamton. Then as we were leaving Binghamton for Buffalo, they started rolling down the runway without closing the door to the outside, realizing their error only when a warning light came on. Next they delayed our flight from Buffalo to Albany because they had mistakenly thought we were going to Rochester first and had to get new flight plans approved. And finally, after we were strapped in and ready to leave Albany for Rochester, they removed all our luggage and gear from the underbelly of the plane because the weight wasn't distributed properly.

The copilot had also insisted on spending five minutes before each takeoff giving us emergency instructions, amounting to the same drill four times in twenty-four hours. When he got up on the final leg of the trip and asked for our attention, I just looked at him and whined, "You're not going to tell us about the fire extinguishers again, are you?" He grinned and said, "Why don't you do it."

"Okay," I said, and proceeded to inform my fellow passengers, in as loud and official a voice as I could muster, that one extinguisher was in the rear on the right and one behind the cockpit, that the emergency exit could be opened by pushing and throwing the plug out the window, and that in the event that life jackets were required during this flight over central New York, they were under no circumstances to be inflated before exiting the plane.

We put our seat belts on and turned our cell phones off, but moments later the pilot climbed out of the cockpit and informed us that all three metropolitan airports—La Guardia, Kennedy, and Newark—had been completely shut down for three hours because the president was flying in. They could take us to Farmingdale, on Long Island, or Westchester, north of the city, but they couldn't fly us any- where remotely close to Hillary's last event, a union rally in midtown Manhattan.

Naturally, this last announcement was met with a great deal of skepticism. Yes, sometimes one of the airports was closed for a few minutes because Bill Clinton was flying in, but never all three, and never for three hours. One by one, everyone whipped out his or her cell phone and started calling Hillary's campaign staff to find out what the hell was going on. Bill Clinton wasn't even supposed to be arriving in New York until the next day. In fact, none of the information the pilot had given us about why we couldn't fly home made any sense, but it did confirm our suspicions that the guys responsible for flying us around on Hillary's last day hated her, and by extension us, and were doing their best to screw up coverage of her final tour on the campaign trail. It was all the more infuriating because our employers were paying $1,000 per person for this fly-around.

After a few of our frantic phone calls to Hillary's staff, the pilot came back out of the cockpit to inform us that, lo and behold, he'd received permission to fly into La Guardia after all. We would arrive too late to cover the union rally, but most of us—including me—had called our editors to make sure other reporters from our New York City offices could get there in time. If it had been earlier in the campaign, some of us might have tried to get to the bottom of this inexplicable series of assertions by the pilots for a possible story. But now we were all just too tired and overwhelmed with other news to care. After months of polls showing Hillary up, Hillary down, and Hillary neck and neck with her Republican opponents in the Senate race—first our tough-talking New York City mayor, Rudy Giuliani, then an affable, hard-to-pin-down Long Island congressman named Rick Lazio—it was clear that the first lady was going to make history by winning this election. Not only were the polls finally showing her with substantial leads, but the Lazio campaign had fallen apart, with one fiasco after another and a round of eleventh-hour attacks by the Republican Party equating Hillary with, of all things, terrorism.

But even if you didn't know anything about the polls, and you didn't know anything about how the campaigns had fared since mid-October, all you had to do was watch Hillary and her staff on that final day to know they were headed for a win. No poker players here; victory was all over their faces. Even the grueling schedules of the past few days hadn't dampened their energy and upbeat moods. On the Sunday before election day, for example, Hillary had a sixteen-hour day with ten events. She started at 7 A.M. to cram in speeches in seven black churches in the Bronx, Queens, and Brooklyn, followed by a Q-and-A for us, a rally for Haitian-Americans at Brooklyn College, and then a flight to Binghamton for a 10:30 P.M. event at the airport. Everyone in the press corps was exhausted and muttering gibberish by the time we got to the upstate rally; I felt like a neglected child—no dinner in my belly, in need of a bathroom, runny nose, chapped lips, dirty fingernails, ink on my face, missing my family, and half-hating, half in awe of the hardworking candidate who was putting me through all this and didn't appear to be half as tired as I was.

We found 350 people, most in down coats and jeans, waiting for us when we got to Binghamton. It seemed like a pretty impressive turnout for such an out-of-the-way place so late on a chilly November night. Just three days earlier, Lazio had held a noontime rally in a waterfront park in Buffalo on a beautiful day, accompanied by Senator John McCain and a couple of big-name local athletes, including former Buffalo Bills quarterback Jack Kemp, who'd also been a congressman, secretary of housing and urban development, and the GOP's 1996

vice-presidential nominee. Despite the star power, only a hundred people had shown up, proof positive that Lazio's campaign was deflating.
As I stood in the hangar in Binghamton, watching the pumped-up
crowd waiting for Hillary late on a cold Sunday night, it hit me that she
was really going to win. She'd focused on the lagging upstate economy
as a theme of her campaign, and she'd spent months traveling around
traditionally conservative regions of the state—places Democrats usually assumed they couldn't win—and all her efforts were about to pay
off. Suddenly the crowd let out a roar, and there she was on the stage.
She'd changed clothes since we'd left the city, from a frumpy purple
plaid skirtsuit that seemed just right for church, to one of her sleek
black pantsuits with a blue blouse the color of her eyes. Her hairdo was
freshly pouffed and sculpted, and I could see, even from the back of the
hangar where the press was forced to stand, that her makeup had been
redone, heavy on the eyeliner for a glamorous look on the local eleven
o'clock news.

But what was even more striking than her appearance was her
demeanor. She was *rockin'*. It was as if this were her first appearance of
the day instead of her tenth in fifteen or so hours. In one of the black
churches we'd attended, the choir had sung "Victory today is mine,"
and in another, the pastor had told Hillary and his cheering congregation, "God said, 'We got the victory!' Our first lady got our vote. We
got the first lady on lockdown. We got the polls on lockdown. When
we pray, God answers our prayers, so it's already yours!" It was clear
that she still felt that way, here and now, in a completely different
place, a place filled with as many white faces, far from the city, as that
church had been filled with black faces in the inner city. She had a
smile as big as a half-moon, her voice was strong, and everything about
her body language said, "I'm a winner!"

She recalled for the crowd how she'd launched her campaign sixteen months earlier (that was the second launching, according to my

private, unofficial count of her campaign's reincarnations) on Senator Daniel Patrick Moynihan's farm at Pindars Corners, not far from the Binghamton airport. "I began this campaign by landing here," she said, "and I didn't want to end the campaign without coming back. . . . I could not be anywhere near as optimistic as I am without your support."

She ended her speech with what had become a trademark joke in the last two weeks, ever since she'd heard Senator Joe Lieberman say it at a union rally in Manhattan.

"This election is like driving a car," she said with the kind of friendly, expectant smile you have on your face when you're telling a funny story with an obvious punch line to an old uncle who could use a laugh. "You wanna go backwards, you put it in R. You wanna go forward, you put it in D! D for Democrat! Thank you, everybody!"

About a third of the audience—the third that was really paying attention, I guess—caught on to where the joke was going and joined in on the "put it in D" line. But all of them roared with laughter and began applauding when it was over.

Our plane was leaving in a few minutes for Buffalo, but I needed to grab some quick quotes from a few spectators. I was trying to elicit quotes about the economy, but the first three people I approached happened to be women, and something else was on their minds.

"She's smart, that's why I'm voting for her," one of them said.

"She's the president's wife, and she's done a lot of good for women," the next one said. "She's a world-class lady, and anyone with half a brain would have to vote for her."

"We need a woman. We need an intelligent woman. She's not a puppet of the good old boys," said another.

So much for the economy. These little declarations of gender pride reminded me of yet another of my colleagues' Hillary spoof-songs, this one to the tune of the seventies Helen Reddy hit "I Am Woman."

I am Hillary, hear me roar
I'm too powerful to ignore . . .

Of course, when I saw the exit polls on election day, the quotes from those women suddenly made sense. Hillary beat Lazio by twelve points—a far bigger margin than anyone had anticipated, including her staff—and she would do it largely by mobilizing women. In the final count, 60 percent of women voted for her, including 65 percent of working women, 75 percent of New York City women, and 55 percent of upstate women. The upstate vote was a particularly impressive achievement for a Democrat; she came within eighty thousand votes of beating Lazio in what is traditionally the most conservative part of the state. And she also racked up the third-highest vote total (in actual numbers of votes cast) of any Senate candidate in New York ever. Only Moynihan, in 1988, and Robert F. Kennedy—another carpetbagger—in '64, collected more votes than Hillary in 2000.

But I had no idea how big her margin of victory would be as I stood in Binghamton, about to fly to Buffalo. Suddenly I saw one of Hillary's press liaisons, Karen Finney, motioning me toward the exit. I shut my notebook and sprinted out the hangar toward the turboprop.

By the time we got to our hotel in Buffalo, it was midnight. Food was waiting for us in the lobby, and as we stuffed our faces, Hillary and Chelsea arrived. Most of us were drinking beer and shoving pizza down our throats, but Hillary headed to a large basket of fruit that we had been ignoring, picked up a couple of clementines after laughingly announcing that she couldn't remember what they were called, and went upstairs.

The first event Monday morning was a rally at Buffalo State College. We got there shortly before nine. Bizarre musical selections like "Sexy Thing" were playing over the sound system; I would have thought by now Hillary's campaign would be paying more attention to background music. They'd never settled on a theme song, but had gotten in trouble when she formally announced her candidacy back in February—the fourth time she'd launched her campaign, according to my count—because a deejay had played Billy Joel's "Captain Jack" to warm the crowd up. With lyrics about masturbation and drugs, it was not the best choice. The February announcement had ended with a much more appropriate selection—Des'ree's "You Gotta Be," an up-tempo, strong-female-voiced song with a chorus that goes

You gotta be bad, you gotta be bold, you gotta be wiser
You gotta be hard, you gotta be tough, you gotta be stronger.

That seemed like a potential campaign theme song, and it was played periodically at events throughout the year. But when I asked why it hadn't become an official campaign theme song, one of Hillary's aides looked at me as if I were an idiot and said, "You have no idea the science that goes into picking out a campaign theme song. It's very complicated." So complicated that they never figured it out.

Then, a few weeks before the election, amid a backdrop of questionable fund-raising practices like inviting campaign donors to sleep in the Lincoln Bedroom and accepting $50,000 from a Muslim group that the Republicans tried to portray as less than kosher, an upstate event had featured the Donna Summer song "She Works Hard for the Money." One of Hillary's advance people had gone running to the deejay and gotten that one stopped midsong, but on the day before the election, nobody seemed bothered much by "Sexy Thing" played at earsplitting volume—nobody except those of us in the press corps who'd gotten about four hours of sleep and felt as if our brains were being electroshocked into operating mode.

The canned music gave way to a live but similarly earsplitting performance by Ten Thousand Maniacs, a band with local roots that had made it big with Natalie Merchant back in the late eighties and early nineties and then drifted into relative obscurity after Merchant began a solo career. Hillary's thank-you lines that day included this one, which sent the press corps into paroxysms of laughter: "I want to thank the Ten Thousand Maniacs for being with me this morning."

Accompanied by Chelsea, Buffalo Bill quarterback Doug Flutie, comedian Bill Cosby, and New York's other senator, Chuck Schumer, the first lady went on to give her standard stump speech, including the old "for more than thirty years" line about her devotion to children's issues, the "You wanna go forward, you put it in D" gag, and another favorite: "If you will work for me and fight for me and speak for me for the next thirty hours, I will go to the U.S. Senate and fight for you for the next six years!" I'd heard that line start about a month ago, only then it was "If you will fight for me for the next thirty days . . ."

Next stop was Albany, for a rally on the City Hall steps. So many people were gathered in front of the building, behind the press area, and along the side streets that I was having a hard time estimating the crowd. Because I work for the Associated Press, my stories are sent out by computer to newspapers and broadcast outlets all over the state and often the country, and they are frequently seen by editors at these other news organizations before their reporters have turned in their own stories. As a result, AP copy—from the lead, to the quotes, to the crowd estimate, to the background material—is often used as a benchmark by editors elsewhere to compare their own stories against. I could always count on a CNN producer, Phil Hirschkorn, to ask me, when a Hillary event was over, "What's the AP lead?" He didn't necessarily need to use the same lead, but if he planned on leading with something else, he might get asked by his editor why his account differed from AP's. By asking me in advance what I saw as the news, he could prepare to argue his case.

Crowd estimates were one of the details we all tried to agree on, so that our stories wouldn't end up reporting a dozen different tallies. Some reporters had a good enough eye to just glance at a gathering of people and come up with a ballpark figure, but I didn't trust myself enough for that. Instead, I had a methodical approach: I'd count heads from left to right, then from front to back, then multiply and round off. Then, using my fingertip, I'd draw small circles in the air around every group of ten people I could see, and hope that I'd come up with the same number as my multiplication method. This event was hard to figure because I couldn't see all the areas where people were congregating. It looked to me as if it could be as high as two thousand, or as low as twelve hundred. I checked with a couple of other reporters and settled on fifteen hundred.

Back in Buffalo, Bill Cosby hadn't been very funny, but here in Albany he had a great line. "This is another joke we're gonna play on Hillary," he told the crowd. "We're gonna vote her into office!"

Then Schumer served up two of his favorites: "She's gonna win because she did it the old-fashioned way: she earned it!" and "Can we have a moment of complete silence? I want to be able to hear a pin drop, because that's the sound you're going to hear Tuesday night at Lazio headquarters!" I'd been hearing those lines for about the last week as he accompanied Hillary on the campaign trail. When he used the lines at a union rally in Manhattan, he thickened up his Brooklyn accent, pronouncing "you're going to hear" as "ya gonna hee-ah," but now that we were in Albany, with his *other* constituents, he'd suddenly located his dropped *r*'s.

Finally it was Hillary's turn, and she came through with even more pumped-up confidence than before: "I'll stay with you, I'll fight for you, I'll stick with you, I'll go to the U.S. Senate and work my heart out for you!" It was as close to a victory speech as a candidate who hasn't been elected yet can make, and it was further proof that she was sure things were going her way.

The rally ended at 2 P.M. We had one hour of downtime in Albany to write and file our stories. I headed a block away to the AP's office in the capitol building. My colleagues there hooked me up to the computer, kindly fetched me a sandwich from the cafeteria, and then I started typing furiously. I had two stories to write: one for the national wire about the final day of this Senate race, a campaign that had, because it involved the first lady, been almost as closely watched as the presidential campaign; and another story for the state wire, focusing just on Hillary's last day. Time flew for the next sixty minutes, and by the time I had to get back on the campaign van, I had only managed to finish the eight hundred words for the national wire. I finished scribbling the state story in my notebook en route to Rochester, our next stop, and dictated it by cell phone to one of my colleagues back in the New York City office.

The next event, in an elementary school in a Rochester suburb called Brighton, was another mob scene, with four hundred people in the room where we were sitting, four hundred more in an adjacent room, and hundreds more outside the building. "This is the last upstate event of my campaign," Hillary told them. It was momentous, I guess, but it didn't feel that way. We were all too tired, too antsy, and too distracted to feel as if something important was happening. I'd more or less stopped taking notes; the speeches were all the same and I'd shot what little energy I had left into writing those two stories. Besides, it was 6 P.M., near-deadline time for most newspapers. Nobody would use additional copy at this hour unless it was really newsworthy—a pie in Hillary's face or the equivalent.

One of the other reporters whispered to me that the Secret Service agents who always accompanied Hillary and frequently harassed us seemed more animated than usual. Someone had heard a few of them in the hallway reviewing the procedures for removing someone from the crowd if necessary. I wondered if they expected some kind of protest and looked around the room. The only people who looked unusual in this white-bread group of middle-class suburban types were three Muslim women, standing near the back, chadors draped around their hair and shoulders. They appeared to be listening intently to Hillary's speech, clapping at the appropriate moments; they certainly didn't look as if they were planning to heckle her. I noticed one of the agents—telltale wire in his ear—hovering not far from where they were, his eyes roving in their general direction, so I positioned myself nearby, feeling slightly ashamed for honing in on them, but also wanting to make sure that I didn't miss anything in case there was news. Ever since the *Daily News* had three weeks earlier bashed Hillary for taking money from members of a Muslim group, anything involving Muslims and this campaign was potentially newsworthy. Hillary had returned the money, but Lazio and the state Republican Party had audaciously suggested in ads, speeches, and telephone calls to voters that the first lady was a friend to terrorists, and various Muslim organizations had complained that the tactics were racist and outrageous. It was just one of many crazy subplots that had emerged during the campaign, so complicated and bizarre that I was certain most voters didn't have a clue what it was really about. With election day hours away, it barely seemed to matter anymore, but that didn't mean I wouldn't have to be on the ball if someone wearing a chador heckled Hillary over it. So I stayed by the three women until the speech was over and felt just a little ridiculous as they applauded and filed out of the room, along with everyone else.

We got back on another van for the trip to the airport and boarded the plane for the last flight of the day, the last flight of Hillary's campaign. A few people were still typing on their laptops or dictating to their offices by cell phone; meanwhile the drama involving our pilots' uncertainty about flying into La Guardia played itself out. Finally the little plane took off, the entire cabin vibrating with the noise of the engine, and we settled back for the last round of Frank Buckley's Travel Game.

"For sixteen months, I've been talking about the issues," one person offered.

"I'm delighted that my daughter, Chelsea, could be with us today," said the next, her voice perfectly capturing Hillary's tone of maternal pride.

"What a day the Lord has made!" said someone else, using the line Hillary opened every church speech with.

"I've been to schools in New York that are among the finest in the country, but I've also been to schools that *no* child should attend!" That was my contribution.

"Miracles happen every day. You just have to look for them," said another person, eliciting congratulations from the rest of us for coming up with such a good one—obscure, yet familiar, and oh-so-Hillary.

Then came the one we'd all been waiting for: "You wanna go backwards, you put it in R. You wanna go forward . . ."

Chapter 2

Evolution Time Line

September 21, 1998. On a day when everyone else in the world is making jokes about cigars and *Leaves of Grass*, I'm trapped in an alternate universe where Hillary's quoting de Tocqueville. I thought I'd be writing a story about her sniffling and sighing and pushing back the skin on her cuticles, but, no, she looks serious, she's nodding, she's actually paying attention while some professor pontificates about banking and investment and blah blah blah. The rest of America is watching a televised videotape of the president's August 17 grand jury testimony on the nature of his relationship with Monica Lewinsky while I'm sitting in a room at New York University with the victim-wife and a bunch of academics contemplating democracy and the global economic crisis. Bill Clinton is on TV describing his "inappropriate intimate contact" in the Oval Office with a girl half his age; Hillary Clinton is describing "what makes life worthwhile: family, religion, spiritual life, free association." She gets a standing ovation and then holds court, shakes hands, signs autographs, is admired. Isn't she strong, they say, hushed and respectful, isn't she poised, isn't she dignified. She's like a widow, a lioness, a doormat, and an Amazon all rolled into one. We are the audience, staring and waiting: Will she weep? Or roar? Or ever stop pretending?

A law professor discusses consumer mentality: "We have to get over the idea that anything the majority is willing to watch [on TV] is something that they ought to watch." Nervous laughter in the room. The first lady's studious face breaks into a smile. A big smile. Now at least I know she knows. She knows how weird this is, but she's not ashamed. Let them whisper in pity and wonder. She will not hide.

Now the president arrives. Everywhere else he is the laughingstock, but in this room, he's presidential. Prime ministers from England and Italy and Bulgaria are here, big men discussing big things while Hillary sits silently in the front row, a first lady listening. The president thanks her for arranging this conference; she has no reaction. He recalls their trip to Africa; she did not use his name, but he is not embarrassed to use hers. He speaks about taxation, investment, and problems with the Asian banking system; everyone takes notes. He says "the treatment of young girls in certain cultures" is "the most perverse manifestation of gender inequality"; no one titters. Am I the only one paying attention?

When it's over, Hillary greets the Italian prime minister but ignores Bill. Their aides escort them out like strangers. They do not look at each other or speak or touch.

I am Alice in Wonderland. I want to shout, *"Can't you see this isn't normal?"*

November 2, 1998. Election day is tomorrow and it's only in the last few days that the polls have shown Chuck Schumer, New York's Democratic Senate candidate, leading Al D'Amato, the Republican incumbent. The White House has made a priority out of a Schumer victory, and that has meant repeated appearances in New York on Schumer's behalf by the president, the first lady, and the vice president. Bill Clinton flew in to host a fund-raiser for Schumer; Gore attended a rally for him in a Bronx park and a party for him in a Park Avenue penthouse where there were bite-sized pastries shaped like the Capitol. At both events Gore told a corny joke about an HMO administrator trying to get into heaven only to be told by St. Peter, "You can only stay three days!"

The first lady has been here twice already, and today she's back, on the stage of a union hall in midtown, headquarters for Local 1199, the Hospital and Health Care Employees Union, on West Forty-third Street, for a final push. We are in a huge auditorium with several thousand people who are cheering and rooting and will not be quiet. Sure, they like Schumer. Yes, they agree with him. And absolutely, they will vote for him. But this outpouring of emotion is not about him. This is for the president's wife. They are in love with her. They are going wild for her. And no amount of shushing and trying to get on with the program will keep down the cheers.

When it's over, I head for the exit with the other reporters. It's getting late and we have stories to file. But a man in a suit with a curly little wire hanging from his ear is blocking our way. "Sorry, nobody leaves till the first lady's out." We are frozen in place. We are not going anywhere. We don't understand. We are not used to this. This isn't supposed to happen at a rally for Chuck Schumer—he's just a normal guy from Brooklyn! We are not good at following orders like this. We explain, we complain, we curse. Now one of us has pushed past the man and rushed through the door. I watch to see if he is taken out by a SWAT team. The agent he pushed aside is angry but does not appear to be pursuing him. Others are heading out now, too. I shrug. Why not? I follow. We run downstairs, schoolkids in a fire drill, no talking, just concentrate, get outta here. There's the street, the cops, the motorcade, the barricades, the shiny black cars with D.C. plates. We dart past it all to the corner. We made it. We are free.

November 6, 1998. Three days after election day, the day Schumer beat D'Amato 54–45, a much bigger margin than anyone had anticipated. Today, another political bombshell: New York's other senator, Daniel Patrick Moynihan, has announced that he will retire when his fourth term ends in 2000. Speculation immediately begins as to who will run to replace him—Robert F. Kennedy Jr., Andrew Cuomo, Carl McCall, Nita Lowey? Kennedy, the assassinated senator's son, a tall, passionate, charismatic man who looks hauntingly like his father and his uncle, is an activist who has largely shunned the political life, working instead as an environmental lawyer on cleaning up the Hudson River and other local issues. Cuomo—President Clinton's secretary of the U.S. Department of Housing and Urban Development—is the son of New York's former governor and has inherited his father's long-winded manner of speaking, but lacks the Reagan-Bush backdrop that made the elder Cuomo an articulate and inspiring icon for sidelined liberals in the 1980s. Carl McCall, raised on welfare by a single mother, grew up to become a top corporate banker, an ordained minister with a gift for public speaking, and now, as state comptroller, the first black candidate to hold statewide office in New York. Lowey, a likable Westchester congresswoman, had made a name for herself on abortion rights issues and by fighting for continued government support for *Sesame Street* and other public television shows.

On the Republican side, there's Mayor Rudolph Giuliani, or maybe Governor George Pataki. Less likely but still on many lists are a couple of Long Island congressmen: Peter King and Rick Lazio.

And a few pundits are crazy enough to throw out Hillary Rodham Clinton's name. A couple of people—including Charlie Rangel, the raspy-voiced Harlem congressman—tell the first lady she ought to consider it. "I thought it was an off-the-wall idea," she later recalls in *Newsweek*.

January 3, 1999. Senator Robert Torricelli of New Jersey, who, as chairman of the Democratic Senatorial Campaign Committee, is responsible for scouting out potential Democratic Senate candidates, says on *Meet the Press* that he believes Hillary Clinton will run for Moynihan's seat. Before Torricelli's prediction, RFK Jr. has made it clear that the family business is not for him, perhaps because he knows that the very personality traits that make him so appealing—his willingness to show emotion and get all worked up about a topic as dry as PCBs—make him ill-suited for the hazing process that is politics in New York. McCall, seeing Giuliani crouching on the other side and knowing that he can run for governor in 2002 as an expert on state finances, has also already taken his name out of the Senate ring by the time Torricelli speaks out. Then, five days after the *Meet the Press* segment airs, Andrew Cuomo says he's not interested either. There's something about the sound of Governor Cuomo, or something about the sound of Senator Clinton, or both, that sends him down a different road. Only Nita Lowey is still hanging around, cheerfully insisting that it's just fine with her if Hillary wants to run, but reminding everyone that she's available in case the first lady doesn't work out.

In retrospect, I like to think of this as the first launching of Hillary's campaign.

January 11, 1999. Chuck Schumer has already been sworn in, in Washington, but the ceremony is being reenacted today, in Manhattan, for his New York supporters, and the vice president has seen fit to join him. Gore is telling the joke again, about the HMO guy trying to get into heaven. Everyone laughs except me; I just mouth the punch line along with him. (I'll hear him tell it again at a fund-raiser in a Long Island mansion on September 21; at a meeting for business executives at Manhattan's Sky Club on September 30; and finally in a televised debate with Bill Bradley on October 28. In the meantime, I have everyone in my office keeping a log of the times they've heard Gore use it, and we've had three more incidents, in Manhattan, Westchester, and upstate. When I finally call our Washington political desk to see if this is worth a story, they tell me that Gore also told the joke during a one-on-one interview with an AP reporter. But they decide to hold off on a story. It's just as well; as far as I know, Gore stops using it after the Bradley debate.)

But Al Gore's lame joke isn't really an issue at this swearing-in for Schumer, because no one really cares about what Al Gore has to say today. Or even what Chuck has to say. Instead, in the balcony where the press corps is sitting, we're all buzzing about Hillary. Adam Nagourney of the *New York Times* had a story over the weekend quoting various Democrats speculating on whether Hillary would actually be willing to make a bid for Moynihan's seat. "Mr. Rangel said that Mrs. Clinton, in a conversation the other day, said nothing to dissuade him from advancing her candidacy," Adam wrote. He then quoted Rangel as saying, "Me being an optimist, I consider that very favorable." This chatter from Rangel seems to push the rumor up a notch. While Torricelli's prediction might have been wishful thinking by the guy in charge of finding decent Democratic Senate candidates and scaring off potential Republican contenders, there's nothing in this for Rangel to pump up a rumor with no basis—unless, of course, he thinks it's true.

As for me personally, I don't believe Hillary has any intention of running for Senate. It looks and sounds like an ego-boosting distraction from the impeachment scandal. Why would she want to get into a fight that she might not win after all the fighting she's been through? Why would she want to spend the last two years of her husband's term on the campaign trail in New York after expending so much effort to stay in the White House? And why would she want to be one lousy voice in a hundred when she could run a university, make millions at a corporation, or command audiences with heads of state around the globe on behalf of all her pet causes? The world is her oyster; New York is a snakepit. I'm convinced she's too smart to come here.

Still, I can't help but think back to that seminar at NYU and the rally in the union hall. They really loved her. And she knew it. And all that applause, without anybody mentioning Monica, must have sounded pretty good to the world's most publicly humiliated wife.

January 12, 1999. Today Bill Bradley establishes his presidential campaign fund. Al Gore formed his January 1. I can understand how a guy who wants to be president needs this much lead time, but the Hillary Clinton for Senate conversation is now at full volume, too, well ahead of any other Senate race and twenty-two months before the election.

January 26, 1999. A Marist poll shows Hil leading Rudy 53–42 in a hypothetical Senate race. On November 7, 2000, after she, Giuliani, and Lazio have spent $90 million on their campaigns, she will beat Lazio 54–42.

February 2, 1999. Bill Clinton attends a fund-raiser for New York Democrats in Manhattan. "It's highly likely," he tells the audience, "that I will increasingly be known as the person who comes with Hillary to New York."

February 12, 1999. The Senate votes today on impeaching the president, and Hillary holds a four-hour meeting in the White House about running for the Senate with Harold Ickes, a former White House deputy chief of staff who helped mastermind both of Bill Clinton's presidential campaigns.

February 16, 1999. The first lady issues a statement: "I will give careful thought to a potential candidacy in order to reach a decision later this year."

February 21, 1999. Hillary has just been featured on the covers of *Time* and *Newsweek*, a first lady on the verge of making history, and today Giuliani is making the rounds of the Sunday political talk shows with appearances on CNN, ABC, and WCBS-TV, a lame-duck mayor itching for a fight. "There'd probably be more of an inclination to do it if she were to decide to run," he says. Since I covered the last Senate race, I've been assigned to cover whatever happens in this one, and I duly put together a Rudy-Hillary story. But we are still twenty-one months away from an election, and I still can't believe she'll do it.

April 19, 1999. Now Hillary is showing up in New York every five minutes, pretending she's just doing her normal rounds as first lady even though she hasn't spent this much time here in the previous six years. Today she attends eight events around the city in fourteen hours. There's a ceremony in Central Park, a meeting about Kosovar refugees, a fund-raiser for a congressman, and a speech on education at Columbia Teachers College that ranks as one of the most boring events I have ever attended ("I dare you to find a sound bite," I whisper to the local cable TV news producer sitting in front of me). Hillary makes herself available for one, and only one, brief interaction with the press, and when she's asked about the Senate, she says the magic words: "I'm obviously still considering, and exploring, and am very interested. But right now I'm very focused on the situation in Kosovo." Yeah, right.

She also talks about how much she's always liked New York and its diversity, from big cities to "rural areas that provide some of the crops you might be surprised are actually grown right here." Well, maybe *she's* surprised that apples come from upstate and potatoes from Long Island, but as for the rest of us, it's old hat, Hil.

Later, she presents an award to Katie Couric at a Manhattan luncheon for women in broadcasting. Katie teases her about apartment-hunting. Meryl Streep tells a story about white-water rafting. "The *other* white water," she giggles. And Nora Ephron makes a crack about the very un–New York wardrobe of a first lady: "You can run. You can live here. And you will never have to wear a turquoise jacket again."

April 20, 1999. Ickes introduces Hillary at a forum on something or other at Hofstra University on Long Island, and she makes a long, boring speech. But there's one bit that stands out, and it even makes a pretty good lead. She talks about the health-care reform effort that the president assigned to her, the one that was a total disaster, the one that consisted of thousands of proposed regulations hatched in secret and then presented to Congress like a fait accompli only to be thrown back in her face by angry lawmakers and a scornful public. And what does she say about all that today?

"I'm not going to try that again, rest assured," she says in a humble, self-deprecating tone of voice. "I come from the school of smaller steps now."

Earlier in the day she visited an elementary school on Long Island in Syosset. Told that Eleanor Roosevelt had once been there, she says, "I'm used to following Mrs. Roosevelt. I don't know that I've been anywhere in the world, literally, that she hasn't been first."

Tonight, there's a gala dinner for the United Jewish Appeal. Giuliani has already pledged to make Hillary's statement from the previous year, supporting a Palestinian state, an issue in the campaign, and tonight she makes the first of many efforts over the next nineteen months to backtrack. It was May 6, 1998, when she'd told a youth conference on peace in the Middle East that "it will be in the long-term interests of the Middle East for Palestine to be a state." Colin Powell could say that in 2002 after months of violence, but Hillary spent the Senate campaign backing away from it. Bill Clinton's position has always been that Palestinian statehood is something the Palestinians and the Israelis need to work out for themselves, and tonight Hillary Clinton repeatedly expresses opposition to any "unilateral moves" in the peace process. An outsider would have no idea what she was talking about, but the seven hundred guests at this dinner applaud, knowing that what she's really saying is that Yasir Arafat better not unilaterally declare an independent state for the West Bank and the Gaza Strip.

April 29, 1999. Hillary's back in New York for the fourth time in two weeks, and I'm already tired of being forced to show up at every event ninety minutes before she does so the Secret Service agents and their dogs can search me and everything I own. I have even learned the terminology for this practice: *lockdown,* as in the "lockdown time is seven A.M.," which means we, the lowly press corps, have to be present and accounted for by then—even if Her Majesty doesn't waltz in till eight-thirty—or else we won't get in the door. I'm also starting to tire of events that have no news, and of following her around for days without ever getting to ask her a question. Even the public's admiration for the wronged wife has cooled; the latest polls show she and the mayor are in a dead heat for a Senate race that's over a year and a half away and that neither of them will commit to.

Today's schlepp involves taking the A train, nearly to the end of the line, to a Queens junior high school in South Ozone Park where the first lady is playing principal for a day. We are ushered into the school office; the photographers complain because there's not enough room to set up their equipment. Besides, they bitch, she always walks past without turning her head. No Q-and-A either, the print reporters gripe. The whole thing sucks.

"Heads up!" someone calls as she walks into the narrow room. We are all crowded behind the counter like students clamoring for a schedule change, jostling to see her, pens poised for a quote we don't expect to get, cameras following her just in case.

Suddenly everything is in slow motion. She's pausing. She turns our way. She looks at us. She smiles. The cameras whir and snap. *She's posing for us!*

I hear her voice. "Good morning!" she says cheerily, like a waitress turning on the charm in the hope of getting a really good tip. "How are you all today?"

She's talking to us! I am stunned. For the first time since she started making these trips, Hillary Clinton has recognized our existence.

And now another shocker. We'd been told that when she went into a library to talk to thirty kids in an eighth-grade social studies class, we'd have to leave the building. But now they're telling us that we are welcome to come along. We follow her through hallways decorated with hand-made signs that say "The first lady is cool!" and "Happiness is a visit from Mrs. Clinton!" And then her aides—largely White House staffers—tell us to pull up a chair, leave our tape recorders on, and sit there for an hour while she chats with the students. Right off the bat, a student has a question for her: What does she think about the bombing of Kosovo?

Damn, I think to myself. Why didn't I plant a question with one of these kids about the Senate race? It hadn't occurred to me that they'd have the nerve to actually ask her something newsworthy, but this kid who asked about Kosovo, this kid's clearly on the path to a career in journalism. "I support the continuation of the bombing," she replied. "I believe it will eventually work. I believe it is a way of punishing the Milosevic regime."

The rest of the session feels like a local-access TV show about what New York City teenagers are really thinking, except that the moderator, instead of being a school counselor, just happens to be the first lady. "I really hope we'll have a chance for me to know if there are things you want me to talk to the principal about, or even to talk to my husband, the president, about," she says in a tell-me-your-troubles-and-I'll-take-care-of-it tone of voice. "We need ideas from young people to provide better conditions for all of you."

The kids include immigrants from around the world—Trinidad, India, Puerto Rico, and Guyana—and she expresses fascination that the school offers a bilingual class for students whose native language is Punjabi. Then she asks the kids about gangs, and a boy mentions that the Bloods and the Lost Boys hang out in front of local grocery stores.

"Most people want to belong to a group," she responds. "They want to be part of something. How do we do a better job of giving kids good gangs to hang out in or more chances to be part of something positive?" There's talk of the school shooting in Littleton, of metal detectors and violence in video games, and a wistful admission from Hil: "I think it's much harder being a young person today than when I was growing up."

We're all scribbling furiously, checking our tapes to make sure they don't run out during this hour-long exchange, even though everybody knows that most of this stuff will never get into print. And while we can't ask questions, we can watch and listen, and that seems like a lot, considering that we thought we'd be out on the street. Something has happened here, and it's not about being principal for a day. I can't get out of my head how charming she was in the principal's office, the way she acknowledged our existence. All of a sudden, Hillary Clinton wants the media. Hillary Clinton needs the media. Hillary Clinton *smiled* at the media, spoke to the media.

For the first time, I think it might be true, what everyone has been saying since January. Maybe she really will run for the Senate. If she's decided she needs to have a relationship with us, there must be a reason.

May 23, 1999. Rick Lazio on ABC's *This Week* says Hillary Clinton needs "an exploratory committee to find Elmira." Two weeks later, the first lady makes a point of saying she'd "been to Elmira." When the *Star-Gazette* newspaper, located, of course, in Elmira, runs an article questioning her veracity, her Washington spokeswoman, Marsha Berry, explains that Hillary had been through Elmira as a child on a family trip between Chicago and Scranton. That is not an obvious route when you look at a map, but maybe the attractions of Elmira were deemed worthy of a side trip by the Rodham family.

May 26, 1999. On *60 Minutes II*, Dan Rather asks her which baseball team she'll root for if she moves to New York. "The politic answer, since I do plan to live in New York, no matter what I wind up doing, is, I'll root for both," she says.

June 2, 1999. I am sitting in the hot sun on a balcony overlooking the Harlem campus of City College. Below me, three thousand graduating students and their families are awaiting the start of their commencement ceremony. Suddenly a cheer goes up, then a ripple of applause turns into a roar, then the students rise and begin to point and crane their necks to see the person they've been waiting for: Hillary.

I look down from my vantage point and fix my eyes on her. She's easy to spot, a small, blond white woman in a purple graduation gown, making her way down a path through a sea of black and brown faces at this mostly minority public university. As she walks from the plaza entrance to the stage, the students wave and reach out to touch her. And then, spontaneously, the chants begin: *"Run, Hillary, run! Run, Hillary, run! Run, Hillary, run!"*

At first she ignores the adulation, shrinks back from the extended arms; I can see that she's surprised by this, a little overwhelmed, doesn't know how to react. But as she continues along the block-long path to the podium, she starts looking at the students who are calling her name. She nods hello, returns a smile, looks relaxed. One woman has written "It takes a village" on the inside of her mortarboard; she holds the cap up and catches the first lady's eye. Now Hillary's pausing to shake the outstretched hands and even stops to allow a large man to wrap her in a hug while her agents hover nervously. By the time she gets to the stage, the aloof first lady who arrived on campus a few minutes before has all but disappeared, and in her place another woman has emerged— a woman who's running for office. When she finally speaks, she says nothing that is all that important, but her tone of voice is totally different from anything I've heard from her before. All of a sudden, there's a roar in her words, a cadence that invites applause, a rise and fall designed to rev up an audience that's already treating her, as Bob Hardt at the *New York Post* will write, like a rock star. Gabe Pressman, a veteran political reporter for WNBC-TV, put it this way: "We've just seen the evolution of a candidate."

Two hours later, we are at Tavern on the Green, waiting for her to speak, and the old Hillary Clinton is back. We are ushered into an adjacent room, ostensibly to interview the Democratic Party chairmen for Westchester and Rockland Counties. But when we try to go back into the luncheon, we are told the area is off-limits until Her Majesty finishes eating. It seems the first lady does not want her picture taken while she dines.

June 10, 1999. "The fact is," she says on ABC's *Good Morning America,* "I've always been a Yankees fan."

The Sound of Hillary Listening

September 14, 1999. I am riding in a car with a photographer for the AP, pulling into a Great Neck, Long Island, parking lot for one of Hillary's Listening Tour events, when I spot a familiar figure gesticulating angrily to a Secret Service agent posted at the entrance to the parking lot. It's my mother-in-law, Leah, and needless to say, I didn't expect her to be here.

The photographer readies his press pass to show to the agent, who is walking toward us as we slow down. I slink down slightly in my seat, but it's no use.

Eagle-eyed Leah, who is about five feet tall and old enough to legitimately say that Eleanor Roosevelt was her favorite first lady, spots me in the passenger seat.

"That's my daughter-in-law!" I hear her announce to the agent in a commanding tone of voice. "She works for the Associated Press!" She peers into the car and explains that she is trying to get into the event, which is at a senior center in her hometown where she has taught an exercise class for the elderly for many years. But Leah's name is not on the list of invited guests, and even the center's director, whom she's known for a long time, has told her there's no way she can get in. So, she wants to know, can she just come in with me?

"I can't do that," I say in a small voice, noticing that she is wearing one of her nicest dresses, with jewelry, makeup, and everything, the way she does for important family gatherings and the High Holidays.

"Why not?" she asks. "Why can't I just come in with you?"

It's so simple from her point of view, but so incredibly complicated from mine. The photographer, meanwhile, is sighing and tapping on the steering wheel, impatient to be inside the building so he can grab a good spot for taking pictures and set up his gear. I tell Leah I'll come back in a minute after we park. We drive nearer to the building and get out. The photographer takes his tripod and cameras inside, while I head back to the edge of the grounds where Leah is still banging her teapot.

"There you are!" she says as I approach, then takes my arm, puffs herself up, and introduces me to the agent in her most imperious manner. "This is my daughter-in-law, Beth Harpaz, who works for the Associated Press. *She's* been covering Hillary for months now."

Then she turns to me and lowers her voice. "You can't just take me in with you?"

I explain that my name is already on whatever list the campaign is maintaining for the press, that my Social Security number is on file with the police department, and that even with all that, I still have to have my bag searched for explosives and sniffed by German shepherds every time I go inside a building where Hillary is speaking.

"For the general public, these things are invitation only," I add. "They're very strictly controlled."

Now Leah is indignant. "I *know* that. I tried all *day* to get in there. I've been on the staff of this senior center for years. I called everyone I know here and *none* of them would help me, not one. They said the list was made up a long time ago and there was no room to add anyone else. I'm never speaking to *any* of them again. Everyone on the board of directors got invited, and because I'm not on the board, I can't get in. It's ridiculous!"

I try nodding sympathetically the way Hillary does when she's listening to people whom she can't really help, but it doesn't seem to calm Leah down. Instead she becomes increasingly agitated, and the Secret Service agent is beginning to look a little alarmed. Sometimes they pass around Polaroids of people who make a fuss like this, and I definitely don't want Leah to get on *that* list.

"Look, you're upset, and you have every right to be," I say in my most reassuring voice, while trying to make eye contact with the agent to let him know that even though she's a little upset, this woman—a widow and grandmother of six who's old enough to be Hillary's mother—is completely harmless.

"It's just awful that nobody could get you inside, but it's not necessarily the senior center's fault," I try to explain. "These guest lists are written in stone."

She lists for me all the people she'd spoken to that day to try to get her in—everyone from the staff of the center to a couple of Hillary's local financial and political supporters whom Leah knows. "Nobody could help," she says, suddenly sounding exhausted.

I look at my watch. It's almost lockdown time, the time after which reporters will not be allowed inside. I lean over, touch her arm, and look her right in the eye. "You have to calm down. I feel terrible about this, but there's nothing anyone can do."

She shakes me off and stiffens her back. "Never mind," she sniffs. "It's a bunch of phony baloney, that's all. This whole Listening Tour is phony baloney. Hillary is phony baloney. I'm going to tell everyone I know what happened here today, and I'm certainly not going to vote for her."

I sigh. "I gotta go." I give her a hug, catch the agent's eye again to make sure he can handle this without resorting to some tactic that we'll all regret later, and am relieved to see him smile slightly and nod. He understands, and it's going to be okay.

I hurry inside. The event, like a lot of these Listening Tour meetings, turns out to be less an opportunity for the public to tell Hillary what's on their minds than a way for Hillary to make known her support for a standard Clinton administration position—in this case, a proposal to use part of the projected federal budget surplus to shore up Medicare and add a prescription drug benefit.

When it's over, she has the most intimate "avail"—journalist's jargon meaning an "availability" for the press corps—that she's ever held with us. At most Listening Tour events, there was no avail, or if she took a few questions from the press, they had to be shouted from the rear of the venue where we were always seated, over the heads of the hundred or so civilians in the audience, with several dozen of us fighting at once for her attention. Inevitably, the people in the audience would turn around and regard us with a mixture of curiosity and horror, as if they were witnessing an uncivilized mob of starving refugees at a food handout.

But this avail, in contrast, is peaceful and well-organized. We are in a small, quiet room, "pencils"—print reporters—seated in a circle in front, so that our heads don't get in the way of the TV cameras and "stills"—newspaper photographers—standing behind. It's mid-September, and I wonder if maybe after spending the summer being followed around by us, she has finally gotten used to us and is signaling her comfort by coming closer, physically, to us than she ever has before.

We'd all been buzzing about a recent article in *Esquire* that was a meditation on Hillary's sex appeal, as well as another item in the *New York Post* that claimed she'd been having plastic surgery consultations in Manhattan. A couple of my male colleagues were arguing over who ought to ask her whether the report was true. "I'll do it," I volunteered, immediately feeling slightly guilty about my eagerness to pose a somewhat sexist question, while at the same time feeling obliged, as the wire service reporter who has to make sure the basics are covered for news outlets that might not be present, to get the plastic surgery question cleared up.

By then I'd been around Hillary enough that I was certain she wasn't considering plastic surgery; still, we needed her on the record about it. Sure, she has her share of laugh lines, but she struck me time and again as a woman who actually had very little personal vanity. I attributed her wide-ranging taste in clothing to a simple desire on her part to don the appropriate uniform for whatever was being asked of her, without really caring much one way or the other—a ball gown for the cover of *Vogue*, pink when she testified before the grand jury, black (or gray or beige) pantsuits paired with a jewel-tone blouse when she was in Manhattan, bright colors in Arkansas and often in upstate New York, and always, *always*, a skirt with matching jacket for church. I didn't much share her taste in jewelry; she often wore big necklaces and a chunky brooch pinned to her lapel. But I thought the hairdo she'd adopted for her New York look was great—a short, simple, blond helmet with a wave on one side that could be pouffed up or sculpted for a more dramatic look. It was businesslike yet sophisticated, up-to-date without being faddish, and age appropriate but not at all dowdy. It was the hairstyle of a corporate lawyer or a busy editor or a Wall Street executive, the hairstyle of a smart, self-assured, influential woman—all the right messages for a woman seeking elective office to be sending. It also permanently replaced the ever-changing coiffures that had set her apart from so many of the previous, more staid first ladies and led her critics to ask whether her positions on the issues might be just as changeable—and somehow, by implication, unprincipled—as her hair.

Of course I felt guilty about sharing the public's and the media's fascination with her appearance. But I often justified it in my head by reminding myself that when I'd interviewed Senator Schumer for a profile, I'd asked him where he bought his suits. (The answer was Gorsart's, a downtown discount place.) It seemed to me that you could tell something about people—were they vain or oblivious to appearances, thrifty or extravagant, old-fashioned or on the cutting edge?—from their preferences in clothing and other aspects of how they looked. And later, when Lazio entered the race, the press devoted almost as much space to discussing his appearance—his grin, his boyishness, the little wavy lock of hair over his forehead—as there had been devoted to hers. (One afternoon on the Hillary van we even debated whether the flecks of gray appearing in Lazio's hair were natural, caused by the stresses of the campaign, or purposely dyed in to suggest maturity. Someone finally picked up a cell phone and called a relative who worked as a hairdresser, who assured us, after hearing a detailed description of the gray, that it sounded perfectly natural.)

Silly as it was, though, I needed to get Hillary's direct comment on the plastic surgery report. I signaled that I had a question for her after a couple of other reporters had asked theirs, and she nodded my way. I mentioned the *Esquire* and *Post* reports, but then tried to camouflage the crass underpinnings of my query—was she going for plastic surgery?—by also asking whether she viewed the media's interest in her appearance as sexist.

To my surprise, rather than appearing annoyed by my question, she leaned her head back and laughed long and hard. It started out like a giggle—"hmm, hmm, hmm"—but ended up almost giddy, like a belly laugh. It was a laugh I'd hear again and again during the campaign when she was asked a potentially embarrassing question; I later realized that it gave her a few seconds to formulate a response—usually one that sidestepped the question—and also suggested that despite the sensitive nature of whatever the question might have been, she had nothing to hide.

But this was my first exposure to the laugh, and I was impressed that she appeared so carefree about this subject. We all waited, pens poised, tape recorders running, until she finally stopped laughing and then started scribbling while she spoke. "I have never talked to anybody about plastic surgery," she said unequivocally. When she'd heard about the *Post* report, "at first I just laughed about it. But I want to set anybody's mind at rest who has any concern about this." She neatly avoided making a judgment as to whether such reports are sexist, saying instead that she hoped coverage of her campaign would focus on "what we just heard from the senior citizens . . . public education, health care, jobs, campaign finance reform, or gun violence."

I left the building when the avail was over to find the Secret Service guy standing alone at the parking lot entrance. My mother-in-law had given up and gone home.

A few days later, at another event, I saw Howard Wolfson, communications director for Hillary's campaign. I told him about Leah, thinking he'd find it amusing, or that he might even get defensive about how tight the Listening Tour guest lists were.

He did neither. Instead he just said, "Why didn't you just ask me? I would have gotten her in."

"What?" I said, somewhat flabbergasted. "Are you kidding? I'm not supposed to ask a campaign staffer to do a favor for my mother-in-law."

He shrugged. "I've done it for other people," he said nonchalantly.

"You have?"

He nodded and walked away.

For a minute I felt terrible. I probably *could* have gotten Leah in and saved her all that angst, but it had never even occurred to me to try.

Then my Righteous Journalist's Conscience kicked in: Wouldn't it be a conflict of interest to ask Howard to do you a favor like that? It was different from asking him to help out with something that made it easier to write a story.

On the other hand, the entire incident was also a perfect illustration of why the Listening Tour was so often described in news accounts as "much-ridiculed." Leah was right; in some ways, the Listening Tour *was* phony baloney. These were not the open town meetings that we had been led to expect, the type of forum that might be publicized a few days in advance with tickets made available to the community on a first-come, first-serve basis. Instead, these were high-security, invitation-only, carefully formatted programs. True, the campaign did not handpick the guests, but whatever local organization had been asked to host the meeting did handpick them. As a result, most of the audiences were friendly to the point of worshipful; typically people would get up and tell sad stories about not having health insurance, or inspiring stories about making the transition from welfare to work, or complicated stories about some local controversy, and Hillary would chirp, "I appreciate your raising that issue! It's something I care deeply about!" Afterward, she'd be mobbed by admirers, many of them carrying just-bought copies of *It Takes a Village* for her to sign.

Each Listening Tour event had a theme—gun violence, education, health care—but especially in the beginning, the press often did not get to ask any questions, and the news value had more to do with the sheer novelty of a first lady sitting around some dingy auditorium in an out-of-the-way place chatting with a bunch of locals than the actual content of anything she said. (The reporters who covered these events did, however, get very good at nodding their heads the way Hillary did when she was listening. Here's how: Without ever blinking your eyes, you bring your chin way up, so that your neck is painfully extended, then you slowly drop it way down to your chest, then you move your head an inch to the left or the right and repeat—sort of like those velvet dogs you sometimes see on taxi dashboards. To make it even more authentic, say, "You know, that's an *excellent* point. Thank you for bringing that up.")

The idea for the Listening Tour was born in the second week of April (1999) in a memo from Mark Penn, who became the campaign pollster and one of Hillary's chief advisers. Penn had just done his very first poll for the first lady's potential campaign, and in the memo to her, he outlined how receptive he'd found upstaters to be to the idea of her candidacy, and how large that group of potential votes was. He also coined the phrase *Listening Tour* to describe how he thought she should introduce herself to a state where she had never lived: as an unpretentious visitor, stopping by the neighborhood to meet people and learn what was on their minds.

At the same time, Mandy Grunwald, the campaign's media consultant and a former aide to Moynihan, was separately suggesting a virtually identical approach—that it was imperative for Hillary to visit all sixty-two counties, and to engage in a preliminary get-to-know-you stage before formally declaring herself a candidate.

But the focus on upstate was not uncontroversial within the campaign. "What the hell is she doing in Delaware County? Why isn't she at Zabar's?" is how one campaign source summed up the anti–Listening Tour sentiment. Harold Ickes, who'd been the first lady's premier confidant as she weighed the idea of running while the impeachment drama played itself out, was perhaps the most skeptical about trolling for votes north of Westchester. "He thought we were spending too much time upstate and that we should be spending more time in the suburbs, where we had the biggest problems," the source recalled. "But if you looked at the numbers carefully, she had more potential, more to gain, upstate."

The pro–Listening Tour contingent eventually came to include Hillary. "She could feel by the kinds of questions people were asking that it was the right thing to do," the source said. "And every time the downstate press ridiculed the Listening Tour, we basically laughed, because we knew that upstate it was tremendously important." But several campaign staffers acknowledged that it wasn't just the press. As one person put it, "There were people in the campaign making fun of it, too."

Another staff member pointed out that sometimes upstaters even came to Hillary's defense if the press started asking questions that had nothing to do with local issues. Shortly after Hillary was quoted in *Talk* magazine blaming Bill's philandering on his childhood, the first lady held a Listening Tour event at a furniture factory in Jamestown. Reporters were all over her, trying to get her to elaborate on what she'd said in *Talk*, "and finally a woman in the audience got up and basically said, 'Someone is finally here listening to us. You guys shouldn't be asking those stupid questions!' " the staff member recalled.

The staffer added that "just the concept of her going to these places got people excited. These were areas that have largely been ignored," both by the political establishment of the state and by the economic boom of the nineties, "and now the first lady of the United States was coming here and listening to their issues."

But wasn't it true that Hillary intended all along to go through with her candidacy, and that the Listening Tour was never about testing the waters? "That's not unfair to say," another adviser said, "but we didn't want the full campaign to start right away. The point of the Listening Tour was to not be seen as presumptuous, but for her to go and earn it."

As for the media's biggest criticism—that the Listening Tour events were overly controlled, rather than being open, town-meeting-type events—campaign staffers insist that for the most part, the Secret Service dictated what was and wasn't allowed in the beginning. "We were in uncharted territory for letting a first lady do the kinds of things that she was doing," an aide said. "To do a completely general public meeting, that wasn't possible. They wouldn't have let us." But some of the controls, the aide admitted, were "because of her comfort level also."

Despite the invitation-only guest lists, sometimes a hostile questioner would somehow get into the audience. At the first Listening Tour event I covered, an education event in mid-July in Westchester where the guest list included teenagers who were active in student government, local educators, PTA moms, and women who'd been stars in a welfare-to-work program, one woman with three kids got up and said that because the first lady is "a Democrat who needs to raise funds, the teachers union is very important." She went on to suggest that, as a result, Hillary wouldn't be willing to buck the unions on issues like kicking out unqualified teachers with tenure. "But as a parent, I know there are some teachers I hope my children will not get," she added.

Hillary—who did, in fact, court and win strong support from teachers unions—smartly sidestepped the fund-raising crack and instead said something about how she believed schools should "invest more authority in the principal in terms of hiring and retention of teachers." A school principal in the audience then came to the rescue, telling stories about parents who, because of the "rumor mill," didn't want their child to have a certain teacher but later came back to report, "My child had an absolutely wonderful year!"

Afterward, the mother of three was mobbed by reporters desperate for someone to say something other than "Hillary really was listening! She was so friendly! She's such an inspiration!" The woman admitted that she was a Republican who planned to vote for Giuliani and added that Hillary "doesn't even live here. She never has lived here." When we asked Howard to comment, he just smiled and said it proved that, contrary to everyone's perceptions, the campaign was *not* controlling the guest lists.

The press corps was then escorted to vans that were waiting to take us to Jones Beach on Long Island, where the first lady planned to have lunch in a restaurant and take a leisurely, impromptu stroll along the shore—or as leisurely and impromptu as a first lady can take when she's trailed by camera crews, print reporters, Secret Service agents, her press aides, and her personal assistants. We spent the ride from Westchester to the beach trying to make sense out of some of the comments Hillary had made at the forum, such as expressing support for making college tuition tax-deductible. It was a strange way for a would-be candidate to make her positions known—throwing out tidbits during Listening Tour events such as this Westchester forum on education, without elaborating or giving us any opportunity to pin down the details. How much money was involved in this tax proposal? Who would be eligible for the deduction? Was this the same proposal Senator Schumer already had on the table? No one—including her fledgling staff, some of whom were on the van with us, as they would always be throughout the race—seemed to know, and without a Q-and-A or a press release—the basics that any normal campaign would provide—it was difficult to write about the proposal coherently. A normal candidate would just hold a press conference on the issue and then answer questions about it, but I got the feeling that her handlers thought it would be too shocking, somehow, for a first lady, a carpetbagger, and a neophyte candidate to simply lay out where she stood, all at once, in a straightforward fashion. Instead, we were being exposed to her opinions one tiny bit at a time, in a roundabout way, as if these positions were organically arising during the Listening Tour programs we were attending instead of being carefully formulated beforehand.

Yet despite all our griping, it was sort of fun being part of Hillary's Excellent Adventure. The campaign had printed up laminated press passes, in full color, bearing a map of Westchester and Long Island and the words "Hillary Rodham Clinton, U.S. Senate Exploratory Committee Listening Tour." As they dangled from chains around our necks where we carried our regular photo IDs, which were issued by the police department, these special credentials served two purposes. One, they made it easier for Hillary's staff to recognize who was part of her pack; and two, they made us feel really cool. You often came across people who kept White House passes or "Trip of the President" credentials in full view long after they ceased to need them, and having one of these Listening Tour passes on your chain when the Listening Tour was front-page news conferred a similar status. It was like being part of the in crowd in high school. Sure, we made fun of the Listening Tour; it was touchy-feely in an Oprah-esque way, but there was also something oddly groovy about it, about the very words *Listening Tour*, that brought to mind the roadies' bus for a rock 'n' roll show instead of a press van. The *New York Observer* captured it perfectly with the caption "Magical Listening Tour" on a cartoon of Hillary singing an altered line from "I

Am the Walrus:" "I am she as you are she as you are me and we are all together."

When we got to Jones Beach, a crowd had already begun to gather, having heard on local newscasts that Hillary was headed to the boardwalk. They burst into applause when she finally appeared, and within minutes she was surrounded by several hundred people jostling to be near enough for a handshake or a greeting. While the Secret Service hovered, she posed for pictures with shirtless men and bikini-clad women. Then she looked out at the sparkling water and blue skies and confessed, like the carpetbagger that she was, that she'd never been to Jones Beach before.

"I've heard about it literally all my life," she said, smiling a dazzling smile, her big eyes as blue as the sky, "from many friends who would come here and spend lots of glorious summer days. I'm just delighted to be here."

But none of the beachgoers seemed to care that this woman who'd never lived in New York and never been to this beach before was thinking about running for office here. The press might get bogged down in petty particulars like that, but these people were simply too starstruck to care.

"I shook her hand!" gushed a beach maintenance worker as he walked away from his encounter with Her. Another woman dreamily told me, "She touched my shoulder!"

Clearly, Hillary wasn't just any old candidate looking for votes; she was a world-class celebrity whose magic touch nearly rivaled the pope's, and these were her adoring fans.

It had been only a week earlier, on July 7, 1999, at a press conference with Senator Moynihan on his farm in upstate Pindars Corners, that Hillary had announced the Listening Tour. Moynihan's wife, Liz, had told the first lady early on, "Whatever you do, don't announce in the ballroom of the Sheraton Hotel on Seventh Avenue in Manhattan like every other candidate!" So instead of the hotel, the campaign was launched on Moynihan's farm, where the senator walked with Hillary down a dirt road toward the scores of waiting reporters, mumbled something about *Plutarch's Lives* and *Pilgrim's Progress*, then declared, "I think she's going to win." (Two months later, when he endorsed Bill Bradley for president, he said, "There's nothing the matter with Gore. But he can't be elected." Say what you will about Pat Moynihan; he knew how to pick 'em.)

Hillary then announced that she was about to embark on a so-called Listening Tour, traveling around the state to learn about New Yorkers' concerns. A day earlier, she had officially formed an Exploratory Committee for the U.S. Senate, a legal entity that enabled her to raise money in anticipation of a likely campaign. Since everybody had already run a slew of stories about her *contemplating* a run for the Senate, and this ostensibly kicked her level of commitment up one notch to *exploring* a run for the Senate, I consider this the second launching of her campaign.

Then came her first real questions from the press. Wasn't she a carpetbagger? "What I'm for is as maybe as important, if not more important, than where I'm from." What about all the scandals? "New Yorkers will make their own judgments about that. I think we've moved beyond all of it."

And finally, this one: "A lot of people see you as the number-one victim of the Monica Lewinsky scandal. I wonder if you see yourself as a victim and if you think you benefit from the sympathy vote?"

Her answer sounded like a response to a different question. "I'm looking forward to meeting with New Yorkers, and I think they'll have a lot to tell me about what they think about me and the positions that I have."

She spent several days "listening" upstate, then embarked on the suburban phase of the tour. The day after the stroll on Jones Beach, she presided over a discussion about gun violence in Rockville Centre, on Long Island. Her cohost was Congresswoman Carolyn McCarthy, a former nurse who had entered politics as a gun-control advocate after her husband was killed and her son injured by a gunman on the Long Island Rail Road in 1993.

Also present was Alice McEnaney, whose son, Jason, had been shot in the groin when he disarmed a gunman holding thirty-six people hostage in a classroom at the State University at Albany. It was a story familiar to most New Yorkers because it was one of the nation's first school shootings, and because of the dramatic heroics involved in ending it.

"On December 14th, 1994, we got a phone call that's every parent's nightmare," Mrs. McEnaney told the first lady. "My son was involved in a hostage-taking at SUNY-Albany. He disarmed a gunman. He had been shot in the process."

"You've really spent a lot of time in the years since your son's murder—" Hillary started to say, only to have Mrs. McEnaney interrupt.

"He wasn't murdered. My son's alive!"

"Thank God," Hillary responded.

Jason, in fact, was in the audience of about sixty people, seated in the first row.

The reporters seated in the back of the room were astounded by the screwup. Had her staff failed to brief her properly, or had she become confused? We looked at each other incredulously.

When the session was over, I called my office. I was torn about whether to lead with her blunder. On the one hand, it seemed a little unfair to make such a big deal out of the type of mistake that anybody could have made. On the other hand, it was just about the only unscripted moment in an otherwise canned event. If that wasn't the lead, what was? The first lady supports gun control? I think we knew that already, and therefore, by definition, that was not the news.

The verdict back from my editors was to lead with it, and to find out whether Hillary had met Jason beforehand or been told that he had survived. Our Q-and-A had been brief and chaotic, one of those situations where people were shouting questions from the back of the room. It hadn't occurred to me to try to confront her about the mistake, and nobody else had either. Howard wasn't traveling with us that day, but the other campaign staff members on hand said he was the only person who could comment on the mix-up. When I finally reached him by cell phone, he was understandably peeved. After all, his job was to spin the news in the most flattering way toward his candidate. "This shouldn't be the lead of your story," he said, and asked who at the AP he could appeal to. I deferred to my bureau chief, Sam Boyle, and Howard called him directly to try to talk him out of it. But it remained in the lead of our story, and Howard, for his part, refused to say whether Hillary had been told before the forum that Jason had survived or that he was in the room. "Mrs. Clinton was sharing her concern for the mother of a gunshot victim and misspoke" was all I could get out of him. "That's it."

The same day, a new poll registered the voters' initial reactions to the Listening Tour and the first week of Hillary's exploratory campaign: Giuliani was now leading her by a half dozen points. Both the *Post* and the *News* had front-page headlines the next day announcing Hillary's "slip is showing," and it seemed that the novelty of following Hillary around on her don't-call-it-a-campaign-trail was already wearing off. Now we were recording the deflating reality of a novice candidate making no news for us on a good day for her—and bad news for her on a good day for us. The free ride from a worshipful public and a respectful press only lasted as long as she gave a flawless performance, and just a week into her Listening Tour, that phase had already ended.

Chapter 4

You People in the Media

November 24, 1999. I am standing on the front steps of the apartment building where I live, shouting into my cordless phone. It's
around nine o'clock, the night before Thanksgiving, cold and windy
and dark, and I am talking to a guy named David Rupert, who dated
Hillary when she was in college. He'd been interviewed in a new book,
Hillary's Choice, by Gail Sheehy, and in an excerpt that was released
before the book came out, he'd hinted that Hillary might have smoked
pot. Hinted it, by saying she hung out one weekend in 1969 with a
crowd in which "some of us were inhaling," but refusing to actually
come out and say she partook. "I don't have to go there but you can
read between the lines," he'd told Sheehy. So one of my editors called
me at home to see if I could track the guy down and get him to clarify.

I'd actually called the guy's house a few weeks before when a different excerpt from the book had turned up in *Parade* magazine. I'd found
that excerpt more compelling; in it he'd said they eventually broke up
because he wasn't ambitious enough for her. "I never stated a burning
desire to be president of the United States," he told Sheehy. "I believe
that was a need for her in a partner."

I remembered the name of the town where he lived and was able to get the number again with no trouble. I spoke to his wife both times and left messages, but while he didn't call me back the first time, tonight, for some reason, he has. So now I have a pencil in one hand, my reporter's notebook in the other, and my left shoulder hunched up to keep the phone from falling. And I am trying to pin him down, one way or another, as to whether he actually ever saw Hillary smoke pot.

"Look, it was very, *very* kind of you to return my call," I say in my most urgent yet polite yet assertive yet ingratiating tone of voice, the tone I reserve for people like this, people who don't know me from a hole in the wall, people who, for some ungodly reason, agree to speak to me when, if they had any sense at all, they'd be slamming a door in my face or hanging up.

"But I just really need you to answer this one question, and then I won't take up any more of your time: Did you ever see Hillary smoke pot? I just need a yes or no answer, and then we'll be off the phone."

I glance up as I talk to make sure my boys haven't gotten run over chasing their soccer ball in the street. There they are, two little blond blurs darting around the parked cars in front of the building, a street-lamp illuminating their game.

"No, no, you can't *do* that!" the big one, Danny, yells to his younger brother, Nathaniel, as the little guy bends over to pick the ball up. "*No hands!* You *idiot!* How many times do I have to tell you? In soccer there are no hands!" Danny runs over and kicks the ball away from Nathaniel's grasp, back toward his own turf. Nathaniel looks up at me, a tearful pout forming on his fat, little mug as he stands in the pool of light from the lamppost.

I am pretending, in this phone interview, to be a normal, hardworking journalist, the type of person who would make a call late the night before Thanksgiving from an office or a car or wherever someone like that would be. If I'd tried to make the call from inside the apartment, the kids would have blown my cover in an instant, screaming for this or that and me with no way to tune them out. So I brought them out on the front steps hoping that they would entertain themselves for just a few minutes without pestering me while I did my job. But now, with Danny yelling at Nathaniel and Nathaniel about to cry, it looks as if I am going to have to intervene anyway and reveal my true identity as a mother tethered to two small children and their incessant demands.

"Maaaameeeee!" the little one screams, then lets out a wail.

I give Danny my angriest look, the one where I make my eyes really big and scrunch my lips up, then put one hand over the mouthpiece of the phone and stage-whisper, *"Stop it now!"* while wagging the forefinger of my other hand in their direction. Then I turn my back on them and, facing the wood-and-glass front door of the building, try to resume my conversation.

"You still there?" I say, stepping back into my urgent-sounding yet sincere reporter's mode. "Sorry about that." We'd been going around in circles for a few minutes now, me restating the question every way I can think of, and him not giving me a straight answer no matter what I say.

"Yes" came the reply in a tone both wearied and annoyed. "I'm still here. But you're not going to get me to say what you want me to say. If Hillary wants to tell you people in the media, or the voters, whether she did or did not smoke pot thirty years ago, or whenever it was, that is entirely up to her."

I stop myself from saying, "Then why did you bother calling me back?" But there's no need to, because he immediately launches into the explanation himself in the form of a "you people in the media" lecture. The one about how we shouldn't be chasing after all these scandals, we should just be sticking to the issues. The one that leaves out the part about how readers are a lot more interested in the scandals than they ever are in the issues. This conversation is going nowhere fast. I stick my pencil in the wire coil of the notebook and turn back to face the kids. Somehow Danny has managed to get the game going again. He's kicking the ball toward Nathaniel and Nathaniel is following it with his eyes, then chasing after it, then pouncing on it—

"No hands!" screams Danny. He looks up, sees that he has my attention, and whines, "Mom, he won't play by the rules!"

Nathaniel's eyebrows start to crinkle again. *"Maaaaameeeee!"* The cry echoes off the buildings across the street. I hear a window go up; someone is undoubtedly about to call child welfare to turn me in.

Danny hears the window, too, and is now grinning with delight at having caused Nathaniel to disturb the neighbors. And Nathaniel is picking the ball up, holding it above his head, and throwing it with all his might into the street, grunting slightly with the force of his toss.

Ever since they'd been old enough to walk, a terrible fantasy had played in my head that they might someday, somehow, get hit by a car, so the ball-in-the-street scenario always throws me into a panic. I cover the mouthpiece of the phone again, call out, *"Don't run into the street!"* and dash down the steps to the curb. I put myself in the space between the two cars parked in front of the building to bar any potential recovery of the ball by the children, and turn my attention back to the phone, figuring there's no point in wasting this guy's time—or my own—any longer. If he was going to divulge anything about Hillary smoking pot, he would have already done it by now. It's time to wrap things up.

"Right, well, again, I appreciate your calling me back," I say abruptly, now in the tone of voice I ordinarily reserve for unsolicited calls asking whether I want to change telephone companies. "Have a good Thanksgiving, sir, and thanks very much for your time." I love calling people "sir." I had managed to learn to say it in such a way that no matter how polite it seemed, it was also somehow an insult, like when a cop refers to a handcuffed punk as "this gentleman."

I put the phone down on the hood of the car next to me. I look up the street, see no oncoming traffic, run across to fetch the ball from the other side where it's stuck under a car, and give it a one-handed toss back to Danny, who smiles proudly as he catches it on the fly.

The boys resume the game and I call the editor in Washington who'd asked me to track this guy down. I read her his quotes and she agrees that they aren't strong enough to put on the wire. There is no point in running a story that raises the question "Did she smoke pot?" if we can't answer it. I'd also already gotten a call back from Howard, one of those "I can't believe the Associated Press would stoop so low as to consider running a story like this" calls. Howard also says that Hillary has already denied ever having smoked pot, so I pass that on to the editor, too. The new Sheehy book is to be delivered to me at my in-laws' house in Massachusetts the day after Thanksgiving, so I tell the editor I'll read it as soon as I get it and call her then.

I'm just about to bring the kids inside with me when I see one of my neighbors coming down the street. He's a lawyer who used to be a newspaper reporter, and I guess he'd been working late and was just now arriving home. He has two boys like me, but his wife doesn't work, and his kids certainly aren't outside playing soccer in the dark the night before Thanksgiving.

"Hi, there. What's going on?" he asks casually as he gets to our stoop.

"Oh," I say, feeling ridiculous all of a sudden, "I'm just . . . just calling Hillary's ex-boyfriend to see if she ever smoked pot."

He knows I'm covering Hillary, so it isn't completely absurd—just mostly absurd. I briefly explain about the Sheehy book, and how I'd happened to have the ex-boyfriend's phone number, and how it's just one of those calls that has to be made right then and there, so I'd brought the kids out and . . .

He looks slightly amused, and maybe also slightly relieved that he's given up journalism for a more civilized profession. We say goodnight and I take the boys inside to begin the nightly struggle to put them to bed.

Their father was working late, as he often did. It was the only way we could manage our schedules. He worked late because he did the morning routine with the kids—waking up, breakfast, dressing them, and getting them to school and day care—and always arrived at work late. I started work early—at 8 A.M.—and was supposed to leave at 4 P.M. for the end-of-day routine: picking the kids up, making dinner, supervising Danny's homework and Nathaniel's bath. I liked to say that when my day at the office was over, my *real* job began.

Of course, once I started covering Hillary, leaving at 4 P.M. became a thing of the past. It was highly ironic to me and several other mothers in the press corps that a candidate who talked so much about the importance of family life, of supporting working parents, of the juggling that women do between their careers and their kids, would actually cause us to spend less time with our children than we used to. One day Hillary showed up more than an hour late for a visit to an emergency day-care center in midtown that serves working parents when their normal child-care arrangements fall through. Because this first event ran late, so did the next one, and I ended up being late in picking up my children that day. "Why are you so late?" the big one whined when he saw me as I forked over the $5 late fee to his after-school program. Only Hillary could highlight the child care-crisis in America while simultaneously causing a child-care crisis in my life.

Even my Thanksgiving holiday ended up revolving around Hillary. *Hillary's Choice* was delivered to my in-laws' house early Friday morning, and I spent the day reading it and writing up a story about it. One of the most fascinating tidbits in the book was a quote from Harold Ickes, who'd become her top campaign adviser, telling Sheehy, "This is a race for redemption. It's really that simple." After her failed health-care reform effort, Whitewater, and the impeachment scandal, winning a Senate race "would permit her supporters to say there was a lot more here than anybody thought: 'You guys were wrong!'" Sheehy quoted Ickes as saying.

The timing of the book's publication was perfect. The Clintons had just closed three weeks earlier on a $1.7 million home with two fireplaces and a swimming pool in Chappaqua, in suburban Westchester. Of course, like many of the Clintons' financial ventures, this one was immediately criticized as unsavory. The first couple—famous, but not rich—had allowed Democratic Party fund-raiser Terry McAuliffe to put up $1.35 million of his own money as collateral for a mortgage. The deal was so widely criticized that Hillary and Bill finally went out and got their own conventional loan from a regular mortgage company. But the uproar didn't hurt McAuliffe, who became Democratic National Committee chairman after Bill Clinton left office.

Then, three days before *Hillary's Choice* was released to the press, Hillary ended speculation that she was about to drop out of the Senate race. At the time, her poll numbers were flagging and she was trying to recover from a series of high-profile mistakes—including opposing clemency for a group of Puerto Rican nationalists without consulting anyone from New York's large Puerto Rican constituency, and kissing Yasir Arafat's wife during a visit to the Middle East. Clinton-friend-turned-foe Dick Morris and other columnists and critics were loudly predicting that she was on the verge of quitting. But in her first press conference back in New York after the trip to Israel where she and Suha had kissed, Hillary allowed an ardent supporter, teachers union chief Randi Weingarten, to ask, "So, is it yes, or is it no?"

Everybody's cameras and tape recorders were going and we were practically salivating, pens poised, ready to take down her response and get it back to our offices by cell phone. "The answer is yes!" Hillary responded, beaming like a woman who's just gotten engaged. "I intend to run!"

By my count, this was the third launching of Hillary's run for office. Like the previous beginnings, this one entailed a lot of brouhaha and happy talk—a mini-celebration by her supporters, a fresh round of profiles and front-page stories about the novelty and history of a first lady running for office. Those who had jumped on the Hillary bandwagon early—such as Weingarten, Moynihan, Charlie Rangel, Bob Torricelli, state Democratic Party chairwoman Judith Hope, and Nita Lowey, who was gracious enough to get out of Hillary's way without a fuss—

looked pretty smart now. And in the weeks before and after the "I intend to run" event, Hillary got the blessing of many others, from former mayor Ed Koch, who had crossed party lines to support Al D'Amato in the last Senate race but became one of Hillary's most visible Jewish supporters, to celebrities like Rosie O'Donnell and Harvey Weinstein. Money was already starting to flow in from unions and Hollywood types, a trend that would continue till the end of her $30 million fund-raising effort. And one other noteworthy name turned up early and often among Hillary's big-money donors: Walter Kaye. Kaye, who had made a fortune in the insurance business, was a frequent and generous donor to many Democratic Party causes and also happened to be friends with Monica Lewinsky's mother. That had led Kaye to recommend Monica for the White House internship. Hillary was happy to accept his support for her Senate campaign, however; he and his wife ultimately donated over $100,000 to the state Democratic Party to be used on her behalf.

The "I intend to run!" event also led to another go-round on the Sunday-morning political TV talk shows by her campaign staff and her detractors. "We're moving into a new phase of the campaign," Howard told *Fox News Sunday*. "She's going to be winding down her first lady obligations and increasingly devoting all of her time to New York and this race."

But my favorite quote from the Sunday shows was from Harold Ickes, when he was asked on CNN about the "race for redemption" statement in Sheehy's book. "I don't recall it," Ickes said matter-of-factly. "I remember Gail calling me and asking me if I would interview for the book. And I told her I would not. I may have had a conversation with her on the phone. I don't recall the quote."

Two months later, I had my own interview with Ickes—and I'm hoping that if anybody asks him about it as a result of this book, he doesn't decide to say that it never happened. I'd called him a few times but never gotten a message back, and I really wanted to interview him for a profile I was writing of Hillary in anticipation of yet *another* launching of her campaign—this one the formal announcement of her candidacy, with the president by her side, in Purchase, not far from her new adopted hometown in Westchester. Since it was impossible to get a sit-down interview with Hillary—even though Howard had been promising one to the AP since September—I figured Ickes was the next best thing. One day I noticed, on the AP Daybook, which is a daily calendar of newsworthy events sent out by computer to all the local media, a listing for a reception in honor of the labor law firm where Ickes worked, Meyer Suozzi English & Klein. I decided to go and see if I could corner him. Only one other reporter was there, Bob Hardt from the *New York Post*. Although I'd seen Ickes on TV, I wasn't sure what he looked like. Bob, who knew him, pointed him out and asked if we could chat. A little while later, Ickes escorted us into a back room, shut the door, and proceeded to pontificate, at our invitation, on why Hillary was running for Senate.

"She has had a very long career of public service," he told us. "Most people don't understand that. Most people look at Hillary through the prism of that of first lady, and all that that has entailed—Whitewater, impeachment, etc. The fact is, if you go back and look at her history, you have a young woman who was very committed to public service."

He added, "Hillary looked around and started thinking about the alternatives. She's not driven by making money. I don't think she wanted to go around just making speeches. Or writing books. She really wanted to continue her devotion to public service. People kept saying, 'The world is your oyster.' She could do this, she could do this, she could do this. There are many things she could have done. But she also understands how short the half-life of a first lady is. The half-life of a first lady is pretty damned short. And the more this society becomes focused on celebrity, the shorter the half-lives of formers become."

I asked him about the Sheehy quote. "I do not see this as a race for redemption," he said emphatically. "You don't undertake something this difficult—you're running in one of the most complex states in the union—against a potential opponent who has some very strong credentials, a very tough race, you don't do that to redeem yourself. You don't go through the agony of coming in, establishing yourself, raising money that it's going to take to run this race, for redemption. You do it because you have a very profound sense that you want to continue a career in public service. Some people have said, 'Why do you want to be in the Senate?' Being in the Senate ain't chopped liver! A lot of people want to be in the Senate. You don't work miracles in the Senate, but if you're in it for the long term, you can do a lot. . . . As she looked over the range of alternatives, this was the alternative she chose."

He added: "She also understands that this is not going to be given to her. She's going to have to work for the trust of the people of New York. There was initially all this talk about the first lady. A lot of people came out to see her just because she was the first lady. There was a celebrity factor. That has worn off now. Everybody understands—first and foremost, Hillary—that she has to work for this, that she has to earn the trust of New Yorkers. If you look at the issues, she is on the right side of a very broad range of issues. But there is the question that haunts many people: Why is she doing this? And who is she?"

I have heard a lot of Hillary's supporters attempt to explain why she ever bothered to go to all the trouble of moving to New York, facing down the carpetbagger taunts, subjecting herself to grillings by the New York media on all the Clinton scandals after spending the previous six years doing the same thing in Washington. And I have heard Hillary's opponents explain that she stayed with Bill out of sheer ambition, and that the Senate seat in New York is nothing more than another step by another power-hungry Clinton to regain the White House in a shower of personal glory. I've even heard Hillary, on numerous occasions, defensively contend that she always wanted to live in New York, and that she sees the Senate as the best way to keep working for the causes that are important to her. Of course, it's easy for us in the media to be cynical about all of that, and I'm not saying I will ever abandon the view that raw ambition and some kind of marital payback played a role in Hillary's decision to run for the Senate. But until I heard Harold Ickes explain it his way, I don't think I fully understood what it was all about. I later realized that Ickes was party to a battle over the direction Hillary's campaign was taking; other campaign staffers told me that he wanted to spend more time cultivating the suburban vote and thought the Listening Tour and extensive efforts upstate would not pay off the way they did. Ickes's political orientation was also slightly to the left of where the campaign was usually headed, and even on internal debates such as how to win over Jewish voters, he wanted an emphasis on traditional liberal social issues instead of having her concentrate on shoring up her credibility on Israel. In the end, it appeared that Ickes had lost many of those battles to other voices in the campaign, and the election results, with Hillary's success upstate, may have proved the others right. But there was no denying that his ability to explain why she was doing it, what motivated her and what she wanted to accomplish, was better than anyone else's. As far as I was concerned, he had explained it even better than Hillary could.

After spending most of Thanksgiving at my sister-in-law's house obsessing over *Hillary's Choice*, I tried to explain to her why reporters found Hillary so annoying. She wouldn't answer questions like a normal candidate, I said. She held this silly Listening Tour, she made all these mistakes, she was involved in all these scandals, she'd never lived in New York, she'd never held elective office . . .

So what, my sister-in-law, who grew up in New York, replied. A lot of New Yorkers agree with her positions on the big issues. They don't care about all that other stuff. They just want someone to go to the Senate who'll represent their points of view. It's like Ted Kennedy—

Ted Kennedy! I nearly shouted. What about Chappaquiddick? Some people think he oughta be in jail!

Actually, even if he'd been convicted, it would only have been for criminally negligent homicide, and he'd certainly be out by now, my husband calmly interjected. (Both he and my sister-in-law are lawyers, and I frequently feel at a professional disadvantage in arguments with either of them, since I am trained to see both sides, and they are trained to prove that the other side is wrong.)

But my sister-in-law had a bigger point to make, and that was that the people of Massachusetts, where she'd lived for more than twenty years, keep reelecting Ted Kennedy because he fights for all the liberal values they support. He might be the whipping boy of the right-wing pundits, but his constituents love him. That, my sister-in-law added, is something you people in the media just don't understand.

It was my second "you people in the media" lecture in a week. I was starting to hate those people in the media myself.

Chapter 5

A Normal Campaign

December 9, 1999. I arrived at O'Neill's Restaurant on Third Avenue at exactly 9:30 A.M., just as Hillary's schedule said. But the Secret Service guy posted at the entrance was someone I'd never seen before. "Sorry, you're too late," he said brusquely when I took out my press pass.

"Too late? It's nine-thirty," I said, looking at my watch.

"You were supposed to be here *before* nine-thirty."

I tried the old "Listen, I'm with the Associated Press. If I'm not in there to cover this, I'll get in trouble, but you'll be in even more trouble, because the only way every newspaper in New York State gets this story is if I'm inside."

It didn't work. "Sorry, I can't let you in. We already swept everybody's equipment," he said, referring to the search they routinely do using bomb-sniffing dogs.

"Equipment? I don't *have* any equipment. I don't have a camera. I don't have a tripod." I plopped myself right down on the floor next to his shiny black shoes, yanked open my knapsack, and started pulling out everything inside. "All I've got is a notebook, a pen, a tape recorder, and my lunch. You wanna see my lunch? Here it is." I pulled the plastic cover off the container in which I'd packed leftover beef stew from last night's supper. It was delicious warmed up, but it wasn't a pretty sight cold with the brown gravy congealed on chunks of meat and potato, all emanating a very un-breakfast-like smell.

Someone once told me that when the agents give you a hard time about searching your bags, just pull out the little case where you keep your tampons and they get so flustered that they give up. I was just about to go for the Tampax when Wire Ear had a change of heart.

"Oh, you're not TV? That's all you had to say. Go ahead." He waved me up a narrow staircase to the second floor. I don't know whether it was a true epiphany on his part that one woman with a small knapsack did not constitute a camera crew, or a judgment that someone who was carrying around greasy leftovers was probably not the type to also be carrying a bomb. Either way, it got me in the door.

Still, it left me whining to myself, as I often did, "Why can't this just be a *normal* campaign?" Other politicians were so happy to have the AP cover them that if you were running late and called ahead, they'd wait for you to arrive before they started.

As usual, the room where the press conference was being held was not nearly big enough for the dozens of reporters who'd shown up. All the seats had been taken long ago. I repeated my "Why can't this just be a normal campaign?" mantra in my head and squeezed against the wall next to Adam Nagourney from the *New York Times*. A few minutes later, I spotted Howard and Bill deBlasio, who'd been named Hillary's campaign manager four days earlier. I'd known Bill for a long time because we'd served together on the board of a day-care center that his daughter and my oldest son attended together. If Howard and Bill were here, Hillary was in the building. It was time to cue up my tape recorder.

The press conference started a minute later. It turned out to be one of those squishy tributes to Hillary by her adoring fans—in this case a variety of Irish-Americans, including the chairman of Friends of Sinn Fein, the publisher of *Irish America* magazine; a representative of the

Ancient Order of Hibernians; and Congressman Joe Crowley, a Queens Democrat who was antiabortion but who appeared by the adamantly pro-choice first lady's side with puzzling regularity. I heard Crowley saying that "when the history of Ireland is finally written, it is my hope the Irish people will remember the Clinton administration. The first lady has been there four times! She was the first first lady to go to Northern Ireland! And when that history is written, remember Hillary Rodham Clinton's efforts!"

Call me cynical, but I sort of doubted that Hillary Rodham Clinton would be prominently featured when the history of Ireland is finally written. And while I understood that these guys were legitimately thrilled by the Clintons' support for the Irish peace process, I didn't have a clue what I was going to do for a lead. I scrounged around in my head, playing a sort of free-association game that sometimes helps me come up with a decent angle. Okay, what do New York readers know about the Irish? Well, there's the St. Patrick's Day Parade. Its organizers, the Ancient Order of Hibernians, had refused to let a gay contingent march. The gay group had sued, but the courts had sided with the Hibernians, saying that as a Catholic fraternal group, it had the right to exclude homosexuals. As a result, for the past ten years, the parade had featured protesters and arrests, with some politicians marching and others—liberal Democrats like city public advocate Mark Green— staying away.

I heard Hillary say something about how every St. Patrick's Day, she attends a celebration at the White House. It occurred to me that this could lead to an interesting little story about the conflicts between her roles as first lady and as Senate candidate. If I could get her to say she'd be in Washington on March 17, I could then state that every other local pol would be in New York, either marching, or making a point of not marching, in the parade.

The Q-and-A was a mess. As usual, there were way too many reporters who had something their station or paper needed to pin down, and there just wasn't enough time to get to everyone. Nobody ever got to ask more than one question, and there was never any opportunity to follow up.

Finally Hillary looked in my direction and I managed to make myself heard. "Are you going to march in the St. Patrick's Day Parade?" I called out.

She paused as if she'd never thought about this before, then broke into a broad smile. "I would hope so!" she cooed.

Within a split second, the demeanor of the press corps tangibly changed. We went from standing around listlessly, barely paying attention, to being on high alert and scribbling like crazy, leaning forward and practically holding our breath to make sure we didn't miss a single word as she finished her response. The change was so stark that even Hillary sensed it. You could see her pausing for a minute, quickly scanning the room and the people standing around her to try to figure out what about her answer had caused everyone in the room to shift gears, almost begging for a clue about what was wrong. But with nothing else to go on, the best she could do was to hastily add to her "I would hope so!" declaration a caveat: "As long as I've got lots of good company . . ."

But it was too late. She'd just made news—unintentionally, which is never how politicians want to do it.

Personally, I was flabbergasted. She was supposed to say she'd be in Washington that day. If she wasn't going to be in Washington that day, she was supposed to demur and say she wasn't sure what her schedule would look like in March, three months from then. A liberal Democrat like Hillary Clinton couldn't possibly intend to march in the St. Patrick's Day Parade! How could she not know about the gay controversy?

Adam was smiling. "Great question," he whispered to me.

I glanced over at Bill and Howard. They both looked miserable. They realized she'd fucked up, and by extension, so had they. Bill, my former friend! Howard, who would probably never return my phone calls again! I started having a conversation in my head with myself. *I*

*hadn't meant to trap her! Honest! I didn't mean to make her look like a carpetbagger! I
thought she knew!*

Then I realized I wasn't supposed to be feeling bad about this. I was
supposed to be feeling glorious! I was supposed to be feeling proud!
How could her staff have sent her to a press conference about Irish-
Americans in New York without telling her about the controversy over
the parade? If there was one thing everyone in New York, Irish or not,
knew about St. Patrick's Day, it was that every year a bunch of gay
protesters got arrested. The protesters usually included several gay
Irish-American politicians, like state senator Tom Duane and city coun-
cilwoman Christine Quinn. I realized just then that neither of them was
up there with Hillary.

I started praying that somebody would *please* ask her a follow-up
question. Maybe she *did* know about the gay controversy. Maybe she
didn't care, which would have been ironic, because Adam had a story in
the *Times* that day about how Hillary disagreed with the president on
the "Don't ask, don't tell" policy. She'd told a group of gay supporters at
a fund-raiser earlier that week that she thought the policy didn't work,
and that she believed homosexuals should be allowed to serve openly in
the military.

So it didn't make sense that she would now turn around and thumb
her nose at the gay community on the parade. On the other hand,
maybe she just felt that she couldn't say no to marching in the parade
when she was surrounded by a bunch of Irishmen.

But it seemed far more likely that she didn't know about the controversy, or that if she *did* know, she didn't understand what a big deal it
was. She'd already made Puerto Rican officials mad over the FALN controversy, and she had spent much of September apologizing, explaining, and pledging to do a lot of consulting with community leaders in
the future. Then in November came the infamous kiss on her official
first lady visit to the Middle East, where she'd attended an event with
Yasir Arafat's wife, Suha. Mrs. Arafat used the opportunity to accuse the

Israelis of using "poison gas" against Palestinians in the West Bank, contending that the chemicals had poisoned water supplies and led to a cancer epidemic. The visit ended with the smooch between the two first ladies that showed up on the front pages back in New York.

Hillary spent the rest of her campaign explaining the incident, variously saying that, in the Middle East, a kiss is like a handshake; that she'd had a bad translation of Suha's remarks and didn't realize until much later how "offensive" they were; and that, as first lady, she couldn't very well cause an international incident by rebuking Suha to her face or refusing to kiss her good-bye.

It all seemed pretty mealymouthed in contrast to Giuliani. Now he was a guy who loved creating international incidents. In 1995, he'd had Yasir Arafat kicked out of a concert at Lincoln Center celebrating the fiftieth anniversary of the United Nations, saying he didn't think terrorists ought to be enjoying the good life in New York. He also made no apologies for marching in the St. Patrick's Day Parade. It wasn't that the mayor didn't support gay rights; he did and had passed one of the strongest domestic partnership laws in the country to prove it. But he also thought the Hibernians had every right to invite whom they chose to their party, and he didn't see the merit of the other side's argument.

But we didn't know whether Hillary had weighed the pros and cons of marching and reached the same conclusion, or if she was simply unaware. Nearly everybody was going to lead with her parade commitment the next day, but nobody had asked the crucial follow-up question.

Now the event was over and reporters were starting to deconstruct what had happened. One said that even if we had followed up, there would have been no way to get her to admit she'd screwed up. But somebody else pointed out that we could have said something like "Mrs. Clinton, are you aware that very few other Democrats march in this parade?" That wording made it clear there was a controversy over the parade without giving away what it was. It would have been the perfect way to test her. I wished I'd thought of that earlier, but it was too late now. If this were a normal campaign, I said to myself, we could stay here until every last question was answered. If this were a normal campaign, we could get her on the phone to clear this up or get another Q-and-A at her next event, later in the day. But this wasn't a normal campaign, and none of that would ever happen.

I walked over to Howard, who was spinning so fast he looked dizzy.

"It wasn't a firm commitment that she made," he was saying to a group of reporters standing around him scribbling madly in their note-books. "I think she said she *hoped* to march. We'll review this when we get closer to St. Patrick's Day. As a general statement of principle, not everything you do is going to make every person happy. And in this particular instance, we'll get back to you with the details as to whether or not she's marching . . ."

Only much later did I learn from a campaign aide what had really gone on. It wasn't that she had never heard of the ILGO controversy, but, said the aide, "she had a frame of reference and that's all. It was not entirely news to her, but she had no sense of the intensity of it, the history, the depth." When she said "I would hope so" in answer to the "Will you march?" question, "she was responding from a generic perspective, from a national perspective—of course you don't want to insult them," the aide said. But at the same time, "some part of her was realizing that something was going awry and that's why she broadened the answer. She knew there was a problem. So she managed to say, basically, 'I'll march if other good, decent people march.' She was acting incredibly cleverly. And we were all absolute idiots for not thinking to brief her on this earlier, and in our discussions of this later with her, we duly noted that we had left her out there on this one, and *she* duly noted that we had left her out there. . . . We all kicked ourselves."

The aide added that the campaign also felt the disclosure of her opposition to "Don't ask, don't tell" had been mishandled. This was, potentially, a huge story—a way of currying favor with gay voters, and a sign that she was willing to disagree publicly with her husband's administration and influence the president's thinking on a controversial issue. Yet she had revealed her position on this issue at a private fund-raiser that was closed to the media, and when someone who'd attended the fund-raiser had leaked it to the *New York Times*, the campaign lost an important opportunity. Not only would other newspapers pay less attention to the story once it had appeared in the *Times*, but it would ultimately get lost in the controversy over the St. Patrick's Day story. "We had no business doing something as important as that at a fund-raiser," the aide said.

That afternoon, Hillary attended a luncheon for a foundation headed by Denise Rich to raise money to fight leukemia, the disease that had killed Denise's daughter. I'd never heard of Denise Rich before and couldn't have imagined how important she'd become after President Clinton left office and a scandal erupted over his pardoning her ex-husband, the fugitive financier Marc Rich. Denise's name came up a few times during the Senate race as one of the Democratic Party's top donors, but no one paid much attention at the time. Even though she'd written a number of Top 40 songs, she wasn't well known to either the press or the public; her visits to the White House and her donations to the Clinton library in Arkansas wouldn't be news for over a year to come.

Nevertheless, when her public relations person approached me at the leukemia fund-raiser that day to ask if I wanted to interview her, I said, "Why not?" You never knew when someone might say something that could turn out to be significant.

I remember being impressed by Denise's elaborate makeup and her dramatic, but slightly spaced-out, demeanor; she tearfully told me about her daughter's life and death, how important this annual fund-raiser was, and how grateful she was that Hillary had agreed to headline it this year. I was completely ignorant of how big a player she was in Democratic circles, and stupidly responded by suggesting that she have

Barbara Bush speak at the fund-raiser the following year because Bush's daughter Robin had died of leukemia, too, in 1953 at age four.

Denise gave me a slightly horrified look. "Barbara Bush?" she asked, her tone of voice suggesting an unspoken "Why would I want to invite her?"

I repeated my explanation about the former first lady's daughter. Denise nodded politely and murmured something about not having known about the Bush family's connection to the disease, but the look on her face remained uncomprehending, as if what she really wanted to say was, "You don't get it." Finally I gave up, thanked her for her time, and walked back to the press area of the hotel where the fund-raiser was being held. It was only much later that I realized why Barbara Bush wasn't a suitable candidate to headline Denise Rich's leukemia fund-raiser. But that day, I didn't think there was anything particularly news-worthy about my—or Hillary's—interactions with Denise. I had the St. Pat's controversy to write about, and that was the news of the moment.

By the time I got back to the office that day, Howard had already called several times and left messages, including a statement he wanted in my story: "She plans to march, and believes all such parades and celebrations should be inclusive." Except that we all knew it *wouldn't* be inclusive, so what the hell did that mean? The whole thing was rapidly devolving into a bucket of spin, and I started wondering if I'd be black-listed from now on as the reporter with the trick questions and have an even harder time than I already did getting my turn at the press conferences. I decided to feel Howard out on the subject, and a few days later I asked him if he was pissed at me for having asked the question.

"Nope," he said breezily. "It was totally fair." That was one good thing about Howard: as far as I knew, he never held a grudge. Even when you wrote a story he thought was unfair, and he called up to complain or sent angry e-mails telling you what for, the next day you had a clean slate. Sometimes he was less than helpful, or unresponsive, and that often made my job difficult. But at least he wasn't vindictive and didn't take things personally. Campaigns have good days and campaigns have bad days, and the mark of a good press secretary is that he treats the media the same way on the bad days as he does on the good days.

Four months later, on March 17, after explaining a hundred times to all her gay supporters that she believed their concerns were important, too, Hillary did march in the St. Patrick's Day parade. And was met with boos and cries of "Carpetbagger!" every step of the way. (Of course, half the people shouting those things were from New Jersey.) She also marched in just about every other parade held on the streets of New York and was wildly cheered at some, such as the Puerto Rican Day Parade and, yes, the Heritage of Pride parade, held to celebrate gay pride. It seems the Puerto Rican community forgave her for the FALN blunder, and the gay community forgave her for marching on St. Patrick's Day. But the kiss with Suha Arafat was not as quickly forgotten. When she marched in the Salute to Israel Day Parade, she was booed nearly as much as she had been on St. Patrick's Day.

All this marching on Fifth Avenue led some of my colleagues to conclude that the campaign had made a commitment early on for her to participate in all the city's major parades, and therefore, even if she had known how controversial the St. Patrick's Day event was, she would have given the same answer. Certainly she didn't want to get trapped in a liberal Democrat's box of just going for minority and urban votes. Just as she made major outreach efforts upstate, to women, to blacks, and to Jews, she didn't want to leave out the white ethnic or the white Catholic vote, and that probably meant marching on St. Patrick's Day no matter what.

But the entire incident surrounding the press conference where I asked the question—the run-in with the Secret Service agent, the difficulty in asking *anything*, the impossibility of posing a follow-up or getting something clarified in a straightforward fashion—left me looking back wistfully on the Schumer-D'Amato Senate race of 1998. I didn't know how good I had had it then. There was no security to go through.

You could walk up and ask the candidates questions whenever you needed to. It *was* a normal campaign.

I was moaning about the contrast one day to Adam, who had also covered Schumer-D'Amato, and he said he thought the media access problem was a simple matter of Hillary running "a Senate campaign on the scale of a presidential campaign."

I realized he was right. The sheer number of reporters—twenty or so on a light day, fifty to a hundred at a big event—made it impossible for Hillary and her staff to respond adequately to our needs. You could tell just from the way phone calls were handled. At the press office for the Republican Senate candidates—first Giuliani and later Lazio— phone calls were answered on the second ring and immediately turned over to someone who could actually answer your question. But I eventually gave up trying to reach the Clinton campaign through their office phone. It was always busy, and even when I got through, I almost always got trapped in a voice-mail system that, as far as I could tell, was never checked for messages. When I mentioned the contrast in phone systems to Karen Dunn, who worked with Howard in Hillary's press office, she said, "What does that tell you about the other side?" Well, either they're a lot more efficient and responsive than the Clinton campaign, or more likely, they don't get nearly as many phone calls. Hillary was the news in this campaign; Lazio was merely The Other, and even Rudy was Only the Mayor.

Hillary's fame and its flip side, her security needs, also made it virtually impossible for her to do what's called retail campaigning in malls and subway stations the way other politicians do. The closest she ever came was shaking hands in Grand Central, which she did three times. Each time, within moments of her arrival, crowds of hundreds of people formed instantly, reaching halfway across the terminal's cavernous waiting room. Near the end of the campaign, she held a meeting in a Chinese restaurant in Flushing with Asian community leaders, and while she was inside, word got out in the neighborhood. By the time she emerged a half hour later, the street outside the restaurant was jammed so tight with hundreds of people chanting "Hillary!" that it was completely impassable. Mounted police were ordered to do crowd control to keep traffic moving.

Shortly after she moved into their new home in Chappaqua, Hillary went to the local Grand Union supermarket. No reporters went along; it was apparently supposed to be a normal grocery-shopping outing. But her description of it afterward made it clear that Hillary simply can't go grocery shopping like a normal person.

"I went to the supermarket in Chappaqua . . . and I could not get up and down the aisles," she told Michael Tomasky in *New York* magazine. ". . . I can't seem to get anywhere without drawing so much attention that I can't really do what I came to do. I suppose I could go to the theater, because the lights go out. But I don't know how to do this. I'm having a really hard time." No wonder President Bush—the father, not the son—didn't know what a scanner was when he visited a supermarket during his administration.

And while most politicians rely on the media to help them communicate their ideas and self-images to thousands and sometimes millions of voters whom they can't possibly meet individually, Hillary was already, by the time she began campaigning, the most famous woman in the world. I almost never attended a Hillary event without running into someone who was doing a story on her for the international press, and by the time the campaign was over, I'd met reporters from Brazil, England, France, Germany, Holland, Italy, Japan, Norway, and Turkey. Why did their audiences care about Hillary? "In France she is a star," Laura Haim, who worked for a French TV station, Canal Plus, told me. "She's powerful, independent, bright, modern. She's what every French woman wants to be." Which seemed *très* bizarre, since so many American women view her as exactly the type of person they *don't* want to be—a humiliated wife.

Every one of these foreign reporters would complain about the lack of access, about her staff's nonresponsiveness, and ask local reporters like me for tips on how they could get an interview with her. How would they get their stories done without a one-on-one? they would fret. And to every one of them I would give the same answer: "The lack of access *is* the story. Hang around for a few days and you'll see what I mean."

In February (of 2000), when she officially launched her campaign with Bill by her side at an event in Purchase (the fourth launching), she decided to do away with her last name. Who needs the formality of a surname when your first name is relatively unusual and your fame is unparalleled? Elvis, Cher, Madonna, Oprah, and now, Hillary! Until February, Howard had always, when speaking to us about her, referred to her as "Mrs. Clinton" (although he called her Hillary in person), and her schedules and press releases always had her full name, Hillary Rodham Clinton, printed on top. But the banner used as a backdrop at the Purchase campaign kickoff read, simply, "Hillary," and from then on, the campaign press releases also referred to just plain "Hillary," no last name required. Later in the year, when the presidential campaign was in full swing, there were even buttons that read "Gore-Lieberman-Hillary." I guess "Al-Joe-Hillary" just didn't cut it, and "Gore-Lieberman-Clinton" was more than the vice president could bear.

Of course, dropping her last name was also a way of trying to make her seem less formal, less reserved, more accessible and friendly. But one of the great ironies of this transformation was that Hillary was on a first-name basis with everyone except the reporters who covered her. She called us by our first names, but we never called her by her first name. To us, she was always "Mrs. Clinton."

I remember interviewing Schumer after he'd won the election but before he'd been sworn in. I started to call him "Senator," then interrupted myself and asked, "What is your title now? 'Senator-elect'?" "Just call me Chuck," he replied. I couldn't imagine Hillary ever inviting us to call her by her first name; and if we had, somehow, it would have seemed disrespectful. John Riley of *Newsday* did it once when asking her whether she'd mischaracterized Lazio's position on privatizing Social Security. "Hillary! Hillary!" he called out forcefully to get her attention. It worked. She looked at him, and so did the rest of us, and then she finished answering his question.

"I've always called people I cover by their first names," John told me later. "Somehow, the notion that you weren't supposed to do that with Hillary had gotten inside me just like everyone else. But there was no rational reason for it that I could see, and it seemed to be part of an aura that caused her to get special treatment and insulated her from a certain type of scrutiny. We could throw jabs and she knew how to duck and move, but it was against the rules to get inside and work the body. It seemed absurd that she didn't get called by her first name, so I consciously decided to do it."

One of my all-time favorite Hillary songs addressed this whole issue of her first name. It was a spoof of a 1995 hit called "One of Us" that asked, "What if God were one of us?" The parody went like this:

What if Hil was one of us? Could she tawk like one of us?

A verse in the original song speculated about what to call God to his face, and the matching verse for Hillary went:

If Hil was her name . . . would you call it to her face?

It was also odd that Hillary never appeared on any Sunday-morning TV talk show during the campaign. She didn't avoid TV entirely; she appeared several times on her friend Rosie O'Donnell's show, was interviewed by WCBS-TV reporter Marcia Kramer on a weekday afternoon show, showed up regularly on the morning talk shows like *Today* and *Good Morning America*, and also did an interview for Lifetime. All of these outlets had predominantly female audiences, so they were strategic choices given her campaign's effort to cultivate support among female voters. But none of them were hardball political shows like NBC's *Meet the Press* or ABC's *This Week*. On those shows Hillary would send her surrogates—Wolfson and deBlasio and Ickes and James Carville and Mandy Grunwald, a former Moynihan aide and now a high-priced, Washington-based political consultant, or sometimes Ed Koch or Charlie Rangel. But she never went herself. Meanwhile, both Giuliani and Lazio made a point of blitzing the Sunday-morning shows. Did Hillary and her campaign simply deem these shows an inefficient way to reach the New York voters who needed convincing? Were they afraid that more national exposure than she was already getting would do even more to mobilize the Hillary-haters around the country who were donating millions of dollars to her Republican opponents? Or were they worried that she'd blunder under questioning by big-gun interviewers like Brit Hume and Tim Russert? Once, a few weeks before election day, I asked her if she was ever going to do the Sunday-morning TV circuit. "I'm going to be talking to the voters of New York and the press of New York," she said.

After the election, several of her campaign aides explained that they always felt the New York–based media had generally given her a fair shake, while the cable talk shows and out-of-town press focused more on the White House scandals, her personality, and other issues. "It was an interesting dichotomy," one adviser told me. "You all reported on who she was as a candidate. You would listen to what she had to say and report it." The rest of the media, the adviser felt, seemed less concerned with the substance of her remarks than her style. Even at the end of the campaign, the adviser recalled, commentators on some of the cable TV shows were still complaining that "she never talks to the press, she's the Queen of England. . . . By then, there was an avail practically every day."

It was true. By the time election day drew near, basic media access had improved dramatically. The avails became more frequent and more orderly; Hillary became more accustomed to answering questions about whatever was in the news that day, and her comfort level with us increased to the point where she was actually friendly and funny. When I and another AP reporter had a private interview with her in February (of 2000) in Buffalo, we had so many questions that had never been asked of her that we could have sat there for hours. (We only got forty-five minutes.) But in July, five months later, when we interviewed her in Corning, there was little new ground left to cover. Yet in the second interview, she was much more personable and at ease with us.

Shortly after the Corning interview, I ran into Jesse Drucker, who had covered the campaign for a few months for *Salon*. I told him about how much nicer she was being to everyone, and he said, "Yeah, but did she *open up?*" Well, no, I had to admit, she hadn't, and I didn't think she ever would.

I was with my sister-in-law when I ran into Jesse, and afterward she said to me, "What makes him think that Hillary should open up to him?" Well, some politicians do reveal their inner feelings, especially in New York, and you're never left wondering how they feel about anything or where they stand. But others don't. Hillary, it seemed, would always be in the latter category. It wasn't just logistics that limited her media access. It was also that the woman who had suffered more public humiliation in the White House than any other first lady in history had gotten through it by holding her head high and telling people that the choices she made in her marriage were her business and nobody else's. She wasn't going to cry or scream or name-call or give out any juicy tidbits, and that applied not just to questions about her marriage but to questions about everything else, too. Some people respected her for it; others held it against her. She'd taken the Queen Elizabeth approach to dignity in the face of dirt, but that didn't always go over big in the land of *Oprah* and *Jerry Springer*.

Early on in Hillary's campaign, AP photographer Bebeto Matthews had been told by Howard that he would let us take some "behind the scenes" photos of her. We imagined an interesting photo array of Hillary in her campaign war room, meeting with her top advisers; Hillary in her van, exhausted after a long day; maybe even Hillary powdering her nose right before she gives a speech. But it never happened. In the fall, we asked again for better photo access, and again, it never materialized.

Lazio provided the contrast for what might have been: his campaign allowed AP photographer Richard Drew to stick to him like glue, riding with him in his personal van and spending time on the bus with his wife, Pat, and their two daughters. The resulting photos—Daddy Rick painting his little girls' fingernails with felt-tip markers, Rick and Pat catching a quick snooze in their seats between campaign stops, Lazio gazing out the window right before election day, looking very much like a man about to be defeated—were widely used in newspapers around the state. Sometimes you'd catch someone on Hillary's staff staring at a photo of Lazio in the paper, as if the person couldn't figure out why that photo had been used instead of a picture of Hillary standing at a lectern. On election night, we had a photographer in Lazio's suite, but nobody saw Hillary until she came out to give her victory speech.

So guarded were Hillary's private moments that when we did manage to observe one, it was unforgettable. "One little nothing moment sticks out in my memory," recalled Liz Moore of *Newsday*. "I had this sit-down interview with her in Nassau County on her Long Island tour. We were in a side room at one of these catering halls. We finished the interview, I got up to leave, and as I'm walking out of the room, she stretches and yawns. It was a normal human thing to do, but it was so shocking to me to actually see her yawn."

In *The Making of the President, 1960,* Theodore White pioneered a much imitated method of observing candidates up close and writing in colorful detail about who they were and how they behaved, not just what they said in their stump speeches. But by 1972, when White was interviewed for *The Boys on the Bus*, he mused that the media's intrusion on the candidates' personal moments had gotten out of hand. Recalling the night George McGovern won the Democratic presidential nomination, White said, "There were three different network crews at different times. The still photographers kept coming in, in groups of five. And there were at least six writers sitting in the corner—I don't even know their names. We're all sitting there watching him work on his acceptance speech, poor bastard. . . . All of us are observing him, taking notes like mad, getting all the little details. Which I think I invented as a method of reporting and which I now sincerely regret. If you write about this, say that I sincerely regret it. Who gives a fuck if the guy had milk and Total for breakfast? There's a conflict here—the absolute need of the public to know versus the candidate's need for privacy, which is an equivalent and absolute need. I don't know how you resolve it."

Hillary resolved it for us. We never did get our behind-the-scenes access, and we never found out exactly why. Was it her elaborate first lady security operation? Her own strong personal reserve and high-walled zone of privacy? Her decision? Her advisers'? Or just the reality that hers could never be a normal campaign? An AP photographer *always* rode on the president's plane. I'd ridden on a plane with D'Amato and Pataki during the '98 campaign, and my colleague Frank Eltman rode on a plane with Lazio and on buses with Pataki and Giuliani during the 2000 Senate race. The candidate doesn't give up all privacy in these situations; there are ground rules involving where the press sits, what's on the record and what's off the record, and when it's okay to take pictures. But that, apparently, wasn't good enough for Hillary. No member of the media ever set foot in Hillary's plane, and we didn't even have pictures of her getting off it. (Not only that, but no member of the press ever set foot in her van, either.) If we landed at the airport with her, we could only assume that the 707-sized jet, with no mark on it but a code number, was hers. But her staff would time the arrivals so we couldn't see her disembarking, or would spin the plane around upon landing so that the side with the door was facing away from us. (Keeping us away from the plane also limited discussion of the controversy over who was paying for it. Like presidents and vice presidents who campaign for reelection, Hillary paid only the equivalent of one first-class airfare for each of her trips aboard a plane that cost around $3,000 an hour to operate. She used the government-subsidized jet because of security concerns, but Republicans were always demanding that she reimburse the taxpayers for the entire cost of the flights, and not just what was required under the law.)

All this lack of access was in stark contrast to what the New York media usually got from publicity-hungry politicians. Ed Koch when he was mayor met with the press so many times each day at City Hall that reporters sometimes wondered how he was getting any work done. Even Giuliani, who has a notoriously antagonistic relationship with the press, gave reporters an opportunity to ask him questions nearly every weekday. That's not to say he made it easy; he didn't. He frequently held the avails in faraway corners of the city while presiding over some other event, instead of at City Hall, where it would be much more convenient for the press to attend. And he often refused to answer the questions he was asked. He also got angry with reporters who asked him about controversial or personal subjects—police brutality or his prostate cancer, for example. But even an angry response or a refusal to respond is something you can report. At least you can let your readers know that, hey, we *tried* to get the answer to this, and this guy you elected blew up at us or went mum. That observation may in fact give the public as much of a basis for judging their leaders as the actual answer to the question.

Gabe Pressman, a WNBC-TV correspondent who began working in City Hall in 1949 and is still covering politics, once told me Hillary was "the least accessible candidate I had ever covered in New York. I think the Secret Service was not the culprit; I think the campaign itself wanted us to hold back from asking her questions. Is there an avail today? No, maybe tomorrow; we had one yesterday. . . . The pope has audiences; queens have audiences. Candidates shouldn't have audiences. . . . My experience covering candidates in New York is that they're available. On the other hand, it's White House style. . . . I think she really believes in her heart that this is the way it's done and that we're an unruly, irreverent bunch."

Pressman blames the press corps for not making a bigger fuss about the lack of access. "We could have taught her in one day—just say, 'Whaddaya mean, there's no avail?' " But in truth, we did complain, and as time went on, some of us—including me—made it a personal policy to stake her out and shout a question on a day when there was no avail. But only sometimes did she stop to answer.

With Schumer and D'Amato, if we had any complaints about access, it was that there was too much of it. The two of them were a couple of publicity hounds vying to outfax each other. D'Amato, like a lot of politicians, had a system where you could reach him twenty-four hours a day, seven days a week, by paging a spokesman. He would then personally call back within minutes, even on a Sunday afternoon or late at night, as if he had nothing better to do.

And when I went to write a profile of Schumer, his press secretary, Cathie Levine—who, like Howard, later went to work for Hillary's campaign—not only had him call me at home to chat, but also supplied his mother's phone number so I could interview her. Mama Schumer told me she'd been amazed when her son had gone into politics because, as a little boy, he'd been terribly shy. Somehow I couldn't imagine Howard inviting me to call Hillary's mother to find out what she'd been like as a little girl.

I did get one five-minute phone call from Hillary once during the campaign. It was when I was writing a story about how she was shedding her image as a cold, aloof first lady by sticking around after every event to shake hands, sign autographs, pose for photos, and chat. The personal contact really impressed voters, and when I asked Howard for comment, he said he'd have her call me.

"Is that Beth?" came a familiar voice on the other end of the line when it rang at my desk. "This is Hillary Clinton!" I was so shocked that it took me a minute to remember why I'd wanted to speak with her.

A lot of reporters and photographers also complained that they were never sure Hillary knew who they were, or that it took her much longer than the average candidate to get to know them. Part of this was due to our huge numbers, but it was also because she held far fewer avails and often positioned herself physically far away from us, forcing us to shout our questions over the audience. I covered Hillary for months before I was certain that she knew my name. In contrast, just a few weeks after I started covering Schumer, when I started to identify myself before asking a question, he interrupted me to say, "I know exactly who you are."

The Schumer and D'Amato campaigns also always made sure the press corps was fed. If we were on the road, there was a break around lunchtime in a place with restaurants, or sandwiches on the plane. The Lazio campaign was also careful, on most days, to keep the press corps well fed. Only Hillary's campaign would start with an event at 7 or 8 A.M. and keep you going without a break for the next eight hours. "I'm starving!" someone would always be wailing by late afternoon, at which point the driver would feel sorry for us and order pizza by cell phone to be delivered to the van, or we would scrounge around in our bags for snacks and end up passing around a half-eaten bag of cookies or split a bagel four ways as if we were trying to survive the siege of Leningrad. I took to packing sandwiches wrapped in tin foil, like a kid on a school trip; AP photographer Suzanne Plunkett and I lived for an entire week at one point on my egg-salad sandwiches as we catapulted from one Hillary event to another.

Once Lazio started making Hillary look bad in this department, not only by providing food but also by renting a big press bus equipped with electrical outlets for laptops, cable TV, and a bathroom, Hillary said something to us about how much more money his campaign had than hers, and that's why he had superior accommodations. "I'd buy you an ocean liner if I could!" she said grandly. But in truth every news organization was billed for the transportation and other amenities—except for the occasional box of doughnuts thrown to us by a sympathetic staff member.

Occasionally, though, the first lady herself took pity on us. Once when we arrived at a synagogue on Long Island where she was making a speech to a women's group, we could see into the temple kitchen from the parking lot and began salivating over the nice sit-down lunch being prepared for the ladies. Hillary's van pulled up a minute later, and as she got out, she looked over and saw us leering at the food.

"What's the matter, aren't they going to feed you?" she called out with a laugh. It was sometime in April (of 2000), and a new poll that day had shown her surging ahead of Giuliani, who was then still in the race, and we had all noticed that she was in an incredibly sunny mood. A few minutes after we got inside, one of the hosts of the event brought over two huge baskets overflowing with bagels and rolls, compliments of Hillary.

When the event was over and we piled back into our van, the driver turned around and handed us another basket chock-full of candy and cookies.

"Where did this come from?" someone asked. The driver said it had been given to Hillary as a gift by the synagogue, and she had had one of her aides turn it over to us.

"You're kidding," I said. The driver insisted it was true, and I dug in. As each reporter climbed into the van and was offered a chocolate, the story was repeated and was met with the same incredulous reaction: "No way." "Tell me the truth." "Are you sure?" "Who told you that?" It was like Halloween on the press van, and none of us could believe that

Hillary was being so nice to us. We were like a pack of ragamuffins who'd been ignored all our lives by a fancy lady living next door until one day she suddenly decides to shower us with goodies. Who knew what might be next? More press conferences? Personal interviews? Phone calls returned promptly by her staff? We could only dream. In fact, just a few months later she actually ventured onto a bus carrying the press on one of her upstate tours, chatted for twenty minutes, and personally handed out cookies from a local bakery with her image on them in colorful icing. I wasn't lucky enough to be in attendance that day, but it was the talk of the press corps for a long time.

In *The Boys on the Bus*, Crouse complains about how Nixon's press secretary, Ron Ziegler, drove reporters nuts with his refusals to give out the most basic information and his red herrings, announcements about obscure developments that were specifically designed to divert attention from what he knew was the news of the day. At one point, Ziegler told the reporters to form a committee to come up with a rule for how the press conferences should end. Ziegler felt that the system in place, in which a wire-service reporter ended the news conferences with a singsong "Thank you," had become too chaotic, with some reporters continuing to ask questions after the "Thank you" was uttered.

I couldn't help but think that those guys didn't know how good they had it. Hillary's press conferences also always ended with a "Thank you, Mrs. Clinton." But it wasn't a reporter who got to say it. It was Howard.

Chapter 6

What's the Lead?

March 1, 2000. "What's the lead?" a voice calls out.

We are riding around suburban Rockland County in a van with four rows of seats packed so tight—three and four people per row—that it feels like a city bus at rush hour. Everyone is busy mumbling into cell phones, shuffling paper in skinny, spiral-bound reporter's notebooks, and fast-forwarding cassette recorders with a high-pitched squeak. We are using the tapes to double-check the quotes we scribbled down illegibly as Hillary talked to the kids inside the Valley Cottage School. And we are glumly calling our offices with the usual disappointing news: there *is* no news.

No, we tell our editors, Hillary's not doing an avail.

No, she didn't attack Rudy.

No, she still hasn't made any comment on the Diallo case, four days after the verdict came down.*

---

*Amadou Diallo, an African immigrant who worked as a street vendor, was shot to death by four white police officers as he stood in the doorway of his Bronx home. The officers were charged with murder and testified that they had fired at Diallo because they mistakenly believed the wallet he was holding was a gun. They then mistook their own gunfire for his, and when one of the four cops tripped on the building's front steps, the other officers thought Diallo had shot him. In fact, Diallo had no weapon and had not engaged in any

And, no, she didn't utter one word about the story that was on every front page in America that day: the fatal shooting of one six-year-old by another in a Michigan school.

"So what's the lead?" the voice repeats.

It's the usual group in the van—print reporters for the *New York Post*, the *Daily News*, the *New York Times*, and me, for the Associated Press; producers for NBC and ABC; a couple of still photographers; and one of Hillary's press aides, Karen Dunn. (Someone from Hillary's staff was always on the van with us, which was usually to our mutual benefit. We could get our questions about the events answered—sometimes—and they could eavesdrop on our conversations and report back to Hillary Central how her message was going over with the media that day.)

Behind us are a couple more vans carrying TV crews, and ahead of us are Hillary and her aides in her van, a shiny black-and-gray custom Ford with tinted windows and white Washington, D.C., plates that begin with the letters *AR*, as in "Arkansas"; it would be months before she'd switch to New York plates. Her van has a raised roof a foot high, and I always wonder what's stored inside. Her aides insist it just provides extra headroom, but I can't help thinking that maybe there's a nuclear hot line up there, just in case the president catches a ride with her, or some kind of satellite tracking device in case she's kidnapped. I once asked Gregg Birnbaum of the *New York Post* what he thought was up there and he said, "I have no idea. I've never been in the van. *No one* has ever been in the van." One of the AP photographers, Suzanne Plunkett, calls it the Hillary Mystery Van. Bob Hardt from the *Post* and Joel Siegel from the *Daily News* call it HRC Speedwagon, a reference to an old rock band, REO Speedwagon. At various points during the cam-

---

criminal behavior; the officers had been on patrol and stopped their car in front of Diallo's house because they deemed the way he was looking up and down his block suspicious. The case prompted widespread charges of police brutality and racial profiling, but a jury accepted the officers' explanation for their actions and found them innocent of murder.

paign, I became obsessed with peeking into the van, just because it was so completely off-limits to us. One day, looking through the window on the driver's side at the backseat where Hillary sat, I noticed a huge, ugly plastic shopping bag from the Duane Reade drugstore. It appeared to be overflowing with items that I could not make out through the tinted glass, but I found it amusing to imagine one of Hillary's aides running into Duane Reade like everybody else in New York, filling a shopping basket with lipstick and Tylenol and little packs of tissues and nail files and panty hose and breath mints and Band-Aids and God knows what else. Even a first lady has to wipe her nose sometimes. Then, of course, I felt like a media vulture. Jeez, couldn't the woman make a trip to the drugstore without *me* trying to snoop around on her?

Back in the van in Rockland County, the voice that has insistently been repeating "What's the lead?" at low volume suddenly changes to a commanding tone. This woman has never ridden with us before, and she doesn't know any of us, but we all know her. She's Mary McGrory, the legendary political columnist for the *Washington Post*. She's old enough to be my grandmother, and although her writing and reporting are as sharp as ever—and I would be the first to admit, better than mine—age has affected her legs and hips. It's so hard for her to get in and out of the vehicle's sliding door that the other reporters have taken to bodily boosting her up from the ground into the seat. This would be utterly humiliating for anyone else, but for McGrory, it's just another reason to respect her. She was already fifty-five when Crouse included her as one of the only women in *The Boys on the Bus*, and she's still slogging along the campaign trail twenty-eight years later, when most of her peers long ago took desk jobs, retired, went into public relations, or became journalism professors.

Still, her question—"What's the lead?"—goes unanswered. There is an embarrassed silence for a minute or two. The daily newspaper reporters never share their leads. It just isn't done. Why is she asking?

Surely Mary McGrory doesn't need any help in figuring out the lead. But I don't care. Half my colleagues already heard my lead as I dumped my notes by cell phone to another reporter back at AP's Rockefeller Center headquarters. Everybody gets the wire, so discretion is pointless.

I don't even need to check my notes to answer McGrory's question. "Hillary Rodham Clinton led several hundred children at a Rockland County elementary school in a pledge against gun violence," I recite from memory in a monotone. A couple of giggles, a wave of relief; now nobody else has to divulge his or her approach to today's story.

"Thank you," McGrory says grandly.

"Hey, I'm AP. I've got no secrets," I say, shrugging. Even so, I'm feeling just slightly ashamed that there's no more news than that. The lead should have been Hillary's comment on one of the top two news stories—the Diallo acquittals or the Michigan classroom shooting. But we can't write about her comments on these stories because we don't have her comments on these stories. We'd been three feet away from her as she chatted with kids inside the Valley Cottage school, but somehow none of us—not a one—had managed to ask her a question.

So instead, the story had to be about this antigun pledge. It wasn't a bad lead; Hillary had asked a group of fifth-graders in the auditorium to promise that they'd never touch weapons or use them in anger, saying, "Would you do that as good citizens for us?" The children shouted "Yes" and "I promise" in response. It made a nice little sound bite for TV and radio, and at least it was about gun violence on a day when gun violence was in the news. But it just wasn't explicitly enough about six-year-olds killing each other to be widely used in newspaper stories. If a story about Hillary is newsworthy enough, it makes it off the AP's New York wire to the national wire. But it was clear that this story wasn't going national.

"What's wrong with us?" Eileen Murphy, a producer for ABC, had lamented as we'd stood in the school, close enough to touch Hillary, stupidly waiting for her to do what we knew she never would—to just turn to us and make this story, this trip, this boring day, worthwhile with a sentence or two about the real news on everyone's mind. "We're still treating her like a first lady!"

She was right. If Hillary had been any other candidate, we would have walked right up to her and asked her what needed to be asked. But we'd been told there'd be no avail today, and we'd accepted it. That didn't prevent me from feeling slightly humiliated. I was so worn down and so exasperated by the lack of access and the lack of news in this campaign that I'd given up fighting, and no reporter wants to admit that. I kept trying to rationalize what was happening, telling myself, "It's not me. It's her." Any other candidate would recognize the news of the day and capitalize on it. Any other candidate would realize that the press and the voters expect you to weigh in on whatever's making head-lines, whether it has to do with the office you're seeking or not. It's how people figure out who you are and what your values are.

But other candidates weren't surrounded by Secret Service agents. Other candidates wouldn't stand a chance of attracting an entourage of reporters if all they were doing was schlepping to a suburban elemen-tary school. Other candidates weren't the only first lady in history to ever run for office.

Some of the reporters covering Hillary had also spent time cover-ing Senator John McCain's presidential campaign, and as we rode away from the Rockland County school where we'd had no access to the first lady, we couldn't help but compare her to McCain, whose access never ended. McCain talked all day long with reporters on his Straight Talk Express bus; he talked so much that he sometimes said things he shouldn't have, and that's why the media loved him. Just a month after Hillary visited the Valley Cottage School, McCain—a Republican sup-porting Giuliani's bid against Hillary—told students at a forum at

Columbia University that if Hillary made it to the Senate, "She would be a star of the quality that has not been seen in the Senate since Bobby Kennedy was elected senator from the state of New York." It was hard to imagine any other Republican saying anything like that about Hillary, even though in private they probably all agreed. And the notion that Hillary would ever make such an unguarded comment about a Republican was unthinkable.

We also agreed among ourselves that if the Senate race didn't work out, Hillary should definitely pursue a career as an elementary school teacher. She'd read Maurice Sendak's *Chicken Soup With Rice* to a first-grade class in the library that day, and the kids had just adored her. She opened her big blue eyes wide, sat on a low chair so that she was nearly eye level with them, and encouraged them to read along with her; she seemed less a first lady than an enthusiastic mom volunteer. But I couldn't help wincing as she read, "Merry once, merry twice, merry chicken soup with rice," pronouncing *merry* the way somebody from Brooklyn pronounces *Mary*. In New York, *merry*, *marry*, and *Mary* all have a distinctly different vowel sound—*merry* has an *eh* sound, as in *bed*; *marry* has an *ah* sound, as in *back*; and *Mary* has a soft *ay-er* sound as in *air*. Not so in the Midwest, where Hillary's from, and where all three words sound alike. "You guys ought to coach her on stuff like that," I cheerfully advised Karen Dunn, who chose not to dignify my gratuitous kibitzing with a response.

Next stop was a hotel luncheon with a Rockland County business group. As she blathered on about issuing technology bonds to help communities finance high-speed Internet connections, I noticed that most of my colleagues had stopped taking notes. This lady was all substance and no sound bites.

Then we piled back into the van for a return trip to Manhattan, only to have Karen suddenly announce a surprise stop: a striking nurses' picket line at Nyack Hospital.

This seemingly innocuous news was met with groans, whines, and muttering. Another hour before we could get back to our offices. Another event with no news. Another example of how disorganized her press office was.

But soon it became clear that while the visit to the picket line was a surprise to us, the striking nurses had been told beforehand. As the vans—ours, hers, and the others in our entourage—pulled up by the sidewalk where the nurses were rallying, I could see that some of them were wearing "Hillary" buttons and carrying "Hillary" signs. This wasn't a sign of disorganization by her press office; this was something they had deliberately concealed from us till the last minute. Why they chose to do this was unclear.

Half the press stayed in the van; there was no reason to expend any energy to cover this. But now I was angry—angry that we had never got our avail, angry that we hadn't managed to ask her for a comment earlier, angry that the schedule was being screwed around with. I was determined to get close enough to her to ask something, anything. I moved through the crowd of nurses as she did, keeping her directly in my line of sight. At one point, I stopped to get the name of a nurse who'd asked her a question, and when I tried to reposition myself near Hillary, a Secret Service agent who'd seen me dozens of times in the past put his hand out and ordered me to move away. If it hadn't happened to me fifty times before, I would have been outraged. After all, I had a credential issued by the NYPD; they had my photo and Social Security number on file. Any nutcase could walk right up to her, and they're acting like I'm the threat. But arguing with him would have been a waste of time; so I simply crossed the street, ran ahead a quarter of a block, stood where I knew she was headed, then rejoined the pack when she reached me.

Her van was moving up the street along with her entourage. Obviously she was preparing to leave. I was a foot away from her, caught her eye, and seized my chance. "Gun violence, Mrs. Clinton?" I shouted.

"Can you give us your thoughts on gun violence?" It was too noisy and chaotic to ask a complicated question specifically about the Michigan shooting; the idea here was to throw out a phrase, as simple and loud as possible, to grab her attention. If she had anything at all to say on the Michigan shooting, this was her opportunity.

She looked right at me for a second and hesitated. I could see that she'd heard me. Then she lowered her eyes from mine, made a slight gesture with her hand as if to say, "I'm done here," and got in her van without a word.

I was disappointed and even felt a little stupid. But at least I couldn't kick myself any longer for not having attempted to get her. Eileen was right; we shouldn't be treating her like a first lady. Even if she wasn't going to answer me, from now on I was going to ask.

The next day, Mary McGrory's column about the trip contained two unforgettable lines: "A splendid elementary teacher was plainly lost when Hillary married Bill and politics" and "The ladies on the Hillary press van . . . call her 'the un-McCain.' " I wasn't sure whether any of us had actually uttered that phrase, or whether Mary had simply captured what we were feeling more articulately than we could say it ourselves.

That afternoon Hillary was scheduled to be interviewed on WCBS-TV by Marcia Kramer. Marcia could be a bulldog in a one-on-one interview. Her claim to fame, in fact, was with Hillary's husband in 1992, when she'd pinned him down on his previously elusive responses to questions about his marijuana usage. "I never broke the laws of my country" gave way, in Marcia's deft handling, to his admission that while he'd once put a joint to his mouth, he'd never actually inhaled.

So I was hoping for a similar bombshell as I arrived at the WCBS studio to watch the taping. Gregg Birnbaum was there, too, but none of the other regulars had bothered to show up. They could just as easily watch it from their offices, but Gregg and I figured it was worth going to the station on the off chance that we'd catch Hillary outside. But as the interview wore on, it was clear no news would be committed. Outside, afterward, we looked for the Speedwagon, but she'd already taken off. Then we spotted Howard and another press aide, Karen Finney.

Gregg started to give Howard a hard time about the fact that it had been five days since the Diallo verdict and we still hadn't had a chance to ask her for a comment—not to mention the fact that there hadn't been any other news coming out of the Hillary campaign in a while.

"What about yesterday?" Howard said, referring to the Valley Cottage School event.

"There was no news in that!" Gregg said.

"Hey, I read a nice little story on the AP wire about it," Howard said with a smile.

Of course, Howard knew that a nice little story about Hillary leading children in pledges against gun violence just isn't news in the *New York Post.* The paper's editorial cartoons typically portrayed Hillary on a broomstick; and while the *Post* ran the photo of her kissing Suha Arafat as the "wood," newspaper jargon for the front page, the paper's exclusive photo of Lazio grinning ear to ear as he shook Yasir Arafat's hand was deemed unworthy of page one and appeared inside instead.

I decided to ask Howard about the Million Mom March, an antigun protest planned for Mother's Day in Washington, D.C. I'd been seeing Million Mom March sign-up sheets at my older son's school and at our local synagogue, and it seemed like the type of event that would be a natural for Hillary.

"Million Mom March?" Howard asked. "What's that?"

I explained and added that I'd called the organizers in Washington, and they'd told me that in an effort to keep it nonpartisan, they didn't want politicians to speak at the rally, but they had invited Hillary to take part in the march and hadn't heard back from her office.

"Hillary's a mom," Howard mused. "She could march. I'll find out and get back to you."

Howard frequently offered to find things out and get back to people, but because so many people were always asking him for one piece of obscure information or another, he often did not follow through. It wasn't that he was lazy or inefficient; it was just that he didn't have time to respond to everyone. His pager and cell phone were constantly going off; he often started his day at dawn by buying the papers and ended it after the 11 P.M. news shows. When he was in the office, he was continuously both on the phone and the computer, simultaneously answering calls and e-mails from the dozens of media outlets clamoring for a little piece of Hillary.

Of course, when he didn't like something someone had written, he'd find them in an instant and complain vigorously by phone or e-mail. Other times he'd actually call to say he liked a story. He once called me up to compliment a lead I'd written for a Hillary story, then added, "You know, it would be even better if . . ." Needless to say, I had no intention of rewriting my lead based on Howard's suggestions.

He also had a dry sense of humor and was generally calm in the face of small crises. Once when he was holding a news conference in City Hall Park in front of a bevy of reporters, an extremely bedraggled and obviously disturbed homeless man walked over, stood next to him, and started to babble. Howard didn't miss a beat. He looked the man in the eye, smiled, and said, "Would you mind just waiting a minute till I finish?" The man took a step back and did just that. AP photographer Bebeto Matthews took a picture of Howard holding court with the homeless man, and another photographer later presented a copy of it to Hillary.

In other ways, however, Howard seemed a little bit eccentric. He was allergic to chocolate, nuts, and a hundred other things and was often sick or inexplicably injured—such as the time he hurt his foot stumbling in a bookstore or the time he showed up at a press conference, his face red and swollen from an allergic reaction. He was terrified of flying and would take the train or drive to upstate cities hours from Manhattan to avoid taking a plane to Hillary's events. He was notorious for paying little attention to his appearance and walked around for the longest time with a huge hole in his shoe. Probably if I knew Howard personally, in the fuller context of his life, some of these quirks might fade into the background, and he wouldn't seem any odder than anyone else. But knowing him only as Hillary's protector and defender meant that on any given day my interaction with Howard was limited to his answering a question about Hillary while I noticed that he had a cold or a limp.

In contrast to Howard, there were a group of women on Hillary's staff that I often thought of in my head as "the lovelies" because all of them had beautiful smiles and charming personalities. In fact, when Howard recruited Karen Finney to work with him as a press aide, he told her simply, "You're charming. I'm not."

At the time, Finney was working as chief of staff to the CEO of Scholastic; she'd previously worked for five years in the Clinton White House, ending up as the first lady's deputy press secretary, before escaping to a seminormal life in the private sector—a life where, as she put it, she actually had time to buy groceries and go out with her friends. She went to Scholastic never intending to return to politics, but Howard—and Hillary—talked her into it.

Karen Dunn, whom Howard had brought in from Nita Lowey's staff, was already working on Hillary's campaign when Finney was hired. Dunn, who is white and stands five feet tall, was momentarily concerned that having two Karens on staff would be confusing. "I don't think that will be a problem," Howard said. "Karen Finney is a six-foot-tall black woman." (Actually, Finney's mother is white and her father is black.) I sometimes felt like the first lady had purposely surrounded herself with all these warm, sweet, pretty young women—the Karens; her two blond personal assistants, Kelly Craighead and Allison Stein; and later another press aide, Cathie Levine—almost as a foil for the largely humorless Secret Service agents who were always telling us where we couldn't stand.

While my relationship with the Karens was generally one of light, friendly banter, probably from all those hours we spent riding around in the vans together, I sometimes felt paranoid about my dealings with Howard, and I was not the only member of the press corps to experience this insecurity. When Howard didn't get back to you about something—a semipermanent condition for a lot of us—did that mean he was ignoring you, or had he just forgotten? Ellen Wulfhorst of Reuters summed it up this way: "I started to think Howard wasn't talking to me. But then I thought, how would I know the difference?"

In other words, most of us had become accustomed to being blown off by Howard, and you couldn't take it personally. For example, standing outside the WCBS studios that day and asking him about the Million Mom March, I could tell immediately that my query had landed in the dead-mail slot in Howard's mind. No one was on deadline about it. No one was accusing Hillary of doing anything evil. It was the sort of request that, if Howard heard anything about it on his end, he would get back to me, but I knew he wasn't going to go out of his way to pin it down.

So I was peeved to hear that two days later, when Hillary finally got around to holding a press conference—her first in a week—she announced that she was going to take part in the Million Mom March! Now it was out there for everyone to write about. (In the media business, nothing is newsworthy when everyone knows it.)

I was angry and confused. Had Howard been lying to me? Had he really not known? And why, since this had turned out to be important enough for Hillary to make an announcement about, hadn't he followed up on it? But I decided not to confront him about it. Instead, I figured I'd just wait until the next time he called to complain about something I'd written and bring it up then.

I didn't have to wait long. That Sunday, Hil was making what her campaign had billed as a "major" speech at Riverside Church, an extremely liberal and politically active church near Columbia University. Riverside was one of the obligatory stops for politicians on the campaign trail, along with ringing the opening bell on Wall Street, eating at a Jewish deli, and appearing at the 92nd Street Y.

Hillary had traded in her black pantsuit for her going-to-church skirt. Her speech turned out to be a lawyerly appeal for better relations between the police and the citizens they protect. She referred repeatedly to a "false choice" city officials had made between bringing crime down and treating New Yorkers with respect. She had made a similar speech the weekend before at a conference for Dominican New Yorkers, so I wasn't really sure why this was supposed to be such a big deal.

I borrowed a cell phone from a photographer and phoned in some quotes from the speech. My own cell phone had a dead battery. Somehow it had been left on—prime suspect, two-year-old Nathaniel.

From Riverside we headed in a press van to Queens, where Hillary was marching in a small St. Patrick's Day parade five days before the big parade March 17 on Fifth Avenue. Unlike the big event, this smaller march in Queens had decided to allow an Irish gay group to take part. Hillary's new line was that she would march in the big parade to show support for the Irish peace process, and she'd take part in the small parade to show support for the Irish gay group. "It's a case of competing values," she'd repeatedly said.

A lot of reporters hate covering parades because they're chaotic and exhausting. You have to fight with the cops to stand where you want; you have to walk a couple of miles, regardless of the weather; and you have to pay attention every second on the off chance that something dreadful happens. I once covered a St. Patrick's Day parade with Mayor David Dinkins in which beer bottles went whizzing by his head—and mine—and that had taught me once and for all that parades can create a lot of news.

But as I tried to get near Hillary, I realized the police were insisting that the media not walk in the middle of the street with the marchers, but instead stay behind the blue NYPD barricades that had been set up all along the parade route to keep spectators on the sidewalk. Our press credentials specifically state that the bearer "is entitled to pass police and fire lines wherever formed," so at first I ignored the officers who kept telling me to get out of the line of march. Finally a sergeant came over and ordered me in no uncertain terms out of the parade route. The AP, the *Times*, the *Daily News*, and the New York Press Club had just negotiated an agreement with the city over the police department's failure to honor our press passes. The pact stipulated that the NYPD would, in future, allow us to cross police lines unless there was an imminent danger, like a fire or a hostage situation. But now I had this sergeant in my face. I asked him whether he was familiar with the agreement, but he simply repeated his order that I get on the sidewalk. The AP later protested the incident at a meeting with police brass, but for me to argue it out on the street would have meant having my press pass confiscated. That was a hassle I didn't have time for, so I did as he asked. One by one every reporter and camera crew was relegated to the same area as the spectators.

But the sidewalk turned out to be a decent vantage point for the story that immediately presented itself. A band of hecklers was walking along the sidewalk, following Hillary and booing her. "Go home!" they were shouting. "Carpetbagger! Go back to Arkansas!" I began interviewing them and discovered that a lot of them were not from the neighborhood, but had made a special trip from Brooklyn or Manhattan for the sole purpose of heckling Hillary. None of them would admit to being Republican goons, but it was all a little suspicious. There were Hillary-hate Web sites and right-wing radio hosts who also loved to trash her; these people could have found out about her participation in the parade from any one of these sources. One lady from Bensonhurst who told me she hated Hillary because she'd been a doormat for Bill's sexual escapades went running down the street, screaming at the first lady at the top of her lungs, *"You're an enabler!"*

That could well be the only example in history in which the phrase "You're an enabler!" has been hurled at a politician with intent to insult.

But as I walked along, I realized that while the traveling band of hecklers was loud, an awful lot of less audible boos and nasty remarks were coming from spectators who did live in the neighborhood and had simply turned out to watch the parade. It seemed to me that this was a story. Hillary's first foray on the streets of New York City had turned into something of a fiasco. In fairness, she was receiving just as many cheers and applause from spectators as she was boos, and she appeared unfazed by the negative reception. But no one had expected this level of hostility. I suddenly realized it was no accident that the story about the emperor's new clothes ends with a little boy speaking the truth at a parade. After all, politicians can surround themselves with yes-men and schedule all their appearances before friendly audiences, but their staffs simply can't control what happens out in the real world. This was Hillary's first full-blown, unprotected exposure to the masses, and it wasn't all pretty.

I found a pay phone and called my office to dump my notes. The national editors wanted to lead with the parade, so that settled my quandary about whether to put the church speech as the lead or the secondary element. Then I hooked up with the press van and headed back into the city.

Shortly after the story moved on the wire, Howard called. I could hear that he was using his deadpan, formal tone of voice as The Man Who Protects Hillary from Bad Publicity.

"I am shocked that on a day when the first lady makes a major policy announcement regarding the police and race relations, the Associated Press would choose to lead with a parade," he said. It was a cross between a Monty Python routine and an ambassador to a troubled nation registering an outraged but scripted protest over human rights.

Of course I had no intention of changing the lead, but as long as I had him on the phone, I figured it was time to talk about the little grievance I'd been nursing.

"Imagine how shocked *I* was to find out, with the rest of the world, that Hillary was marching in the Million Mom March, after I specifically asked you about it and you promised to get back to me," I said, trying to strike the same tone of voice.

"Oh. So this is payback?"

"No, it's not payback. I've just been wondering why you didn't get back to me about it, and this seems like a good time to bring it up."

"I honestly didn't know. When she started talking about the Million Mom March at the press conference, it was a total surprise to me."

In other words, it wasn't that Hillary had Howard keep information away from us; it was that Hillary didn't tell him either.

We had a few more polite go-rounds about the day's story and said good-bye. I knew he'd be as friendly to me the next time I saw him as he always was, and even though I hadn't changed my story in response to his complaint, I wanted him to feel that he could always make a case for his point of view. Every now and then he'd point out an error or ask to have the campaign's point of view portrayed in a different way, and after all, I wanted to be fair, and I wanted to be accurate, and I was willing to listen to any feedback he wanted to give me. On the other hand, I was not a mouthpiece for the campaign. Just because Hillary's people think she's made news doesn't mean I have to agree.

I often told my seven-year-old son what I'd covered that day. I didn't want him to grow up feeling that work was this horrible thing that only took me away from him; I thought it was good to let him know that while I missed him, I was also doing interesting things at my job. He knew all about "Hillary, the president's wife," as he liked to call her; he could pick her out of a photo with a hundred other people in it.

That night I told him that Hillary had made a speech in a church about how the police could do a better job taking care of people. I thought he'd think one thing she mentioned was pretty cool: a new technology that enables cops to scan an area with a laser light and pick up any images shaped like weapons. This would prevent the kind of situation the Diallo cops were in, where they started shooting because they incorrectly thought the guy had a gun. So I described this scanning device to Danny, expecting him to say, "Wow! Neat!" Instead he looked at me very seriously and said, "Do you think they could give that to teachers?" What a crazy world we live in when a seven-year-old thinks teachers should have weapon detectors.

When I went into work the next day, I was surprised to see that the *Post,* the *Times,* and the *Daily News* had agreed with Howard and led with the Riverside speech. I agonized about it for a little while, but in the end I decided I'd made the right choice for the AP. I was writing for an audience of upstaters and out-of-staters, and a statement made ten days after the Diallo verdict just wasn't that important to my readers—especially when it sounded like a retread of what I'd led with the previous weekend when she'd spoken at the Dominican conference. On the other hand, for the first lady to walk down a street and get booed—by anyone for any reason—seemed like news to me.

A few days later, Hillary had a 5 P.M. event at a gay community center in Greenwich Village, but when I got there, it was nowhere near about to begin and looked as if it was going to run very late. It was the day after Super Tuesday, I was tired from having worked late the night before, and I wanted to see my boys, so I decided to skip it. I collected a few phone numbers from people in the audience so that I could make some calls later on and find out what had happened, and I headed home.

When I walked in the door, I saw my answering machine blinking. Bebeto Matthews, the AP photographer, had called to let me know she'd been heckled. A couple of people at the meeting had started screaming at her because she had agreed to march in the main St. Patrick's Day Parade. Damn it! I was angry with myself and slightly panicked that I had missed this. I was responsible for making sure that Hillary was always covered; then finally news happens and I'm not there. But Bebeto had taken some notes, gotten a quote and a name, and I was able to reach some of the people whose numbers I'd taken. I managed to piece together a little story even though I hadn't been there.

She had apparently handled the situation well, asking the hecklers to allow her to deliver her prepared remarks, and then discussing their concerns afterward. She explained that while she was disappointed that the parade does not include a gay contingent, she wanted to support the Irish peace process. "It's a case of competing values," she'd said.

Before I called the story in to my office, I beeped Howard.

"Did you guys run a tape?" I asked when he called back, knowing that the press staff often carried a microcassette recorder to take down her statements.

"Yeah," he replied.

"Can you get me a quote off of it?"

"No."

"Why not?"

"She took it with her."

"Well, can't you get it?"

"Not until tomorrow."

Gee, thanks. But it was my own fault for not sticking around. On the other hand, I was home with my kids. It was a case of *my* competing values—Hillary versus Danny and Nathaniel. I called my office, dictated a short story, and made dinner.

The next day Peggy Noonan's new book came out: *The Case Against Hillary Clinton*. Yet another Hillary hate book—there were so many, it was hard to keep track. Noonan spends part of the book talking about Clinton victims, and after the last few weeks, I was starting to feel like a Clinton victim myself. When I followed Hillary around all day, there was no news. The one time I skipped an event, news happened. If I reported something unflattering, Howard complained. If I wanted to report something that made her look good—the Million Mom March or the way she handled the gay meeting—Howard couldn't help. Noonan's book contended that the Clintons simply hate the media, don't trust them, and stonewall on giving out even the most benign and basic information. That would certainly explain some of what I was experiencing. It might also explain why it sometimes seemed that Howard was being kept in the dark. Why tell your press staff what's going on and take the chance that they might actually tell the press?

My regular days off at the AP were Friday and Saturday, and I tried hard to preserve my schedule just because I felt that my kids deserved to have a mother a couple of days a week no matter what Hillary was doing. Usually if she had any public events either of those days, someone else from my office was assigned to cover her, but if I knew in advance that an important news event was scheduled, I went to work. The St. Patrick's Day Parade obviously counted as a big deal, so I arranged for my younger son to spend the day at his day-care center and asked a neighbor's baby-sitter to pick my older son up from school.

Hillary held a brief news conference before joining the march to restate her "competing values" line. She was wearing a green scarf, and all along the parade route, volunteer supporters wearing "Hillary" pins with little shamrocks were in place to cheer.

But it became obvious almost immediately that this was going to be an even bigger fiasco than the Queens parade. The booing was loud, strong, and persistent. It was so bad that at no point did she veer over to the sidelines to shake hands with spectators. There were a lot of people from the suburbs, a lot of Catholics, a lot of Giuliani supporters, and a lot of people related to cops; this was not a Hillary crowd. The cries of "Go back to Arkansas!" and "Carpetbagger!" were so pervasive that the radio reporters didn't need to seek anybody out for a sound bite; they just walked along the parade route holding out their microphones to catch the ambient sound. As for the problem we'd had with the cops at the previous parade in Queens, it had disappeared. We were allowed to march in the street with Hillary without being hassled.

Hillary, meanwhile, kept a smile frozen on her face and left her arm up in a friendly wave for the entire two miles of the parade route. She had to hear the boos and see the angry looks she was getting, but she never let her reaction show.

It was a gray, freezing, windy day, with intermittent rain and snow, and by the end of it, a lot of people in the press corps—including me—were worn-out, shivering and wet, hair blown to pieces. But Hillary looked beautiful. She didn't have a hat or a muffler or an umbrella, but somehow her makeup had remained perfect and her hairdo was untouched. I had another of my flashes about alternative careers should Hillary's Senate bid fail. Forget becoming an elementary school teacher. She could sell hairspray! Whatever had kept her hair glued in place that blustery day was definitely industrial strength and deserved a wider audience.

I went back to the office and spoke with the reporter who'd covered Giuliani. The mayor had been cheered the whole way and spent so much time shaking hands with supporters that he'd had to take little sprints every block or so to catch back up with the line of march.

Somehow I couldn't wipe the smile off my face. I was tired and cold and wet, but I felt absolutely exhilarated. Another colleague who'd taken some of my notes when I'd called in earlier told me she'd never heard me sound so happy as when I was describing Hillary's reception from the crowd. I explained to her that I wasn't happy because Hillary was being booed; I was just grateful to have a real story for a change. I don't wish Hillary ill; I personally couldn't care less if New Yorkers love her or they hate her. But I finally had news. And I knew what the lead was. And this time I knew Howard wouldn't be calling to complain.

The Trouble with Rudy

April 27, 2000. There's a story in the *New York Post* reporting that the mayor had been in the hospital the day before undergoing tests for prostate cancer. It wasn't a front-page story; after all, the guy wasn't fatally ill, he was just having a test. But shortly after I arrived at work that day, around 8 A.M., the mayor's press office announced he'd be holding a news conference later that morning. Our City Hall reporter, Timothy Williams, would cover it in person, but if it was televised live, as big news from City Hall frequently was on CNN or NY1, I was going to put a few paragraphs on the wire using whatever he said on the tube. In the meantime, I called Bruce Teitelbaum, the spokesman for Giuliani's Senate campaign and a tense man under the best of circumstances. He answered his cell phone immediately but sounded miserable. "Hullo," he muttered. I identified myself and asked if he could give us any information about whether the mayor's health was going to affect his Senate campaign. Slowly, deliberately, and glumly, he replied, "I . . . have . . . nothing . . . to . . . say."

The news conference, as we expected, was televised. In his usual businesslike mode, the mayor stood at the podium in the Blue Room at City Hall, where press conferences are usually held, and confirmed that he'd not only been tested for prostate cancer, but that he actually had the disease. It was caught in an early stage and was treatable, he added. But the very first question, of course, was how this would affect his Senate campaign.

We'd all assumed he was going to say that it wouldn't affect it at all. After all, Joe Torre had an equally demanding and stressful job, and he'd led the Yankees to a World Series victory while undergoing prostate cancer treatment. Bob Dole had prostate cancer, and five years later he ran for president.

But, incredibly, Giuliani admitted that he wasn't sure if he would stay in the race.

"I don't think it's fair to answer questions about the Senate race right now," he said. "Should I do it? Would I be able to do it the right way? I hope that's the case, but I don't know."

That "I don't know" was bigger news than anyone ever expected to come from this news conference. Why would any politician in a cut-throat race like this one—he and Hillary had been neck and neck in the polls for months—admit that a treatable illness might force him to drop out of the race?

He also talked about his father, who had died of prostate cancer, saying words that would be quoted in the months to come after a biography of him by Wayne Barrett revealed that the elder Giuliani had been a small-time hood: "I think about my father every day of my life." And he claimed that the illness had given him a new perspective on life. Was the cold, brusque, take-no-prisoners Rudy morphing into someone kinder and gentler?

A lot of reporters who cover the mayor believe that he is an extremely careful and calculating politician, that his temper tantrums at the press and sometimes callous remarks about people and institutions he despises—such as when he suggested blowing up the Board of Education—are not impulsive, uncontrollable outbursts but deliberate maneuvers designed to appeal to certain segments of his supporters. So there were two ways to look at his admission that cancer had left him uncertain about his prospects for remaining in the race: he had screwed up by answering honestly when he should have put up a brave front and denied that it would affect his aspirations; or he was making a play for the voters' sympathy because Hillary had effectively made his belligerent personality an issue in the race. She'd contended over and over that his inability to compromise and get along with people who disagree with him made him unfit for the Senate, a place where you can't get anything accomplished if you don't make deals with your enemies. We had a lot of fun in the van quoting her favorite pronouncements on the subject. "I reject the politics of division and destruction!" we'd say as dramatically as we could. "I want to lift people up, not pull them down!" But it was a smart tack for her to take, because she couldn't attack his competency—too many voters gave him credit for bringing down crime, cleaning up Times Square, and making New York a more livable place—the kind of place where squeegee men no longer stalked cars at major intersections, subway riders no longer sneaked cigarettes in the stations, and Forty-second Street theaters no longer advertised peep shows. In a city where Democrats outnumber Republican voters five to one, Rudy had swamped his Democratic opponent, Ruth Messinger, in his '97 reelection campaign. Yet he wasn't completely acceptable as a hero in his own party, largely because of his liberal views on abortion, gun control, and gay rights. He'd also crossed party lines at times to endorse Democrats who he thought offered more for city residents than Republicans; his endorsement of Mario Cuomo against George Pataki in '94 had caused a rift between him and the governor that had never healed.

But the same personality that allowed Giuliani to do whatever he thought was right, regardless of public opinion or political alliances, also provided fodder for Hillary's contention that he'd have trouble forming alliances in the Senate and that he was not sensitive enough to the concerns of minorities and the poor.

Some of the pundits suggested that Rudy was trying to counteract that impression by using the cancer announcement to portray himself as vulnerable. But others said he had made a fatal campaign error, that his fund-raising operation—which had brought in $20 million already, with $9 million still unspent when his cancer was made public—would be crippled by the uncertainty and that voters would view him as damaged goods.

But there was a third school of thought. What if Rudy really didn't want to continue the Senate race? What if he'd gotten into it thinking it would be an amusing cakewalk over Hillary, only to find that it was more like a wrestling match that required a lot more of his time than he wanted to devote to it? What if he had no interest in spending the rest of the year hobnobbing in upstate diners and county fairs and factories? What if he was tired of the fund-raising and the polls and having the national media bugging him just as much as the local press did? Hillary had set a goal of visiting every one of New York's sixty-two counties and had been swooping in with her entourage to obscure little places like Penn Yan, a tiny Finger Lakes town whose previous claim to fame was being home to the world's largest buckwheat pancake. Rudy, in contrast, couldn't even be bothered to show up for a "Women for Rudy" fund-raiser that had been scheduled in Rochester a few weeks before his cancer announcement. When the Yankees' opening game got rescheduled for the same day as the Rochester event, Rudy had bagged the ladies' lunch and gone to the stadium. Republicans and upstaters had been grumbling ever since that the mayor wasn't showing a lot of enthusiasm for campaigning north of the Bronx. Maybe the prostate cancer was the excuse he'd been looking for to bow out.

When the mayor's press conference was finished, Timothy Williams took our main story over and wrote a more comprehensive version than what we'd hurriedly rushed onto the wire in the first few minutes. I was assigned to put together a sidebar interviewing the pundits and offering some analysis. Interestingly, the pollsters all predicted that voters wouldn't give a fig about the cancer, that they understood it was a highly treatable condition instead of a death sentence. But the political consultants I spoke with all looked for the deeper significance in why Rudy had cast doubt on the likelihood of his continuing with the campaign. Nelson Warfield, a former New Yorker and onetime press secretary to Bob Dole, won my everlasting esteem by unequivocally predicting, two hours after Rudy had pronounced the words "I don't know," that he would drop out. Warfield told me he didn't think the mayor wanted to be senator anyway, and the cancer would allow him to get out of the race gracefully, without making it look as if he was slinking away from a fight.

Hillary was upstate that day. She steadfastly refused to make any prediction about how the mayor's illness might affect the race, saying only that she would pray for his speedy recovery. Minutes after Hillary's reaction hit the wire, the mayor's top City Hall press aide, tough-talking Sunny Mindel, called Timothy to complain that Hillary hadn't yet made a sympathy call to Rudy. Timothy relayed the complaint to the Clinton camp, and two minutes later, Sunny called back to say that Hillary had just spoken to the mayor. It was one of the few conversations the two ever had. Later in the day, Hillary's aides said she'd been trying to get through to City Hall all along but hadn't been able to reach him.

I led my sidebar that day like this: "Whether or not he remains in the race, Mayor Rudolph Giuliani's admission Thursday that he has prostate cancer has changed the dynamics of the U.S. Senate campaign in New York. Political experts predict that his fund-raising will be hampered, rival Hillary Rodham Clinton will tone down her attacks, and New Yorkers may change their views on Giuliani's candidacy. While some voters may feel sympathy toward a tough guy whose cancer suddenly makes him vulnerable, others could worry about his long-term health, or wonder if his refusal to commit to the campaign reveals a deeper ambivalence."

Because the news unfolded so early in the day, I actually made it out of the office in time to pick my kids up from school and make dinner. That evening was one of the few nights I was planning to go out. I belong to a ladies' book club on my block, and once a month I head out to a neighbor's home to chat about whatever novel we'd picked to read. That night we were discussing one of Anthony Trollope's Palliser novels, *Can You Forgive Her?* It was a tough read, much harder than our usual fare, which tended to be more popular recent books like *The Poisonwood Bible*. Because the book club meetings were just about the only thing that ever took me from home at night aside from the occasional Hillary event, they were somewhat sacred "Mommy's night out" events, not to be disturbed by my kids or my husband. So when my office started calling that night to reach me about the Giuliani story, my husband didn't think it was worth going up the block to fetch me from the book club. By the time I'd gotten home around nine-fifteen, they'd called three times. It seems one of Giuliani's campaign press aides, Juleanna Glover Weiss, didn't like my lead and had called my office asking that it be changed. She complained that it sounded as if Rudy was going to drop out. The editor on duty was reluctant to change the story without checking with me, but Juleanna kept calling back, so the editor kept trying me at home. I was confident that my lead hadn't gone beyond what Giuliani himself had said; but it was clear from Juleanna's calls that the campaign staff was very worried about their future. I told the desk to call her back and offer to insert any comment that she wanted to make, but not to change the lead. I wanted to be fair and reflect their point of view, but they certainly weren't calling the shots on this.

The mayor's campaign was run very differently from Hillary's. Hil's offices on Seventh Avenue just north of Macy's and Madison Square Garden were cramped and incredibly hectic; the tiny room that you walked into when you opened the door was plastered with an ever-changing exhibit of blown-up photos of Hillary in various poses on the campaign trail: Hillary holding a baby, Hillary talking to black women,

Hillary meeting old people. It was like the anteroom for some sort of religious cult worshiping a blond lady with blue eyes and a big smile whose holy garments consisted of black pantsuits. The press staff worked out of an impossibly small room that just barely fit their desks and a TV. In contrast, Giuliani's campaign offices, downtown just a few blocks from City Hall, were spacious and open. The walls at Giuliani Central were mostly bare—no photo lovefest here—but for one outstanding feature: a digital neon clock that counted down the minutes to election day, with the red numbers for seconds changing so fast that they were just a blur. The clock later turned up in Lazio's headquarters, but it never seemed to fit in; nobody over there was uptight enough. Actually the person whom the clock most reminded me of wasn't even Rudy, it was Teitelbaum. The man loved to gesture as he spoke, and sometimes his hands would move so fast that he looked like one of those many-armed statues of Vishnu. Teitelbaum had two assistants: Kim Serafin, a pretty twenty-something who was a former actress, and Juleanna, a former CNN producer who had joined the campaign six weeks after her second child was born. It was hard enough covering the campaign as I did, with a two-year-old in day care; I couldn't imagine actually working for one of the candidates with a newborn at home. And while nearly all the women on Hillary's staff wore shapeless, dark pantsuits, Kim—whose hair was dyed so blond it was almost white—favored tight pants and tops that didn't quite cover her belly button. I hasten to add that both Kim and Juleanna were extremely good at their jobs; let it not be said that anyone on the Giuliani side was discounting a woman's ability because she had either a baby at home or a cover girl's style.

Rudy had said he would take a week or two to decide on a course of treatment for his cancer and that the implications of that would determine his political future. Between the day he divulged his cancer and the day he pulled out, "every tiny little Podunk press avail he had was packed with press and TV cameras from Japan to Sweden," Timothy recalled. "It was bizarre, frustrating for the beat reporters, and he wouldn't tell us anything."

At one of these throwaway avails—this one held in Bryant Park to announce an annual celebration of Jewish heritage—the mayor showed up an hour late, surrounded by a half dozen of his top advisers, to deliver another shocker: he was planning to separate from his wife, Donna Hanover.

"He seemed genuinely sad: muted, hurting, visibly pained," Timothy recalled. "It was very odd to see him like this. Usually he is quite loud. That day, he barely spoke above a whisper, which made the setting oddly intimate because the reporters that were there had to crowd around close to him to hear what he was saying. This is a guy who usually refused to answer the most innocuous personal question, and here he was laying himself bare before us."

When asked about the prospects for his Senate campaign, the mayor answered, "I'm not really thinking about politics right now." It all only seemed to add evidence to the theory that he was leaning toward dropping out of the race.

Timothy asked Giuliani if he had told his wife that he was planning to make this announcement. "He kind of stuttered and ultimately said no," Timothy recalled. "They had discussed separation, but she didn't know he was going to go public."

Giuliani also used the press conference to confirm another rumor that had been kicking around: he had an ongoing relationship with another woman, Judi Nathan.

Just a few hours later, Donna Hanover summoned reporters to hear her side of it in a tearful, dramatic news conference outside Gracie Mansion, the mayor's residence.

"Today's turn of events brings me great sadness," she said. "I had hoped that we could keep this marriage together. For several years, it was difficult to participate in Rudy's public life because of his relationship with one staff member. Beginning last May, I made a major effort to bring us back together. Rudy and I reestablished some of our personal intimacy through the fall. At that point he chose another path. Rudy and I will now discuss the possibility of a legal separation."

What a bombshell! The "staff member" Donna said Rudy had had a "relationship" with was obviously Cristyne Lategano, Giuliani's former press secretary. Lategano had sold sneakers in the Super Runners Shop on Third Avenue in Manhattan before volunteering on the mayor's '93 campaign; she had managed to catch his eye and eventually got herself installed as his chief press aide, despite her lack of experience. An article in *Vanity Fair* eventually alleged what many local reporters suspected but had been unable to get any hard evidence for—that she and the mayor were romantically involved. Cristyne and Rudy both vociferously denied the rumors, and she left the mayor's staff after six years and parlayed her City Hall connections into a job heading NYC & Co., the new name for the old Convention & Visitors Bureau. A short time later she married a freelance golf writer. In the days that followed Donna's dramatic press conference, Cristyne again denied that they'd been anything more than coworkers putting in long hours. And Rudy— who had started to actually seem like a nice, thoughtful, introspective guy after his cancer diagnosis—blew up at reporters who shouted questions about his philandering after Donna had dropped her little grenade.

"Don't you guys have the slightest bit of decency?" he barked to the City Hall press corps. "Shhhh! Do you realize you embarrass yourself doing this in the eyes of just about everybody?" To a questioner who asked about sleeping arrangements at Gracie Mansion, he shouted, "Oh, get out of here! Get lost, get lost, that's a sneaky way of trying to invade somebody's personal life."

Of course, everyone had known for years that the mayor's marriage

was for show. The only real mystery was why he and Donna hadn't gotten divorced. Because both of them are Catholics with two school-age
children, Andrew and Caroline, one school of thought was that they
stayed together for faith and family. But there was a less charitable theory: that Donna wanted to stay in the marriage because being first lady
of New York City provided her an instant publicity niche that she
could use to further her acting ambitions. When she'd met Giuliani, he
was the chief federal prosecutor for New York, crusading against mob-
sters and white-collar criminals like Ivan Boesky; she was a local television news reporter. After he was elected, she continued her career. She
became the host of a cable show on the Food Network; she got good
reviews for a supporting role in a movie about Larry Flynt and landed
parts on the soap operas *One Life to Live* and *All My Children*; and she had
been on the verge of appearing in a Broadway show called *The Vagina
Monologues*—a frank, funny feminist diatribe that one could easily imagine Rudy shutting down as obscene if it had been staged in a public
venue like Central Park or City College instead of a private theater—
when Rudy's cancer was made public and she postponed her participation in the show.

Donna had not campaigned at all for her husband when he was
running for reelection as mayor in 1997, and she was just as invisible
during his Senate campaign. But there was one notable Donna sighting
before Rudy dropped out of the race. She and Hillary both received
awards from the Women's Leadership Network, and for a few brief
moments, they were in the same hotel ballroom at the same time.
Hillary sat on the dais from the beginning of the event until the end,
while Donna magically appeared from behind a curtain when it was her
turn to speak, made a self-congratulatory speech thanking New York
for allowing her to prove that you could be a working mother *and* the
city's first lady, and disappeared again behind the curtain. I'd expected a
handshake, maybe even an air kiss, between the two of them; after all,
they had so much in common—namely bad feelings toward Rudy and

sticking out marriages to philandering men. But as far as I could tell, they barely made eye contact, much less exchanged greetings.

Throughout the campaign, I papered the wall behind my desk with cartoons about the candidates, headlines, and quotes. The one I chose about Donna came from the Food Network Web site's "Donna Hanover: Personal Profile." Under the heading "Sage advice," she wrote: "Work hard at several projects. That way, no matter what is going wrong, something will be going right!"

As for Rudy's new squeeze, he'd been parading Judi Nathan in public for several months before the media caught on that she was more than just some random supporter. She'd accompanied him to the St. Patrick's Day Parade and the Inner Circle show, a spoof on city politics staged by reporters, but not until a few days before the prostate cancer revelation, as the mayor ostentatiously strolled around Manhattan with her while photographers snapped away, had it become obvious what was going on. But going public with Judi wasn't careless behavior; this was a social announcement from a guy whose sexual health and disintegrating marriage were about to become national topics of discussion.

Getting Hillary to comment on the news about Rudy's marriage was even harder than getting her to comment on the news of his cancer. It became a sort of game. Every time she spoke to the press during the three weeks between the time the mayor announced he had cancer and the day he dropped out of the race, we'd try a dozen different ways to get her to say something. How was it affecting her campaign? Wasn't it hard to continue campaigning with all this uncertainty, or, conversely, wasn't it easier to continue campaigning when the other side was imploding? Did she have any advice for the mayor? Who did she think would replace him? It didn't matter; she gave the same answer every time: "I'm just going to keep on doing what I've been doing all along, which is to keep focused on the issues." It was undoubtedly the right tack to take, both politically and as a matter of good taste, not to mention as a woman who had survived a screwed-up marriage of her own. And the more she soldiered on, keeping her campaign commitments at fund-raisers and union rallies and ladies' luncheons, the more respectable she looked in light of Rudy's soap opera. In fact, rather than being unsettled by the chaos on the other side, she seemed, if anything, to be radiating a calm, sunny confidence.

But internally, the campaign was not looking forward to losing Rudy as an opponent. "By the time Giuliani got out, we didn't want him to get out," one insider told me. "Hillary was very comfortable with Giuliani as her opponent. She knew who he was and how to deal with it."

And the mayor's lack of interest in upstate New York made the campaign feel increasingly secure. "Every time Giuliani said, 'Who cares about the Listening Tour?' he was basically saying to upstaters, 'I'm not going to listen,'" the Clinton campaign adviser added.

Finally, on Friday, May 19, just over three weeks after the mayor had made his cancer public, he announced his withdrawal from the race. The main reason, he said, was that he couldn't decide on a course of treatment with the simultaneous pressure of making a decision about the Senate race.

Rick Lazio, a Long Island congressman who looked younger than his forty-two years, had seemed absurdly presumptuous when he'd declared an interest in running for the Senate months earlier, only to be ordered by Governor Pataki to get out of Rudy's way. (Ironically, on election day, the governor's wife, Libby Pataki, complained in a radio interview that the mayor had "hung around way too long" before bowing out. "He was just jerking people around," she said. "It was terribly unfair. . . . It really did cut into the time Rick could have used.")

But when Rudy dropped out, it looked like Lazio was off to a fabulous start. He'd already quietly raised $5 million for a campaign nobody imagined he'd ever wage; and as a fresh-faced, likable, happily married suburban father with no political baggage, he was the perfect replacement for the mayor, whose cancer, messed-up marriage, and acerbic personality added up to one big pile of negatives.

In fact, while Hillary had certainly had her share of screwups—the Suha kiss, the St. Patrick's Day controversy, the FALN flap—at least her mistakes only looked like the foolish blunders of a neophyte. The mayor's troubles, in contrast, looked egocentric and sometimes even heartless. He tried to shut down the Brooklyn Museum because he didn't like a painting of a black Madonna decorated with elephant dung and pictures of bare bottoms. He demonized a black man, Patrick Dorismond, who was fatally shot in a confrontation with police, by saying that Dorismond had a "propensity to violence" and allowing the release of Dorismond's sealed juvenile record for a robbery arrest at age thirteen. And he ordered police to take any homeless person found sleeping in a public place to a shelter; those who refused to go would be given a summons or arrested. "Streets do not exist in civilized cities for the purpose of sleeping there. Bedrooms are for sleeping," the mayor declared. I wondered whether Rudy was aware of a slightly different declaration by nineteenth-century essayist Anatole France: "The law, in its majestic equality, forbids the rich as well as the poor to sleep under bridges, to beg in the streets, and to steal bread."

The mayor had also been involved in nearly two dozen lawsuits contending he had violated the First Amendment by closing City Hall Plaza to the public and denying permits for various demonstrations. He'd lost nearly every case. All of these controversies made it easy for the Clinton campaign to deflect criticism of her missteps by picking on his.

The mayor's personality was also a good issue for Hillary's people to focus on because, in truth, she and Rudy did not much disagree on a lot of the real issues that normally divide Democrats and Republicans. But all that changed once Lazio entered the race. His views, while hardly right-wing, were much more conservative than Giuliani's: he opposed mandatory gun licensing, late-term abortion, Medicaid-funded abortions, and civil unions between homosexuals. Republicans, meanwhile, were thrilled to finally have, in Lazio, a candidate who was actually willing to campaign outside the five boroughs. By the end of his first forty-eight hours in the race, Lazio had visited nearly as many upstate cities as Rudy had during the previous three months.

Rudy made his big announcement about dropping out of the race on a Friday, which was my usual day off. It was the day I kept my younger son home from day care, picked my older son up at three o'clock instead of sending him to after-school, went to the library, and hung out in the playground, just as I imagined stay-at-home moms doing. My husband called me midday to give me a heads-up that Rudy was going to make the big announcement that afternoon, but my boss was nice enough not to call me in. I thought about volunteering to help out with the coverage, but I knew Hillary's news conference was already in the capable hands of someone else from my office, and I decided that, for a change, I'd pick the kids over Hillary and get the details of the story from TV news and the papers, just like everybody else. Danny had a play date that afternoon with a friend, and I didn't want to let him down. I bought the kids ice cream after school from a Mister Softee truck, and by the time we got home, Rick Lazio had scheduled a press conference for the next morning to launch his own campaign.

Some have suggested that given Rudy's brilliant leadership after September 11, he'd surely have beaten Hillary had he stayed in. What people forget is that before September 11, he often looked like a bully for picking on, say, the homeless or a museum. it wasn't until he was facing a real enemy—the terrorists who attacked the World Trade center—that his strong personality, courage, forceful speech, and determination made him a real hero. Rudy more than earned a place in history books for that, and New Yorkers who lived through that awful time—even those who once hated him—remain thankful he was mayor, not senator, when the towers were hit.

Wooing the Jews

July 16, 2000. It's a slow Sunday afternoon and I'm sitting in the newsroom reading the thick weekend papers. The only news out there is an accusation from a new book alleging that Hillary called someone a "fucking Jew bastard" in 1974 in Arkansas, but while the *New York Post* and the *Daily News* have stories about what we're all already referring to as simply "FJB," the networks, the *New York Times*, *Newsday*, and the AP are holding off reporting it. The accuser, Paul Fray, who worked on Bill Clinton's congressional campaign, says in this book, *State of a Union*, that Hillary called him an FJB the night Bill lost the race. But there are two big problems with the story: Fray's a Baptist, although he apparently had one Jewish grandparent, and more important, he's not returning our phone calls.

The *Times* has also chosen this particular day to run a story about how the Senate race has become incredibly boring now that Rudy is out and Lazio is in. So boring, in fact, that, according to the *Times*, Howard Wolfson, Hillary's chief press aide, has nothing better to do than to sit around playing rotisserie baseball. I have already e-mailed Howard to suggest that he use his newfound free time to respond more promptly to my e-mails.

Then the phone rings. "City desk," someone answers. "Hey, Beth, it's for you."

"This is Beth."

"Beth, it's Karen Dunn."

"Hey, Karen! What's up?" I figure she's calling to let me know when they're releasing the summaries for Hillary's campaign financial filings. I figure she's definitely *not* calling to talk to me about FJB.

"We're holding a news conference," she tells me. "At Hillary's house. In Chappaqua. Fifteen Old House Lane."

"You're holding a news conference?" I repeat stupidly. "At Hillary's house?" I'm certain I have heard her wrong.

"Yup. Three o'clock."

It's one-twenty. The campaign office is in midtown, and like me, none of the Clinton staffers have cars. Chappaqua is a forty-minute drive.

"How are you getting there?" I ask, figuring that if they're going up to Westchester in a cab, I could run over and go with them.

"Um, I'm not sure. We might try to get a van together."

Yeah, right. I've waited for vans at Clinton campaign headquarters that never showed up, and I've been on campaign vans that got lost or were driven by lunatics. I didn't have time for that kind of nonsense now, not with just an hour and a half to get to Chappaqua.

"Never mind, I'll figure it out on my own somehow. I assume this is about the book?"

"Yes."

"Okay, we'll be there. Hey, listen, I know you're not really focused on this right now, but what's happening with the financial filings?"

"I see you have a story out on the wire saying we'll have them today, but we won't."

"Fine, see ya."

I hang up and start typing furiously. "Add to the Sunday Day Schedule. Three P.M. Hillary Rodham Clinton holds news conference regarding allegation in new book; 15 Old House Lane, Chappaqua."

"I got news," I call out to the editor.

"Yeah?" She looks up.

"Hillary's holding a news conference. At her house. About the book."

Everyone in the newsroom is looking at me like I'm out of my mind. "I'm going to move this day schedule item," I say, typing the commands to send it out on the AP local wire to every newspaper and radio and TV station in the metropolitan area. Then I start typing a lead for the digest, which is a preview of the top stories we're working on that gets sent out on the wire each afternoon.

"CHAPPAQUA, N.Y.—Hillary Rodham Clinton holds a news conference at her Westchester home to respond to allegations contained in a new book that she used an anti-Semitic obscenity in 1974. Slug: NY Senate-Clinton. By Beth J. Harpaz. Associated Press Writer."

I store the lead in my computer, tell the editor the file name, and start dialing for Metro-North. There's a train at one fifty-four, arriving two forty-eight. I have less than a half hour, but if I take a cab to Grand Central, I can make it.

Meanwhile Suzanne Plunkett, an AP photographer on desk duty for the day, is trying to get my attention to make sure she heard me right, that there's a press conference at Hillary's house. She makes a few phone calls to rustle up a photographer, but after striking out decides she should go herself. "Let me see if I can get somebody else to run the desk here and I'll drive you up," she says.

One of the other reporters, trying to be helpful, points out that my counterpart covering the Lazio campaign, Frank Eltman, is already up in Rockland County with Rick. "We can beep him. He can probably get there in time," she says.

I'm thinking, no way am I passing up a chance to go to Hillary's house. I don't care if I have to walk there. This is practically the longest fucking campaign in U.S. political history, and after covering it for almost a year and a half, if anybody gets to hear Hillary talk about this stuff at her house, it's going to be me.

"Don't bother. There's a train in fifteen minutes. I can make it."

I type another message, this one for the national editors, who had earlier asked when we were going to get the financial filings. I send them my lead for what's developing and note that the financial filings won't be released today.

The photo editor is still on the phone, trying to get somebody to spring her so she can come, too. But I can't wait any longer and take the chance that I'm going to miss the train. I throw a notebook and my tape recorder in my bag and run out the door.

When I arrive at Grand Central, somebody is ahead of me at the information booth asking for very complicated directions to Little Italy, and the clerk is telling her the wrong train to take. Ordinarily I would butt in like any good New Yorker and straighten them both out, but now I'm desperately rushing to make this train. Two minutes to go. Finally the woman leaves, map in hand, and I get my track number. I run downstairs, jump on the train, and sit down. I buy my ticket from a conductor and put my head back.

Suddenly I am in a panic. This couldn't be right. I must have misunderstood Karen. Hillary couldn't possibly be holding a press conference about this. There's no way she would dignify this kind of accusation by talking to us about it. And she couldn't possibly be doing it at her house. The only time she's ever talked to anybody at her house was when she and the president moved in, and the press was camped out in their cul-de-sac. She's way too private and way too paranoid to actually invite us there. And it couldn't possibly be happening on such short notice. Sure, the Clinton campaign makes a lot of last-minute schedule changes, but not like this.

In my head, I go over my conversation with Karen. AP policy is that we don't take schedule items over the phone. Everything's got to be faxed or e-mailed, to make sure they're legitimate and to make sure that there are no misunderstandings over the phone about times and dates. I made a rare exception today because I know Karen's voice, I've talked to her a thousand times on the phone, and neither she nor I had time for a fax. Did I somehow misunderstand? Checklist: She definitely told me this was about the book. She definitely gave me Hillary's address. She definitely said three o'clock. Now I'm getting paranoid. How can I be sure it was Karen? Well, she knew about the financial filings, and she knew we had a story on the wire that said they'd be out today. Of course it was her. I'm just losing it.

We're at Valhalla. Did I miss my stop? No map on this train, it's not like the subway. I strain to hear the announcements. I look around. Any other time I've covered Hillary in Westchester or Long Island I've run into other reporters on the train. I don't see any familiar faces. Now we're in Chappaqua. I have to go to the bathroom, but it's ten to three. I have no idea how long it will take to get to Old House Lane. I figure I can use a bathroom when I get there. I get in a cab and give the driver the address. He turns around and smiles.

"My cousin lives on Old House Lane," he says knowingly.

"Yeah?"

"Whenever the Clintons are there, they have the dogs sniff the school bus for bombs."

"Really?" If true, that would be an interesting way to figure out just how often Hillary's slept in Chappaqua. Anytime it seemed likely she was there overnight, if you asked her press office for confirmation, they'd say they didn't know. "Like how many times would you say?"

"Oh, only ten or twelve, probably."

Scratch the school bus theory. I don't know how many times she's stayed at the house, but I'm certain it's more than ten or twelve.

"And my cousin invited the Secret Service agents over for a barbe-cue one day, but they never came." The driver is clearly miffed by this. I wonder whether the Secret Service agents realize how rude the locals thought they were. I wonder whether the locals realize how strange it would be for the Secret Service agents to walk off the job at Hillary's house to go have a hot dog across the street.

We turn off a two-lane road onto a tree-lined side street. I see other reporters and Secret Service agents milling about. I pay and get out. I see one of the advance guys, Steve Feder.

"Steve," I say. "I really have to go to the bathroom."

"Sorry. No way."

"I promise not to look in the medicine cabinet."

He shakes his head.

"Isn't there a Secret Service bathroom I could use outside the house?"

"Nope."

"Jeez, the least you could do is set up a Porta Potti in the woods for reporters."

I throw my bag down in the pile of cameras, tape recorders, and knapsacks that have to be "swept," as the agents say, for bombs. One guy with a wire coming out of his ear kneels down and starts turning on our cell phones one by one to make sure they're not really explosive devices. Another agent comes over and asks me, "Have you been magged?"

That's short for magnetometer, a handheld scanner they use to detect metal objects. I hold my arms up and the agent waves the device up and down my body.

I see our photographer, Suzanne. "You made it!"

She smiles. "I can give you a ride back."

"Great."

A car drives up with US CONGRESS plates. Inside I spot Con-gresswoman Nita Lowey, a Jewish Westchester Democrat who would have run for the Senate seat if Hillary hadn't. From where we're standing, you can barely see the whitewashed wooden shingles of the house beyond a narrow, wooded path. A gate blocking access to the path is opened and Lowey's car drives in.

"Why is Nita Lowey here?" someone asks.

"Some of her best friends are Jewish, I guess," the answer comes.

Then another car drives up. Howard Wolfson gets out, and so does Adam Nagourney from the *Times*.

Gregg Birnbaum from the *New York Post*, who has just come from covering Lazio at an Irish festival, is there, too. He says Lazio absolutely refused to comment on FJB.

"I blocked his path to his van door and told him, 'I'm not letting you out of here till you say something about it,' but he wouldn't do it," Gregg says.

Now Liz Moore from *Newsday* has arrived. She's one of the only other reporters on this gig who, like me, has kids. "I was having a family barbecue when I got the call for this," she says. "My six-year-old doesn't get it."

"I know what you mean," I say. "My kids think I spend all this time with her because we're related. Aunt Hillary."

We start talking about what to ask her. Nobody dwells on whether we believe her or not. Our personal opinions are almost irrelevant. The only thing that matters is the material we have available for our stories—quotes, photos, background, and facts. Personally, I don't think she's capable of using that kind of language; she's too uptight. But every time I mentally try to sort out the evidence, or lack thereof, in my head I see President Clinton on national TV, wagging his finger and twanging, "Ah did not have sexual relations with *that woman!*" I remind myself that I believed him, too.

We are each given a copy of a two-page document written in cramped, nearly illegible cursive. After a moment we realize that this is a letter to Hillary from Paul Fray, the man who accused Hillary of calling him an FJB. But the handwriting in the letter is so bad that as we try to decipher it, we begin reading it aloud, with each of us picking up the recitation when somebody else can't make out a word.

"This is like a seder," Adam mutters.

"Yeah, except that instead of there being four questions, there are four thousand," I add.

The letter is bizarre, begging Hillary's forgiveness for "things I said against you . . . without factual foundation," declaring that he is living in squalor, asking her to come and read to his grandson. It's dated July 1997.

"Isn't it great that she could find this letter on five minutes' notice but she couldn't find the law firm files?" someone says.

A couple of TV crews are here now, and we're led through the gate down the narrow path to the house we've been glimpsing through the trees. I'm wondering if maybe they're going to let us in the house. I mean, why else would she summon us all up here if she's not going to let us inside?

We end up on a lush lawn by the side of the house. A simple perennial garden is growing a few feet away, with orange daylilies and purple coneflowers, very understated and wild-looking. A weatherbeaten white wicker couch with a faded floral pillow seat is the only object in the garden. It looks like the kind of thing you'd buy from Pier 1 for a hundred bucks. I'd imagined Hillary's taste ran more to fussy French cast-iron benches.

This is my first look at the house. It's surrounded by big trees and positioned on the property in such a way that you can't see the whole thing from where we're standing. It's impossible to tell how big it is or the layout, or even where the doors are. It doesn't look all that fancy; I've certainly seen more imposing homes in Westchester. One of the cameramen starts filming a background shot of the yard and the house. Karen Finney, tall Karen as opposed to Karen Dunn, who's short Karen, puts her hand on his shoulder and shakes her head. Before the campaign, Finney worked in Washington as a press aide in the first lady's office, and she tends to be the most protective of Hillary of all the campaign staffers. I actually consider it a game to find a way around whatever Finney is trying to shut down. If she says no avail, what I love more than anything is to stake Hillary out and get a question in. If Finney says I can't go interview someone who's part of the first lady's entourage, I make it my business to walk halfway around the building and find another entrance that puts me right next to the person I want to talk to. I don't take her limit-setting too seriously, and she doesn't take my hurdle-jumping personally. She does her job, and I do mine. Right now, for example, she thinks she's being prudent by stopping a cameraman from shooting the house, while I think it's ridiculous that they drag us up here for this and then won't let us take pictures. As if some terrorist is going to figure out how to bomb this place because there was a shot of the shingles for five seconds on the eleven o'clock news.

"Anybody know what kind of house this is?" I ask. I grew up in Manhattan, and suburban house types are beyond my frame of reference. I knew we'd reported it in previous stories about the Clintons' purchasing the house, but now I couldn't remember the right term. "Ranch, cape, colonial?"

"I think it's a Dutch colonial," Liz says. "And are those peony bushes over there?"

"Peony season is over," I say.

"I know, but I think those are the bushes without the flowers."

I shrug. We are all scribbling these little details down in our notebooks.

Now it's clear that we're not going to be allowed inside. The TV crews are setting up in a semicircle, so the house will be behind Hillary and in their shot when she comes out. Stills—the newspaper photographers—are crouching on the ground in front of the camera crews. I try to decide: Do I want to be on her right, where Adam and Gregg are sitting on the wet grass, and get better sound on my tape recorder because I'm closer, or do I want to be straight ahead of her, so if I ask a question, she can't ignore me? I opt for straight ahead.

"Heads up!" someone calls. We turn on our tape recorders.

Here she comes, with Nita by her side. Oddly, they are both wearing lightweight, cream-colored pantsuits. Accidental or coordinated? I remind myself that with the Clintons, nothing is accidental.

Nita starts by expressing her outrage that anybody could think Hillary is capable of saying such a thing. I wonder what she was saying about Hillary back when the first lady big-footed her out of the Senate race. Then it's Hillary's turn. She says she's called us here to state unequivocally that she never made this remark. Her eyes are puffy and she looks exhausted.

Then she starts answering questions. No, she doesn't remember being in the room with Fray when he says she made the remark. I think to myself: It never sounds good to hear a Clinton say "I don't recall."

No, she never responded to the letter that was handed out, but she's releasing it to us to prove that the people accusing her of this have no credibility.

She starts looking around. This news conference is almost over and I still don't understand why we're here. My turn to jump in.

"Mrs. Clinton," I call out. "Are you aware that a lot of news organizations—including my own and many others represented here today—had not planned to do a story on this because of the questionable nature of the material? Your being here guarantees that this is news for all of us. Why are you doing this?"

This is a somewhat self-serving question. I'm basically pointing out that the AP, the *Times*, and *Newsday*, not to mention the networks, haven't joined the tabloids—at least not yet—in running a story that cannot be confirmed by anybody except the sole guy who's making the accusation. Am I ass-kissing here? A close call. But I really, really don't understand why she's doing this press conference. And I really, really want her to know that whatever headlines her statements generate, on the wire or anywhere else, are her doing, not ours.

"You know, Beth," she begins. It's stupid, but it's always a thrill when she uses my name. And no doubt she realizes how ingratiating it is, which is why politicians always try to use first names when talking to people. When I used to tell nonjournalists I was covering her campaign, they'd often ask, "But does she know you?" It was only after she started answering my questions by using my first name that I could confidently respond, "Yeah, she knows me."

She goes on to say that she's been accused of a lot of things over the past eight years, "including complicity to murder," a reference to the Vince Foster case, and that she had a policy of ignoring most of the allegations. But she said she couldn't ignore this one and decided to hold a press conference so that "anyone who tries to get someone else to believe this will at least have to say, 'Well, she says it's not true.' "

All of a sudden she brings the side of one hand down with a chop into the palm of her other hand for emphasis and raises her voice. "You're darn right it's not true!" she says, for the first time sounding really angry and upset after fifteen minutes of emotionless denials. "It's absolutely false! I'm just sick and tired of this kind of politics."

I realize Peter Moses, a producer for Channel 9 news, has just now squeezed himself next to me so that he is now directly in front of her, too. Peter is the ultimate "How do you feel?" TV guy, the kind of person who doesn't mind sticking his mike in the face of someone who's crying to try to get a quote. Watching him do this sort of thing makes me glad I don't work for TV; on the other hand, I have to admit, I kind of admire it.

He has that impish look on his face now that means he's about to pounce. He grins naughtily and calls out in a singsong tone of voice to Hillary, "But why aren't you *angrier?*"

There's a low groan from a couple of the other reporters. At times like this, Peter reminds me of my son Danny, who has a big personality, a devilish sense of humor, and a tendency to act on impulse. Months later, when I ask Peter about this particular incident, he tells me he'd gotten "a lot of grief" from some of the other reporters who accused him of trying to make her cry. "I just wanted to see if there was any real emotion under the veneer," he says. And personally, I don't have a problem with him doing it—I'm just glad it wasn't me who asked it.

His question elicits a glare from Hillary. "I *am* angry. I'm *very* angry. But you know . . ."

Now her voice starts to break and she looks away from us for a moment. She's about to cry! Hillary the Ice Queen is letting us see her inner feelings! She wouldn't let us in her house. That would be asking too much. We could never sit with her in her van or hang out and chat the way we do with other candidates. But she has invited us onto her property and let us come as close as she possibly can, physically and emotionally. Her eyes are now welling up. This is amazing! Hillary is going to shed a tear! I don't know whether to feel sorry for her or happy for me, because this is news.

Then I see her swallow. The sob, however close it might have come to spilling out, is gone. Back to the cerebral first lady who never shows her real feelings. "Her Majesty's a pretty nice girl, someday I'm gonna make her mine," the Beatles once sang, and sometimes that's how I feel about Hillary at those rare times when she seems to be lifting the curtain and letting us in on her inner feelings. It's what all journalists want to do to the people they're interviewing: get inside their heads. But I knew I wouldn't be making Hillary mine today, now that the sob is gone.

"I learned a long time ago that the people who generate this kind of stuff are really hoping to divert attention from what's important in a campaign . . . ," she begins. Yeah yeah yeah. The press conference is over. I start to stand up.

"Down in front!" somebody screams in my direction. Hillary and Nita are walking through her garden toward a gate, behind which, I assume, is the swimming pool, and my head is in the way of a camera shot. I crouch down and crawl over to Suzanne.

"Wow!" she says. "I think we saw a tear."

"Really?" I say.

A *Daily News* reporter comes over. "A tear? You sure? You gonna look at your film now?"

Our photographers all use digital film and can edit and transmit their pictures onto the AP wire by satellite computers from anywhere— a war zone, a highway, anywhere. But Suzanne had left the computer in the office and wants to get back. I still have to go to the bathroom. I see Howard, grab him, and beg him to let me use the Secret Service facilities.

"I'll see what I can do." That's Howard's response to everything. I could see it wasn't going to get me a bathroom today.

I walk back with Suzanne to her car. Everybody had been forced to park a quarter mile down the road. "You still need a bathroom?" she asks.

"Nah." Now I just want to get back. I replay my tape, transcribe the quotes, pull out my cell phone, and start dictating to a reporter back at the office—a "rewrite," as in the old newsroom movie scene, where a hard-bitten cop reporter in a fedora picks up the phone and says, "Hello, sweetheart? Get me rewrite."

By the time we reach the office, the story is nearly ready to move on the wire. Somebody has grabbed a quote off CNN from the author of the book, Jerry Oppenheimer, and a fax has come in with a statement from President Clinton. I throw a little into the story from each of those, tinker with the lead, and hand it to the desk. Eight hundred words and no room for the Dutch colonial or the purple coneflowers. Too bad.

It won't be until the next day, after learning that the president had interrupted the Camp David peace talks to personally speak with the

Daily News about the controversy, that I realize what's really going on. As long as the story was only in the *New York Post*, a Rupert Murdoch–owned paper with unabashedly conservative columnists and editorials, the coverage didn't matter that much. But once the story appeared in the *Daily News*, which politically takes more middle-of-the-road positions, the campaign went into crisis mode. By giving the *News* an exclusive interview with Bill Clinton, the campaign is also punishing the *Post*, its rival tabloid. The next day it also occurs to me that Hillary is consciously portraying herself as a victim here, a victim of one of the many people who knew Bill and Hil back in Arkansas and periodically grab the media's attention with an allegation about something they did years before they were in the White House.

Now why would Hillary want us to view her as a victim? Because the last time everybody felt sorry for her, during the Lewinsky scandal, her poll numbers were sky-high. But I'm not thinking about any of that now; I'm still too wrapped up in the thrill of the day's news, in the excitement of having gone to Hillary's garden and nearly witnessed her crying.

I walk over to where Suzanne and an editor are looking at a couple of photos up on a computer screen. Hillary looks mean in one, mad and tired in another, and puffy-eyed and resigned in a third.

"No tears?" I ask.

"No tears."

I still need to use the bathroom. Now that the story's done, I can.

The next morning we're all up bright and early to watch Hillary address a group from the New York Academy of Sciences. As usual, she's amazing, chatting knowledgeably about the human genome and high-speed Internet connections and medical research and technology-based economic development. None of us understand any of it, but it seems to go over big with this audience of engineers, researchers, professors, and high-tech financiers. Of course, there won't be any news from this; we're just here in case she says anything else about FJB. I sit next to Bob Hardt, who covers the race with Gregg for the *Post*. Bob likes to say that the two of them are like Laurel and Hardy. Bob is bald, round, droll, and deliberate and wears seersucker suits with a straw hat; while Gregg, wiry and hyper with a brown beard, favors dark sunglasses and has a large collection of blazers, my favorite being a herringbone number the color of gourmet mustard. Both of them are savvy and smart and have saved my ass on any number of occasions with quotes I missed or background I didn't have.

Today Bob is playing with the newest toy to make the rounds of journalists: a PalmPilot. In *The Boys on the Bus*, reporters covering the Nixon-McGovern race shared tape recorders, filed their stories via Western Union telegrams, and flung TV film into helicopters to get it back to their stations in time for the next broadcast. Today, everybody has his or her own beeper, cell phone, and tape recorder; TV crews transmit live via satellite; and there is no sound in this world as comforting to me as the clack-clack-clack of Adam Nagourney typing away on his laptop during a Hillary news conference. One day as I sit next to Adam on a campaign van, he even plugged his laptop into his cell phone and sat there reading his e-mail as if it were no big deal. And now Bob's doing the same with his PalmPilot. While he's at it, he checks the departure time for a ferry we are supposed to take out to Ellis Island for Hillary's afternoon event, and he even uses the tiny pointer to see what's in that day's *Washington Post*. "Hey, they used your story on the Chappaqua news conference," he tells me.

Karen Finney comes around and whispers that Hillary will do an avail on Ellis Island at 1 P.M. Hooray! That will be news for sure. But when we get to Ellis Island, there is no sign of her Senate staff. Instead, this is all first lady stuff, with her aides from Washington informing us that the Q-and-A has been postponed until after a ceremony about federal grants to renovate more of the island's historic buildings.

We sit through the ceremony, most of us barely taking any notes because we know the real reason we're here hasn't happened yet. Afterward we are rounded up by the White House staff and told to take our positions and prepare our equipment for the Q-and-A. Then, for no apparent reason, they decide to move us, from one spot in the grassy field where we have set up, to another, and then another. Finally, the last time they tell us to move, the TV guys flat out refuse. The cameramen are happy with the light the way it is, but the White House people are worried it will be in Hillary's eyes. There's a brief standoff; finally the Washington aides simply disconnect everyone's cables from the multiple-feed box, which is hooked up to the microphone Hillary will be speaking into, and drag the mult and the mike where they want it. While everybody hooks up again, the White House staff erects a series of metal barricades in front of us. Twenty-four hours earlier, we'd all been sitting in Hillary's garden, close enough to touch her. Now we are going to have to shout our questions from thirty feet away, roped off like criminals in a maximum-security prison. These people from the first lady's office were making Howard and the Karens look like the best friends we ever had.

And after all that, we still had to wait, and wait, and wait. Nobody'd had anything to eat or drink for hours, and once again, I had to go to the bathroom with no facility in sight. I'm certain my grandparents were treated better than this when they came through Ellis Island on a boat from Russia about a hundred years ago. Liz Moore from *Newsday* helps me pass the time by telling me her nanny horror stories, like the one who had her boyfriend half-living in Liz's house and the other one who kept crashing Liz's car. Somebody asks me if I think Hillary's making us wait on purpose. I don't think she's doing it deliberately to piss everybody off; I think she probably had people to meet, and a lunch to eat, and autographs to sign, and, well, if we all end up standing in the hot sun for one or two or three hours, so what? Finally, around three in the afternoon, we get our avail. Today's spin is all about Hillary proclaiming herself a victim and snidely suggesting that FJB was part of a larger Republican plot against her. Of course, there was no evidence to suggest that FJB had anything to do with the GOP; the author of the book where the allegation surfaced told me himself that he's a Democrat who voted for the Clintons, and the guy who made the accusation, Paul Fray, was one of Bill Clinton's campaign workers.

I use the ferry ride back to listen to my tape and transcribe the quotes, then I call some of it into the office while walking to the subway. When I get back to my desk, I find that the quote of the day has come not from Hillary but from Lazio, who's changed his "no comment" to an "I don't know what to believe." I also call Gail Sheehy, who'd interviewed Fray for the biography she'd written the year before, *Hillary's Choice.* She tells me Fray's wife had told her the FJB story but she'd left it out of her book because she didn't believe it.

I spend the next day working on a story about Fray. I'd read somewhere that Fray had been disbarred, but when I call the Arkansas State Supreme Court to get the records, all they can do is fax me the date his license was revoked; they claim that the reasons for the revocation aren't public information. So I ask one of AP's news researchers, Rhonda Shafner, to see what she can find, and within the hour she's obtained the records through an Internet-based research service that provides legal documents. The Arkansas Supreme Court Committee on Professional Conduct revoked Fray's license because, in 1977, he made a false entry on a court docket to change a DWI conviction for one of his clients to a dismissal. When he applied to have his license reinstated, he gave as evidence of his good moral character the fact that he'd obtained a master's degree from a Baptist divinity school. The judges denied the reinstatement of his license, but in their written opinions, they noted that Fray had suffered a brain hemorrhage a month after making the false entry in the court docket, and that he behaved in a "bizarre" and "forgetful" manner "before and after" the hemorrhage. Some of this behavior, the judges wrote, was caused in part by medication to which

Fray had become addicted, although they noted that he later went into rehab. None of that was in the book containing the FJB allegation. I am reminded that conveying the truth in any story has as much to do with what you leave out as what you put in.

Gregg Birnbaum, meanwhile, has arranged for Fray to take a lie-detector test and reported the results in the *Post*. "There's no doubt in my mind that Mr. Fray is truthful," the polygrapher who administered the exam in Arkansas told Gregg, even though another polygraph expert deemed the results "inconclusive." Fray also told Gregg that despite the controversy over FJB, he hoped Hillary would win. "She will make an excellent senator," he said.

Although I am occasionally contacted by readers or other reporters who are intrigued or upset or moved or amused by something I have written, my story about Fray did not appear to have much impact—I suspect because every journalist took the story in a different direction (witness Gregg's approach versus mine), and there was no consensus on what the next-day story was. When everybody's lead is different, it's hard for the public to sort out what's important.

One week after the FJB story broke, Hillary spoke at the Hampton Synagogue, a modern Orthodox synagogue in Westhampton Beach, an exclusive summer resort on Long Island. It was a very Hillary thing to do. Going to a Reform synagogue on the Upper West Side would have been too easy; she wanted to prove her mettle before a group that didn't already love her. On the other hand, it would be too risky to go to a real Orthodox shul in Brooklyn; she might get booed. So instead she goes to a congregation run by Marc Schneier, a prominent rabbi who heads an organization to promote ethnic cooperation and who wrote a book proclaiming that relations between blacks and Jews have never been better.

Schneier originally told me that reporters attending the service couldn't bring cameras, tape recorders, or even notebooks. But when I arrived, Finney greeted me with the news that the edict had been changed. We were now allowed to take notes, but not use electronic devices. Gregg gave me a sly smile, then patted the breast pocket of his jacket. "I'm bringing a tape recorder in anyway," he said.

"What makes you think you're going to pick up any sound if it's in your jacket pocket?" I said.

"I was practicing last night with the television, standing different distances away with it in my pocket. It worked."

I laughed and started singing "Secret Agent Man." Gregg later told me that he'd gone to RadioShack the day before and bought a tiny little microphone, the size of a pencil. A couple of other reporters decided to smuggle in tape recorders, too, but were less discreet; one of them was confiscated by a Secret Service agent on the way in. But I felt okay relying on my pen and decided that I didn't want to disrespect the rabbi's request. Gregg took a different line: "I am sure G-d will forgive that small transgression," he told me.

Finally we saw Hillary arriving. Her motorcade parked around the corner; it wouldn't do to drive up to the front door of an Orthodox synagogue on a Saturday. She was wearing her church skirt instead of the pantsuit and was accompanied by Karen Adler, an adviser to the campaign on Jewish affairs. After the FJB story broke, Adler had sent around a memo to some of Hillary's Jewish supporters, asking them to call reporters for the *Forward* and the *Jewish Week* to proclaim Hillary's great love for the Jewish people. The memo also instructed them to conceal from these reporters that the campaign had asked them to make these calls. A couple of moles were on the list, and all the papers and the AP promptly reported that Hillary's campaign had asked her Jewish supporters to "lie" for her. When we finally got to ask Hillary about Karen Adler's role in this, she just smiled and said, "I think she realizes she made a mistake." I'd read in various books about the Clintons that anybody who screwed up on one of Bill's campaigns would get a chewing out from Hillary that they never forgot, but it seemed to me that Adler's presence at the Hampton Synagogue showed that Hillary did not, in fact, hold much of a grudge against a bumbler.

Hillary's remarks before the congregation concerned her own upbringing in a devout Methodist church, her visits to Israel, and the Camp David peace talks, which were going on that weekend between Yasir Arafat and Prime Minister Ehud Barak. She was careful never to mention Arafat's name; she condemned terrorism without accusing the Palestinians directly; and she condemned bigotry, without bringing up FJB.

And then it was over. Finney and Howard told me there would be no avail, but I figured I had nothing to lose by trying. When she emerged, I asked her if she could just take a minute and summarize her message. Her aides were gesturing her to hurry up and come along, but I could see she was wavering. "We weren't allowed to use tape recorders inside," I added quickly. "I just want to make sure we get it right."

She looked at Howard. "Didn't we tape it, Howard?"

Howard shook his head. How odd, I thought, that she doesn't know about the ban on recording devices; she had to realize there were no TV crews inside. But I could see she was about to say something. I realized the TV crews needed to be in on this, too, so I asked if we could just step across the street where they were lined up.

"No, no, we can't do that," Howard jumped in.

So we did it there instead. She didn't say anything new, but I felt a tiny victory in having gotten her to say anything.

After she left, Howard got an earful from a couple of TV people about not letting her cross the street. "It's disrespectful," he insisted. Seemed like splitting hairs to me—it's okay if she talks into a tape recorder on one side of the street but not into a microphone on the other?

A couple of us stood around for a few minutes going over our notes. This was a time-honored practice in the absence of a tape recorder. If you got three or four reporters together, you could get a virtual word-for-word transcript of anything, because even if one person missed a phrase as it was being said, somebody else had caught it. Besides, if you're not 100 percent sure of a quote, as long as everybody reports it the same way, you're safe.

Gregg walked by and patted the breast pocket of his blazer, where the tiny microphone was hidden. "See ya!" he called out with a smile.

Over the next few days, the Camp David peace talks collapsed without any agreement. Arafat reiterated his threat to declare a unilateral Palestinian state, which the Clinton administration immediately condemned. Then Hillary issued her own statement in which she called for a withdrawal of all U.S. aid if the Palestinians took it upon themselves to declare statehood in the absence of a peace agreement. I checked all the stories we had on the Camp David talks; Hillary had definitely gone beyond her husband in advocating a cutoff on aid. That afternoon she had an appearance at a nursing home in Manhattan. I hoped we'd get a chance to ask her about it.

The nursing home event seemed endless. She showed up late, then watched old people getting physical therapy, then made a speech to a group of nursing home residents and union members who work as attendants. Karen Dunn came to the back of the room where the press was standing and told us we could ask questions when she was done talking. It wasn't an ideal setting; we were separated from her by an audience of two hundred people, and her speech had been about issues related to the care of the elderly. "I have a question, but it's not about any of this," I whispered to Karen. "That's okay," she assured me. "Go ahead and ask it."

A couple of reporters had wandered up to the front of the room and jumped in first with two questions about nursing home care. I looked at Karen and she nodded at me. So I called out, from the back, a question about Hillary's stand ending U.S. aid to the Palestinians. "Are you going beyond your husband's policy in making this statement?"

"I may be, but it's what I believe," she replied.

Then another reporter asked her what she thought of the peace talks. She spent several minutes praising Barak. "What about Arafat?" Eileen Murphy of ABC called out.

All of a sudden there was an impatient murmur in the audience. "Health care!" called out one lady.

"Yeah! We want to talk about health care!" shouted another.

Now the entire room was filled with cries of "Health care!" It looked as if the media were about to be run out of town by a bunch of old ladies in wheelchairs for daring to ask about the Israeli peace talks. We looked at each other, shook our heads, and rolled our eyes. Hillary shrugged a little, smiling, as if to say, "See? This is what the *people* want from me." She could have said, "I'll just answer that last question and then we'll get back to health care." But she didn't. Finally one voice could be heard above the others saying that a lady in the audience desperately needed to ask Hillary something. The woman then launched into a convoluted story about an unpaid medical bill she had from some type of facility, and what was Hillary going to do to help her? Hillary promised to have someone on her staff look into it, and I just sat down on a bench under a window in the very back of the room and put my head in my lap. It was all just too weird.

There were a few more questions and mini-speeches about health care, then it was over. Suddenly the Karens came back to round us up. They were sorry about what had happened; Hillary was going to do an avail with us in the room now so we could finish asking our questions. The "What about Arafat?" question got answered, along with everything else on our minds. It turned out just fine, but it was very funny that her clumsy attempt to combine a news conference with a senior citizen event had nearly inspired a riot among the cane-and-walker set.

Not to be outdone by Hillary on the Jews, Lazio was to speak at the Hampton Synagogue the following Saturday. Frank Eltman went out to cover it; I took the day off and left my house bright and early with my kids to head up to Rockland County to spend the day with my old college roommate and her family. I got home around 7:30 P.M. and found the answering machine blinking. There was one message from my office: "If you're home, call the office. If you're not, consider yourself lucky." And another message from Karen Dunn to call her as soon as I could.

Turned out Hillary had tried to upstage Lazio's synagogue appearance by going on a radio show early that morning to proclaim that the U.S. embassy in Israel should immediately be moved to Jerusalem from its current location in Tel Aviv. Coincidentally, or more likely not so coincidentally, President Clinton was quoted in the *New York Times* that day saying that he would review the issue of moving the embassy before the end of the year. Again, Hillary was going a baby step further than Bill, almost making it look as if she were pushing the administration's policies. (Since Israel's seizure of East Jerusalem in the 1967 Six Day War, the Palestinians, backed by the rest of the Arab world, have sought to reclaim that part of the city and its Muslim holy sites. Placing the U.S. embassy there would be a way of recognizing Israel's claim that the city is indivisible.)

Out in the Hamptons, Lazio had accused Hillary of "flip-flopping" on the embassy relocation. Back in December, she'd said she did not support the immediate move of the embassy. So my office had put a story on the wire leading with Lazio accusing Hillary of reversing her position.

Hillary's campaign went into overdrive. Karen Dunn called seven—count 'em, seven—times to complain and in the end spoke to every single person who was in the office that day in an effort to get a sympathetic ear. She questioned why we'd chosen to lead with one of Lazio's countercharges, which we didn't usually do, instead of with what she saw as the actual news—Hillary's statement on the embassy.

"*We* need to change this lead," she said at one point.

"Which *we* did she think she was talking about?" one of my colleagues later asked me. And Howard called once to say he didn't like the headline on the version of the story we were putting out on the broadcast wire.

Despite the campaign's complaints about the story, it didn't sound to me as if there was anything technically wrong with it. Lazio had made the accusation, and it was perfectly legitimate to report what one candidate says about another, as long as you give all the facts surrounding the accusation so that readers can make up their own minds. On the other hand, I'm not sure I would have led that way; to me it was more interesting that every time the administration made a pronouncement on the Middle East, Hillary was taking a stand that appeared to be just a little more pro-Israeli.

What the entire episode really showed was how much Jewish voters matter in New York. Jewish turnout is typically just 12 to 14 percent of the electorate, and Jewish Democrats outnumber Jewish Republicans about six to one. But a small group of several hundred thousand politically moderate Jews are considered swing voters. Most of the ultra-Orthodox typically vote Republican—although Hillary did manage to corner endorsements from a couple of Hasidic sects—and Lazio would never get the unshakably liberal Jews for whom pulling the GOP lever was anathema.

But the past few Senate races suggested that a Democrat who couldn't get more than 60 percent of the Jewish vote couldn't win. Mark Green and Robert Abrams, both of whom failed to beat D'Amato, did not reach the 60 percent mark. Both were liberal Jewish Democrats but both ran flawed campaigns. In contrast, Chuck Schumer, also a relatively liberal Jewish Democrat, had captured closer to 70 percent of the Jewish vote, and he had beat D'Amato.

Ironically, just as Jewish issues became flashpoints in Hillary's campaign—the Suha kiss, FJB, the Muslim fund-raising—D'Amato's use of a Yiddish word had helped Schumer win. At a private meeting with Jewish leaders shortly before the '98 election, Al called Chuck a "putzhead," which generally connotes a bumbling fool but literally means "penis." Someone who was at the meeting tattled on D'Amato, and Schumer accused him of using a "Yiddish slur." At first D'Amato denied it, but then Ed Koch and a few others who'd been at the meeting confirmed that D'Amato had said it, making him look not only like a liar but also like a pretty crude guy. Schumer effectively used the incident to make the case to voters that D'Amato—who had a reputation for making outrageous comments and who'd been rebuked by the Senate Ethics Committee for allowing his brother's lobbying firm to use the senator's office to help a client—could simply not be trusted to tell the truth or to behave appropriately. D'Amato was popular in the Jewish community for taking on the Swiss banking industry over Holocaust reparations, but that wasn't enough to make up for "putzhead."

Polls showed Hillary's support among Jews at between 50 and 60 percent. That actually wasn't bad for a non-Jew with the FJB allegation and the Suha kiss in her carpetbag. But the conventional wisdom was that she'd have to do better than that to win the election, and that's what all these trips to synagogues, pronouncements on Israeli policies, and phone calls from the campaign were about. (In the end, she got a little more than half the Jewish vote—about what she'd had all along, which led me to believe that her repeated attempts to portray herself as a great lover of all things Jewish, and her enemies' attempts to portray her as an anti-Semite, had canceled each other out.)

Hillary also had a way of getting herself in trouble on issues related to Israel. There was the comment she'd made back in '98 that a Palestinian state was "very important" to the long-term prospects for peace in the Middle East. There was the Suha Arafat kiss. And then, in July, just four months before the election, there was the FJB allegation.

Shortly after the Hampton Synagogue appearances, I ran into Frank Eltman, my Lazio counterpart, at the office. We talked on the phone constantly—often one or both of us on a cell phone that pooped out before we could complete the conversation—but since he was always out covering Lazio and I was always covering Hillary, we hardly ever saw each other. When we did, we couldn't stop chatting. We were like two soldiers hanging out in a VFW hall or a couple of addicts in a twelve-step program. It was as if nobody else in the world understood what we were going through. But this time Frank said he had something funny to tell me and motioned me over to where he was sitting. Then he started singing softly, to the tune of "Anything you can do, I can do better":

Any Jew you can woo, I can woo better.
I can woo any Jew better than you.

I started laughing hysterically. This was simply the funniest campaign song I had ever heard. And the scene it conjured up from *Annie Get Your Gun* was perfect: Annie, or rather Hillary, and her male opponent in a sharpshooting contest, trying to outdo each other. The next time I covered Hillary, I sang it for everyone on the van, and we all agreed that it was not only hilarious, but also because it was a duet, it perfectly captured the dynamic between the candidates and the Jewish voters they were after.

Of course, what neither Frank nor I realized when he first shared his little spoof with me was that the shooting contest between Hillary and Rick—and their jostling for Jewish votes—had only just begun.

Looking back on it after the election, it was so hard to pick out a favorite moment from the Jew-wooing effort. Was it the day Hillary held a press conference with Elie Wiesel, aka "my good friend Elie Wiesel," to express outrage over anti-Semitic statements from a textbook used by the Palestinian Authority? Needless to say, this was not a pressing issue in the New York Senate race.

Or maybe it was the day she went to a YWHA in the Bronx with Hadassah Lieberman, aka "my good friend Hadassah Lieberman," and said that she'd been to Israel five times. That event had been preceded by a speech to a meeting of the National Council of Jewish Women and a visit to a Hebrew day school on Long Island, prompting Joel Siegel of the *Daily News* to ask as we got back in the van, "Does anybody know how to say 'pander' in Yiddish?"

One of Hillary's Jewish events seems much more memorable in hindsight than it did at the time: her visit on August 8, 2000, to New Square, a Hasidic village in Rockland County. Neatly uniformed students from a New Square school for girls stood in rows to greet the first lady, who'd traded in her black pantsuit for a dress on that occasion. Hillary also met that day with the village's spiritual leader, Rabbi David Twersky. Despite disagreeing with her on the voucher issue, Twersky endorsed Hillary's candidacy. As a result, on election day, Hillary got exactly 1,400 votes from the village, while Lazio got exactly twelve. The monolithic nature of the vote was not unusual; Hasidic voters typically follow their rabbis' lead. Even their support for a Democrat was not particularly noteworthy; this particular sect often flip-flopped between parties, supporting Bush for president in 1992, Clinton for president in 1996, D'Amato for Senate and Pataki for governor in 1998, and Gore for president in 2000.

But New Square's support for Hillary became extremely newsworthy after Bill Clinton gave clemency to four men from the community. The men had been convicted of ripping off millions of dollars in government grants for poor college students by establishing a phony school in Brooklyn; most of the money had been illegally funneled to real schools in New Square that were not eligible for government funding. Bill Clinton commuted the men's sentences from more than five years in prison to less than three years after meeting with Twersky and a delegation from the village in the White House on December 21, six weeks after his wife's victory. Hillary was present for the meeting, but later insisted, when asked about the appearance of a political payback, that the president had made the decision to grant the clemency without any input from her. "I had no opinion at the time," she said.

Bill Clinton's pardon of Marc Rich, who'd fled the United States to avoid prosecution for illegal oil deals with Iran, had a Jewish connection, too: Ehud Barak, then Israeli prime minister, had lobbied for it. It was ironic that Hillary had to fight accusations of anti-Semitism before she was elected because of the Suha kiss and the FJB scandal, because once she took office, she and her husband had to fight the perception that they'd done too many favors for the Jewish community.

Another memorable episode in Hillary's campaign for Jewish votes occurred when she visited a nursing home for Holocaust survivors with Tom Lantos, aka "my good friend Tom Lantos," a California Democrat who is the only Holocaust survivor to serve in Congress. Three weeks before the nursing home event, Lantos had told the *New York Post* about the existence of the photo that showed Lazio shaking hands with Yasir Arafat. The photograph was taken during a visit to the Middle East by a delegation that included the Clintons, Lantos, Lazio, and many other U.S. government officials. Lantos said he'd decided to tip the *Post* off to the picture because he was angry that Lazio had criticized the president for shaking Fidel Castro's hand during a United Nations gathering in New York. But the photo also made a nice comeback to people who'd criticized Hillary for kissing Suha Arafat. Lazio didn't just appear to be shaking Arafat's hand in the interests of avoiding an international incident; he had a grin on his face from ear to ear and looked, in his boyish way, really excited to be meeting a famous person.

But the incident from the nursing home event that lived on and on in campaign lore was when Hillary said Lantos had been "ka-velling about his grandchildren." *Kvelling* is a Yiddish word that means gushing with joy and pride, the opposite of kvetching. Hillary had used the word appropriately, but her pronunciation was all wrong. *Kvell* is properly pronounced as one syllable, with the *kv* blend taking no longer to say than the *fl* in *flute*, but Hillary could only say it improperly, as *ka-vell*.

I thought maybe she was taking her cue from Sally Field, who'd bantered with a Jewish union organizer in the movie *Norma Rae* by muttering, "Ka-vetch, ka-vetch, ka-vetch."

I later found out that the first lady had had a *My Fair Lady*–style coaching session with her Jewish staffers during a routine conference call, but it hadn't done much good. It had been her idea to use the word *kvell*, but she'd known she needed a lesson on how to say it. She'd impressed her Jewish aides with her pronunciation on a few other occasions, getting the guttural *ch* in *chutzpah* just right during one of the debates with Lazio, and casually, but correctly, using the word *shul* (Yiddish for synagogue) at an event at the White House one day. From her point of view, using these words showed that she had a certain comfort level with Jewish culture and maybe even earned her a brownie point or two for trying to fit in.

But mastering the pronunciation of *kvell* right turned out to be a lost cause.

"*Kvuh, kvuh,* it's one syllable, can't you hear it?" the aides had told her.

"*Ka-vuh, ka-vuh,*" she'd replied. "That's what I said!"

Hillary's Favorite Color

August 2, 2000. "Scalia or Thomas?" somebody is saying. "Come *on*, what do you say? Scalia or Thomas?"

"I'd do 'em both," a woman answers in a deadpan voice.

"Thomas," says someone else with a snicker. "Could be interesting."

I look up from my breakfast. We are sitting in a diner on the second day of Hillary's three-day tour of Long Island, and I am feeling slightly bummed out. I had planned to finish three stories while she was out here, the first a straightforward piece about her campaigning on Lazio's home turf, the second a feature story about the political instincts of her daughter, Chelsea, who's campaigning with her, and the third, a fun, light feature story about the candidates' "favorites"—favorite junk food, favorite color, favorite book—that I'd been trying to complete for a month.

The first story wrote itself with no trouble yesterday, but here it was, not even nine o'clock in the morning a day later, and my prospects for finishing the other two stories were already looking bleak. Yesterday Chelsea had come off like a totally political animal, thriving on the attention of the public and the press, but today she seems bored and unenthusiastic. And Karen Finney, Hillary's press aide, who had promised yesterday to help me get the answers from Hillary for my favorite list, has just informed me that she didn't have a chance to do anything on it yet.

I'm on one side of the dining room at a big round table with a few other reporters and campaign workers, while Hillary, Chelsea, and some of the locals are eating and chatting at a different table on the other side of the room. The first lady and her daughter are eating fruit, but most of the reporters have ordered the most unhealthy breakfasts possible: runny eggs, white toast, sausage, bacon, and of course, lots of coffee, since we all got up at dawn to watch Hillary greet early-morning commuters at a Long Island Rail Road station in Hicksville.

I tune in to the conversation at the table and realize I have no idea what my colleagues are talking about.

"Scalia or Thomas? What does that mean?" I say. "Why are you talking about George W.'s favorite judges?" Hillary was always pointing out in her speeches that Bush was an admirer of the most antiabortion judges on the Supreme Court. It was one of those sound bites that every reporter who covered her could intone, from memory, along with her.

"Death is not an option," replies one of the other reporters in a tone of voice that suggests I am an idiot. "You have to have sex with one of these people—Scalia or Thomas—and death is not an option. So, like, Schumer or D'Amato?"

Groans. "Yuck!" No one makes a pick. "Okay, Koch or Giuliani?"

The offerings rapidly devolve. Next is a choice between two of Hillary's advisers, and then a choice between two of the TV reporters who are not with us today.

"This game is totally bizarre," I say. "You realize that, right?"

It is explained to me that this is one of the many pastimes I have missed out on by staying home during Hillary's upstate trips, where she is on the road for up to a week at a time. The press has so much downtime and so little news that demented games like this one arise out of the mud. Just in the last twenty-four hours I have also learned how to play Punchy Bug, in which you punch the shoulder of the person sitting next to you in the press van every time you see a Volkswagen. And I have been taught a new song to the tune of "Someone's in the kitchen with Dinah":

Someone's in the Senate with Schumer
Someone's in the Senate I know
Someone's in the Senate with Schumer
Strummin' on the old banjo
And singin' H, I, LL-A-R-Y. H, I, LL-A-R-Y-I-I-I . . ."

This ditty is usually performed in an operatic basso, just as, I am told, it was first sung to Hillary and the press corps by an admirer—a lounge singer named Spiro—during a minor league baseball game in Jamestown. Since then, of course, my colleagues have improved upon it with such intelligent variations as "Someone's in the shower with Schumer." I add this lovely selection to the ever-growing repertoire in my brain that already includes "Any Jew you can woo, I can woo better" and "What if Hil were one of us? Could she tawk like one of us?"

We finish our breakfast. One reporter picks up the tab for our whole table, which includes meals for the Karens. It's too much trouble to get separate checks, so the person who thinks he can get reimbursed most easily by his employer pays for everyone.

A couple of us wander across the room to where Hillary is sitting and stand a few feet away, close enough to eavesdrop but far enough away so that we can pretend we are nonchalantly hanging around. From where we'd been sitting, we could see Chelsea speaking animatedly to her tablemates, most of them local officials—county Democratic Party committee members, delegates, and so on, so we were curious to know what she'd been so excited about. But by the time we get there, either the conversation has petered out or Chelsea's antennae are up. She stops talking, stands up with her mother, and they bid their good-byes.

As we follow them out of the restaurant to the waiting vans, I check out their dirty plates. I'd been slightly dubious of Finney's report that they were eating fruit—especially when we were all feasting on cholesterol and fat—but there are indeed leftover blueberries in bowls where they'd been sitting. We were forever writing details like this down in our notebooks, but at the end of the day there was hardly ever any room for it in our copy.

"By the way," says Finney with a smile, "in case you're wondering, yes, Hillary paid for their breakfast, and, yes, she left a tip." Hillary's tips had been an issue ever since the *Washington Times* made a headline out of her staff's failure to leave one for a waitress in an upstate restaurant where the first lady had been given a complimentary meal. The embarrassed campaign later mailed a savings bond to the waitress, a single mother.

Next stop after the diner was a day camp. Chelsea sat at a wood-sculpture table with a bunch of little girls and absentmindedly made a tall pile of wood shapes. Then she wandered over to the pool where her mother was watching a relay race. But when Liz Moore of *Newsday* good-naturedly asked her if she thought the kids would vote for her mother, Chelsea stared straight ahead and walked away as if some terrible line had been crossed.

She'd been friendlier a few weeks earlier when she'd accompanied her mother to a press conference on the steps of City Hall, her first appearance on the campaign trail in nearly a year. I'd asked Hillary during the Q-and-A if Chelsea was going to be showing up regularly from now on, and she'd said that was entirely up to Chelsea. When the event was over, we all ran over to where Chelsea was standing to see if she'd elaborate. Finney introduced us and we shook hands, but when I started to ask Chelsea whether we'd be seeing a lot of her in the future, Finney physically inserted herself between us, saying firmly, "Now, Beth, I think her mother answered that already."

"Hey, I'm a mom, I understand these things, and I think I heard her mother say that what Chelsea does is up to her," I said.

Chelsea perked up immediately. "You have children? How old are they?"

"Seven and two, and they know all about *your* mother," I said with a smile. "They can pick her picture out of a photograph with a hundred other people in it."

"They're smarties," Chelsea said sweetly, then turned to head off with her mother's entourage.

Suddenly I felt like a dope. I'd wasted the two-minute window I'd had with Chelsea by talking about *me.* I'd rather talk about my kids than just about anything else, and Chelsea had been savvy enough to figure that out. One of the most basic rules of journalism is that when your source starts asking about you, you have to turn the conversation back to them. I hadn't done that, and now it was too late.

"Sorry about that, Beth," said Karen. "I just didn't want it to degenerate into a whole avail."

"Yeah, yeah. You do your job, I'll do mine," I said, feeling that I hadn't done it very well at all. The whole notion that Chelsea could come to a press conference and not take questions was infuriating enough. If she wanted to be private, fine, but don't stand five feet away from a pack of reporters and then let a campaign staffer protect you from the media.

Soon after that, the White House announced that Chelsea planned to take off the fall semester of her senior year at Stanford to campaign with her mother and spend time with her father during his last months in office. I took Hillary at her word that this was Chelsea's decision, but it certainly didn't hurt the first lady to have her daughter along. After all, Lazio had two adorable little girls who often accompanied him on his campaign trips. "Vote for my dad!" they'd shout as the photographers snapped away. One day, when Lazio was being interviewed on ABC's *This Week*, I sat in a TV studio with his wife, Pat, and the girls, waiting for his segment to start. Molly and Kelsey were like two little kittens, tumbling over each other in the hallway, using a rubber band they had found to play cat's cradle, hiding under the buffet, nibbling at the food, and then handing their dad a handful of crumbs when he came in the room. And Pat seemed like such a nice, normal person. I was shocked at being allowed to sit in a room with her and her kids. I couldn't imagine anything like this happening on the Hillary campaign. Sit in a room with Chelsea and watch her mother on TV? Have a normal conversation with someone who's related to Hillary? Not have your bags searched and your movements restricted when you walk in the door? As Pat and I griped to each other about the amount of homework our kids got in school, I couldn't help but think that there was a whole other world over here in Lazio Country that those of us on the other side of the Hillary Border couldn't imagine.

It also occurred to me that Chelsea could never be in her own little world the way the Lazio girls were, oblivious to all the busy grown-ups around them. Chelsea was always *on* when she was out with her parents, on display as the only child of important people, and instead of having a sibling to giggle with, her confidants were the people who'd been hired to protect her and make sure her needs were met. It was more like watching a princess venturing out among the common people than Take Your Daughter to Work Day.

Which isn't to say Chelsea didn't act as though she loved it. On the first day of the Long Island tour, at an outdoor rally in Great Neck, the twenty-year-old first daughter really did seem enthusiastic and had displayed an impressive ability to work the crowd. She hadn't even tried to stay by her mother's side, but instead waded into her own section of the reception line, posing for photographs, shaking hands, signing autographs, leaning down to greet old ladies in wheelchairs and babies in strollers. "Thank you for letting me spend some time with your child," I heard her coo to one parent. She had the perfect posture, clasped hands, and ever-present smile of someone who was accustomed to being stared at, and she seemed comfortable accepting the adulation of dozens of gawking strangers who jostled to meet her. It wasn't poise exactly, but more like a series of poses. Now she's in her chatty mode, relating to a teenager. Now she's in her respectful mode, nodding and listening to an old man. Now she's in her dutiful-daughter mode, gazing with love and awe as her mother gives a speech.

And while she didn't have conventional good looks, she was strikingly pretty: a halo of honey-golden curls moussed into waves, heavily powdered face, and a handsome figure in formfitting slacks and a short-sleeved knit top. At first glance, she closely resembled her father, her eyes and nose conjuring up his. But her big, friendly grin, with perfect teeth shining out of a heart-shaped, brightly lipsticked mouth, was exactly like her mother's. A lot of my colleagues complained that Chelsea wore too much makeup, but I'd always say, "Come on, give her a break. She's only twenty."

I'd put some of the Chelsea material into the straightforward spot story I'd dictated yesterday about Hillary starting the three-day visit to Long Island, and I'd hoped to get even better stuff today. My brain was bouncing around phrases like "bred in the bone . . . her father's footsteps . . . like father, like daughter . . . the Clinton gene for pleasing the crowd," and I'd asked the photographer who was working with me to save whatever he didn't transmit yesterday to go with the story today.

The only problem today was Chelsea. She simply wasn't cooperating with the story that I was writing in my mind. Yesterday she'd taken the initiative to work the crowd, approaching bystanders with her arm extended. Today, at the train station, while her mother positioned herself so she could catch commuters on their way to the platform, Chelsea had hung back, standing fifteen feet away with a couple of aides, saying hi only when one of the people rushing by happened to notice her. She was perfectly polite and friendly when approached and even borrowed my pen to sign a couple of autographs. But it was clear that her heart wasn't in it. Then at the restaurant and the day camp she'd made it clear that she was also off-limits to all of us. The real Chelsea had obliterated the Chelsea I'd profiled in my head, and my story was nowhere. And naturally, although we requested a Q-and-A with Chelsea, we didn't get one. While I could see why they didn't want to have Chelsea answering our questions, it also seemed unfair that they could trot her out as a big campaign prop but then deny us the right to get a few quotes.

I didn't know then that the day she'd spent working the line, chatting with everybody, would be one of the few days that she accompanied her mother and didn't seem like a robot. In October, she and her mother went to a senior citizens residence in Queens, and the lady who was emceeing the event sweetly asked Chelsea, who was doing her usual plastered-on smile and robotic-clap routine, if the audience could just hear the sound of her voice. The first daughter stepped up to the microphone and, sounding more like Ginger on *Gilligan's Island* than a senior at Stanford, uttered a breathy "Heh-low," then stepped away. The audience was silent for a moment, expecting the oddly orphaned greeting to be followed by some conventional phrase like "It's so nice to be here" or "Thank you for your support for my mother." But that was it. Just "Heh-low" and nothing else. For the rest of the campaign, you could hear reporters covering Hillary muttering "Heh-low" to themselves at all hours of the day and night. On a long, boring string of meaningless events, even the grumpiest, hungriest, most exhausted journalist could manage a smile in response to that little "Heh-low." Part of what made it seem so funny was imagining the talking-to Hillary had given her afterward, kind of like the way anybody's momma would react if their kid had blown a chance to impress the grandparents.

We were back in the van now, headed to our next stop, a news conference where Hillary was to be endorsed by Planned Parenthood. I usually get a lot of work done on the van rides, using the few minutes that I'm out of Hillary's presence to organize my notes, listen to my tape, and call my office by cell phone. But so far I had nothing to report. I'd gotten up at five o'clock that morning, taken a six o'clock train to get to Hillary's LIRR meet-and-greet by seven, schlepped to a diner and a summer camp, but I had absolutely nothing.

"What's the lead?" I whined to Bob Hardt of the *New York Post*.

"There is no lead," he responded matter-of-factly. "We're in a news-free zone."

The other reporters assured me that a lot of downtime was normal for Hillary's trips. Although I'd covered her in New York City and its suburbs nearly every time she'd had a public event since September of '98, months before she'd even started running for office, I wasn't used to this type of on-the-road campaign swing. The AP's upstate staff usually covered her road trips, and because I hated being away from home and my kids overnight, I was just as happy to spend most of my time a train ride away from Brooklyn. On this particular swing through Long Island, most of the other reporters were staying overnight in hotels on the island where Hillary and her staff were camping out, while I took the train home at the end of the day and came back first thing in the morning.

The other reporters had told me Hillary was much more relaxed and friendly out of the city, and I could see it was true. During a lull in her morning meet-and-greet at the train station, she'd wandered over to chat with a few of us, greeting us by our first names, as she always did, and exchanging pleasantries. But we were not supposed to ask newsworthy questions at moments like this; these were just rare chitchat moments, the type of thing you got all the time with normal candidates, but which seemed truly memorable with Hil because they were so infrequent.

The Planned Parenthood event turned out to be mildly newsworthy. Chelsea sat on a stage with her mother's supporters, her back perfectly straight, her hands on her lap, and a bright smile on her face as one of the emcees looked at her and said, "We all feel like hugging her. We all watched her grow up." Then Hillary got up to speak, and when the applause died down, I recited the first words out of Hillary's mouth right along with her: "Thank you. Thank you *so-o-o-o-o* much. I'm delighted, and just really honored, to be here . . ."

Today Hillary followed her usual opening line with a salute to New York's history as a leader on reproductive rights, from Margaret Sanger's first birth-control clinic to the legalization of abortion, to her standard assertion that "this election is about choice. It's about protecting every woman's right to choose. It's also about whether we choose to build on the progress and prosperity of the last eight years. . . ."

George W.'s favorite justices came up, of course, and I suppressed an urge to shout "Death is not an option!" Then there were the standard anecdotes from her childhood: the father who didn't own a credit card (of course, not many people did in 1950, but that wasn't part of her speech), and the church youth group that either went to hear Martin Luther King Jr. speak (she told that story to black audiences) or organized teenage girls to baby-sit for the children of migrant farmworkers (she told that story at ladies' lunches). Today it was the baby-sitting anecdote, and as Hillary got to the part of the story where her mother took it upon herself to provide a christening dress for a little Mexican girl from a poor family, I noticed Taina Hernandez, a cable TV news reporter for NY1 who was sitting next to me, shaking her head in disgust. "I hate this story," she muttered. "It's so patronizing."

Next up was the list of problems Hillary had personally witnessed in New York's schools, including the textbook she said was still being used in an upstate classroom that included the line "Someday America will send a man to the moon." I repeated that one along with her, too, more out of habit than anything else. Listening to these speeches was a little like going to a prayer service over and over. Even if you didn't believe in it, sometimes you just couldn't stop yourself from reciting the words along with everybody else.

Finally we got to the meat of the message: an attack on Lazio, or, as she always referred to him without using his name, "my opponent." Lazio had voted against the Democrats' version of a "patient's bill of rights," which would have given patients the right to sue their HMO. The Republicans rejected the legislation as nothing more than a boon to trial lawyers, and Hillary said that Lazio "just had gone crazy" any-time she pointed out his vote on the issue. "I just don't understand," she added with feigned incredulity. "He's either going to accept his record or he's going to have to continue to try to run from it."

I realized at that moment that my tape had run out. There was no point in turning it over now; I had certainly missed the crucial "gone crazy" quote. Although my messy note-taking was good enough to get a couple of simple sentences down verbatim in a brief interview, I didn't trust myself to get it all right in longhand in a long-winded speech like this unless I could check it with a few of my colleagues. And while a lot of other politicians—from George W. Bush to David Dinkins—handed out prepared texts to the press hours before they gave their speeches and then delivered them word for word, Hillary never once provided copies of her speeches beforehand. She also ad-libbed so much that a prepared text wouldn't have done us much good anyway. Sure, there were a few passages we all knew by heart—the thank-yous, the baby-sitting story, the man-on-the-moon textbook, but the stuff that made news—quotes like "gone crazy" that we would actually end up putting in a story—was not likely to have been typed beforehand into her notes.

Her tone of voice suggested that we were nearing the end. "I am pro-choice," she declared, "and I will never vote to confirm a justice to the Supreme Court who would vote to overturn *Roe v. Wade*. My opponent won't say that simple statement."

There was one more detour before the end: the lessons she'd learned from her first lady travels to maternity wards around the world. I'd only heard this one twice before, and it was actually kind of interest-

ing, so I tuned in. In Brazil, she said, the maternity wards were full
of poor women maimed by botched abortions that they'd sought
because they couldn't support any more children. In Romania, where
the secret police followed pregnant women to make sure they didn't
obtain abortions, the orphanages were full of unwanted children. And
in China, population control was achieved through forced abortions
and government-mandated sterilizations. "Any government interference
in a woman's right to choose must be stopped and prevented wherever
it occurs," she concluded, then headed into her wrap-up: "The presidential election will be a tough fight. Mine will be a tough one as
well. . . . But with your help, we can win this." By now, people were
clapping and her thank-yous were lost in the din.

I started asking around to listen to someone's tape for the "gone
crazy" quote. Technical difficulties with the small battery-operated tape
recorders we all carried were common, and most reporters were pretty
good about sharing. Liz Moore let me borrow hers, and I taped the section I needed directly onto my own cassette. Then I called into the
office. Lazio had just gotten an endorsement in Manhattan from the
corrections officers union, and after consulting with Frank Eltman, who
was covering Lazio, we decided to use his endorsement from the prison
guards and Hillary's from Planned Parenthood for a combined lead. I
also dumped the "gone crazy" attack quotes, and Frank said he'd take
care of getting a response from Lazio's people.

Then I gave Frank the bad news that Finney had made no progress
in helping me to complete the "favorites" story. This was of particular
interest to Frank because he'd had no trouble getting Lazio's staff to
help him finish his list a month earlier. The idea for the story was not
particularly original, but it had grown out of a meeting we'd had with
some of the AP staff from upstate who'd told us that a lot of the local
papers were becoming bored with the daily campaign stories. The story
that got more play than just about anything else we'd done in recent
times was Frank's account of Lazio falling in a Memorial Day parade

and splitting his lip. At least it was a story about something real happening, instead of just another talking head. We brainstormed a little and somebody said it was too bad we couldn't ask Hillary the famous "boxers or briefs" question that a seventeen-year-old girl had asked Bill Clinton on MTV. The closest we could come to that, someone else had mused, was to ask her if she wore "cotton or nylon."

I knew I'd never have the nerve to ask Hillary the "cotton or nylon" question. It would have been like asking the Queen Mother if she preferred seamless bras or underwire. Sure, I had no problem asking Hillary about a political controversy, but an underwear controversy? Call me a coward; I couldn't do it. So in the end Frank and I came up with a list we thought would be interesting for readers without blowing our credibility with the candidates. I decided I'd try to get through my list in July, when I and an upstate AP staffer were granted a sit-down interview with Hillary in upstate Corning. Lazio's staff wasn't willing to make him available for a similar sit-down, but they did the next best thing: one of his press secretaries took the list and had Lazio answer all the questions while Frank's tape recorder was running, then gave the tape back to Frank.

I waited until we'd gotten through all the serious questions during the Corning interview—Travelgate, how she'd changed as a candidate during the past year, etc.—and then I explained the "favorites" idea to her. She laughed and seemed amenable, so I started with the list, expecting a one- or two-word answer to everything. Instead I got a whole megillah. Most people have a quick answer to "How do you take your coffee?" Not Hillary. Sometimes she takes her coffee black, she explained, other times with lots of cream, sometimes she likes espresso, sometimes cappuccino. You just couldn't pin Hillary down—at least not on her java habits. Then there was the question about the worst job she'd ever had. Lazio had given a two-word answer: "Mosquito control." No explanation. No elaboration. But Hillary's worst-job story was a virtual parable of youthful righteousness. She'd been traveling with a friend around the country after college and had ended up in Alaska, where she got a job on a floating dock processing salmon. She was issued a raincoat, rubber boots, and a spoon and was instructed to scoop the guts out of the fish. But she decided the fish didn't look all that healthy, and she sought out the manager to pass on her concerns. Her complaints apparently spooked the owners, or maybe they really did have something to hide, because when she returned for her next shift, the whole fish-processing operation had disappeared without a trace. Strike one for Hillary the Moral Crusader! It was a good story, and oh-so-Hillary, but it took so long for her to tell it that by the time she was finished, Howard Wolfson told us the interview was over. That left me with seven or eight questions I hadn't had a chance to ask.

So Frank had his list done in an afternoon without even being in the candidate's presence. I'd had a coveted private sit-down with Hillary and hadn't gotten through half of it. I sent Howard an e-mail asking for help in completing it. No response. A few days later, I sent him another e-mail with the same nonresult. When I found out about the Long Island trip, it seemed as if it might be the perfect opportunity to get someone on Hillary's staff to help me out the way Lazio's staff had assisted Frank. I felt kind of silly about it, of course; it seemed ridiculous to go to all this trouble to find out Hillary's favorite color. On the other hand, it was infuriating to me that it had become such a big deal when the questions were so short and straightforward and the Lazio list was long done.

I was thrilled when Finney readily agreed to help me complete the favorites list on the first day of the trip. But when she told me the second day that she hadn't had a chance to pursue it, I started obsessing and even getting paranoid about it. Such a simple problem, yet I was so powerless to fix it. I began fantasizing that I would have to ask the questions one at a time at Hillary's press conferences. Everyone else would be asking about education policy or her stand on Israel, and I would be shouting out something about her favorite movie. Or maybe I would have to ask her on one of those rare occasions when she strolled over to say good morning before an event formally began. "Good morning, Mrs. Clinton," I imagined myself responding. "As long as you're standing here, do you mind if I ask you what your favorite junk food is?" I realized all of this would make me the laughingstock of the New York press corps and she would never answer anyway.

On the final day of the three-day Long Island swing, Frank and I decided to trade beats. Lazio was doing a campaign stop at a kosher pizzeria in Borough Park, Brooklyn, an Orthodox Jewish neighborhood, and "Jews in the news"—my pet name for the many stories we wrote about New York's diverse and politically active Jewish community—was one of my favorite subjects, so I wanted to be there. Frank, meanwhile, lived not too far from where Hillary was starting her day on the island and was just as happy to follow her around. Besides, we discovered it was helpful to trade beats every now and then and shake off whatever symptoms of the Stockholm syndrome you get when you're covering the same candidate all the time. Sure, you get annoyed with them, but you also spend so much time at rallies filled with their supporters where the party faithful get up and sing their praises that sometimes it's good to talk to some of the people who hate your candidate's guts.

I got a ride out to Borough Park with a photographer and figured I might as well use the time to harass Finney again about the "favorites" list. I didn't have her cell phone number with me, so I called Karen Dunn on hers, knowing that the two Karens are usually in the same vicinity. Dunn said Finney couldn't come to the phone just then. I tried again a few minutes later, but she was still tied up.

Then, as we waited for Lazio to arrive at the pizzeria, I noticed Gregg Birnbaum from the *Post* talking to Howard on his cell phone. Frank had jokingly pointed out to me earlier that Hillary didn't really understand Long Island culture because she'd spent three days there without ever dropping by a mall, so I figured I'd yank Howard's chain.

"Ask Howard how Hillary expects to win the Jewish vote without hitting the Miracle Mile," I called out to Gregg. The Miracle Mile, located in the wealthy suburb of Manhasset, is a strip of designer boutiques and upscale stores, made famous in Billy Joel's "It's Still Rock and Roll to Me" with the line "Are you gonna cruise the Miracle Mile?"

"Beth wants to know why Hillary didn't go to the Miracle Mile," Gregg told Howard. "Something about it being a national Jewish landmark."

I laughed. "And ask him when I'm going to get the favorites list finished."

Gregg repeated the question and then passed on Howard's response: "He says you should have done it when you had the chance."

I stopped laughing and started obsessing again. When I had the chance? What was that supposed to mean? Now they were not only not cooperating with me, they were being mean about it!

Lazio's arrival interrupted my paranoid thought process. He got out of his van and was immediately surrounded by a small mob of ladies in housedresses with shopping carts and men in yarmulkes. Most of them had no idea who he was, but they could tell he was somebody important because his picture was being taken by a gaggle of photographers. And when they found out he was running against Hillary, his stock went up.

"Ooooh, I can't tolerate her!" one of the shopping-cart ladies said to me.

"She's an anti-Semite!" added one of the men.

Clearly Hillary's battle for the Jewish vote wasn't going to be won on this corner. Not only did they believe the FJB story, thinking Hillary had really used the term *fucking Jew bastard* in an argument in Arkansas twenty-six years ago, but they also viewed her as far too sympathetic toward the Palestinians.

But even though the locals were happy to meet the man who was running against Hillary, they couldn't be persuaded to sit next to him once he got inside the pizza place. Perhaps it was because they weren't really sure who Lazio was, or perhaps it was the presence of a dozen of us, following him around, scribbling in notebooks and carrying cameras. Either way, this provided a somewhat comic touch to the event: Lazio sitting all alone at a table for six, digging into an eight-slice pie by himself.

All of a sudden Lazio noticed the Democratic Party's tracker, Eric Schultz, a young guy with a video camera on his shoulder who followed Lazio around like a stalker and reported back on his activities to Hillary's supporters. Eric was a college student who'd taken the semester off from Washington University to help out with the campaign and was sent out every day to try to blend in with the TV crews and capture as much of Lazio as he could on videotape. Sometimes Lazio's staff would put their hands over his lens or wave American flags in front of it, and they did not permit him to attend events that were held in private venues. But in public places, they more or less tolerated his presence. Frank told me that sometimes Lazio even pointed him out to his supporters, saying, "Let's all say hello to Mrs. Clinton!" The Republicans did not have a similar spy on their side taping Hillary's every move, but the need probably wasn't as acute, since any screwup by Hillary would be duly recorded and publicized by all of us.

As Lazio fixed his gaze on Eric in the pizza place, a big grin appeared on the congressman's face, as if he'd just come up with a really clever joke. He grabbed a slice from the pie and held it out in Eric's direction. "Here, have something to eat!" Lazio said to him boisterously while everybody laughed. "You been working so hard following me around, you must be hungry!" Even Eric had to smile, although he turned the slice down.

Lazio shook a few more hands outside the restaurant, then held a brief Q-and-A. Since Hillary was always pointing out George W.'s admiration for Scalia and Thomas, I was thinking about asking Lazio to name his favorite Supreme Court justice. I'd mentioned this to my husband the night before, and he'd predicted that Lazio would pick Sandra Day O'Connor. O'Connor, a Reagan appointee, was part of the court's conservative majority, but she'd voted to uphold *Roe v. Wade* on the grounds that outlawing abortion would have grave consequences in a society that had come to take it for granted. She would be the perfect pick for a candidate like Lazio, who wanted voters to view him as pro-choice without losing his Republican credentials.

I waited until a couple of the more serious questions had been asked; in case the press conference was cut short, I didn't want to feel that I had used up everybody's valuable time with a throwaway. But after a few minutes it seemed pretty clear that Lazio would stand there until everyone had what he or she needed. No Howard on this gig shouting a firm "Thank you, Mrs. Clinton!"

So I tossed it out: "Who's your favorite Supreme Court justice?"

He thought about it for a moment, then answered, "Sandra Day O'Connor."

Bingo! Predictable, yet politically perfect. Then it hit me that I had gotten Lazio to answer a favorite question a day after it had occurred to me; meanwhile I was still trying to get my Hillary favorites pinned down after weeks of trying.

Back at the office I got a call from Frank, who'd been to a press conference on a Long Island beach with Hillary. He told me he'd asked Finney about the favorites list and that she'd blown up on him. "I'm issuing a cease-and-desist order on this subject!" she'd told him. Apparently an AP photographer whom I'd also enlisted in my cause to get the list done had asked her about it, too, and she was starting to get annoyed by all the pressure.

But if Finney wasn't going to help me, how would I ever get it done? It occurred to me that maybe Hillary had been asked all these questions in other interviews and I could just research all the answers myself. A few days later I had some spare time in the office and hooked up to the "Ask Jeeves" Web site.

"What is Hillary Rodham Clinton's favorite color?" I typed in the search box.

"I have found answers to the following questions," the Web site responded. "Is 'What's your favorite color?' a good opener for a first date? Where can I find biographical resources from Britannica.com on Hillary Rodham Clinton? What is the traditional Western symbolism behind black? Who is the first lady of the United States?" Obviously "Ask Jeeves" wasn't going to be much help.

I started to make up desperation scenarios. I would tell Howard I was about to get fired unless I got the favorites list done. I would threaten to write a story about how the Clinton campaign was putting up roadblocks to my finding out Hillary's favorite junk food. I would hold up signs at campaign rallies that read, "Why won't Hillary's staff identify her favorite book? What are they trying to hide?"

Just then the phone rang. It was Frank: "I forgot to tell you, Karen Finney told me to let you know that she got the favorites list done with Hillary on the ride between Northport and Montauk."

Joy! My insanity began to recede. I beeped Karen, she called me back, and we finished the list in about five minutes. Hillary's favorite color turned out to be yellow; her favorite snack foods are chocolate and fruit; and her campaign staff really was trying to be helpful.

Brenda Bombeck

September 6, 2000. The phone rang late that night. It was my mother-in-law, Leah, who, despite her early run-in with Hillary's Secret Service agents and the phony-baloney Listening Tour, had remained very interested in the Senate campaign and my coverage.

"Beth? My friend just called to tell me that Hillary was on the Channel 2 news talking about how you potty-trained Nathaniel. How is that possible?"

"*What?*" I said. "What are you talking about?"

"My friend Bea told me she saw Hillary on Channel 2 news talking to the Associated Press reporter about potty-training, so she figured that had to be you, and she called me. Why was Hillary talking about that on TV?"

"Well, she asked me how my vacation was," I said, slowly trying to remember the rest of the conversation, "and I told her I'd potty-trained Nathaniel, but I didn't realize the cameras were rolling. . . ."

My mother-in-law's friend Beatrice Hart had been right. The lead item on the WCBS-TV news had been a story about "The New Hillary," by their political correspondent, Marcia Kramer. The anchor's lead-in was, "She's shedding her old image and showing voters the kinder, gentler Hillary," and the entire piece was about how she'd invited us all to go have coffee with her one morning after she'd held a press conference with Robert F. Kennedy Jr. to get his personal endorsement. The event was held in a relatively remote area of Riverside Park, on a narrow path with the Hudson River on one side and a fenced-in, grassy hill and the West Side Highway on the other side. It was difficult to find from the street, and because it was a weekday morning, there were few passersby, making it an ideal location for a Casual Hillary Moment. She couldn't be mobbed here, and the Secret Service agents appeared to be as relaxed as they ever were, displaying none of their usual obsessions with controlling where we were standing or moving. That day just happened to be my first day back on the beat after a vacation in Maine, where my sister and I have a small summer cottage in a rural area. Most of the reporters covering the Senate campaign had skipped their summer vacations and were instead planning exotic vacations for after November in the Caribbean, Morocco, and Spain; but Danny would be in the middle of the school year by the time this was over, and it didn't seem fair to deprive him and his brother of our annual trip to the country just because I was covering Hillary. Besides, the opinions of our friends and relatives in Maine often provide a dose of reality from our big-city mind-set. I asked one of my aunts, who lives in a small town in Maine and worked in a shoe factory for many years while raising seven children, what she thought of the presidential candidates, and she replied, "Well, I don't know who Gore thinks is going to vote for him if he raises the tax on cigarettes." Now there's a point of view you'd never hear on the Upper West Side. For the privilege of hearing that sentiment alone, it was worth getting out of the city.

And fortunately my bureau chief had no problem with my leaving the campaign coverage in the excellent hands of some of my colleagues while I was gone. Besides, I figured that between the Democratic Convention in Los Angeles, which was being staffed by other AP reporters, and Hillary's own vacation foray upstate I probably wouldn't miss too many important developments in the campaign anyway as long as I was back the day after Labor Day.

I was glad to see the other reporters that day in Riverside Park; I'd come to think of most of them as friends. A couple of them asked me what I'd done when I was away, and to the two mothers of young children in the group, Liz Moore of *Newsday* and Andrea Bernstein of WNYC-AM radio, the National Public Radio affiliate, I explained that I had taken advantage of my rare sojourn as a full-time mommy to toilet-train my two-year-old. Liz had just done the same with her youngest, and Andrea proudly announced that her two-year-old was using the potty, too.

A few minutes later, after the press conference with RFK Jr., Hillary motioned to us to follow her a few steps away to a café located right in the park with a big table overlooking the water. "C'mon," she said, "let's go have coffee!" She was in a relaxed, expansive mood; she'd made small talk with Marcia about taking a lot of vitamins to get through the final weeks of the campaign, tried on Andrea's headphones, and waved to a couple of people gliding by in a boat on the sparkling blue water. She sat down with the café proprietor, who earlier that morning had walked over to where she was holding the news conference and introduced himself as someone who strongly supported her campaign. A couple of reporters sat down around the table while the rest of us stood, not really sure what to make of it all. All of a sudden as Hillary looked around at us, her eyes fixed on me. I guess after covering her for nearly two years, she'd noticed my absence over the past few weeks and took note of my return. "Hi, Beth!" she called out cheerily. "How was your vacation?"

Since I'd just finished telling the potty-training story, it was still on the tip of my tongue. "It was great!" I responded without hesitation. "I potty-trained my two-year-old!"

"You did what?" she said.

All of a sudden it hit me that I should probably have given a more conventional answer like "It was so relaxing!" But now it was too late.

"I potty-trained my two-year-old," I replied in a small voice.

Hillary looked at me expectantly, as if she still wasn't sure she'd heard me right. Then she repeated it back to me. "You potty-trained your two-year-old?"

I swallowed and nodded. A second ago, chatting with the other moms in the press corps, it had seemed as if talking about potty-training was the most natural thing in the world. But now that Hillary had repeated it back to me, I was starting to feel ridiculous. I mean, I had just told the first lady that I potty-trained my two-year-old! What an absurd thing to do! What the hell was wrong with me?

But I needn't have worried. Now that Hillary realized she'd heard me right, she looked around at the small group and said emphatically, with a big smile, "This woman deserves a round of applause!" Then she turned back to me. "Boy or girl, Beth?"

"Boy," I answered, not sure whether it would be better to disappear from the face of the earth right now or soldier on.

"Boy? That's even harder!" she replied, laughing, then turned her attention elsewhere.

When I finally got to see a tape of the Channel 2 segment "The New Hillary," I saw why Marcia had included the exchange. The point was that Hillary was trying to make connections with us, to humanize herself, and that when she dropped the formality and the regal air, she could be warm and funny and caring, and, yes, even at ease in a conversation about potty-training. I still felt slightly foolish, but I also couldn't help but wonder: If it had been Chuck Schumer or Al D'Amato or Mayor Giuliani that I was covering instead of Hillary, and one of them had asked me how my vacation had been, would it have seemed as natural to respond as I did? And if I had, would they actually have bothered to continue the discussion as if it were a perfectly legitimate topic, the way Hillary did, or would they have put me in a slot in their minds for keeping track of mentally unbalanced reporters and moved on to someone else?

I later talked to Marcia about why she had chosen to focus on how Hillary had reached out to us, instead of leading—as I had in the story I wrote that day for the AP—with RFK Jr.'s endorsement.

Marcia said Hillary's informality with us that day "came at a time when people were beginning to wonder about that, and it gave her a humanity that maybe she hadn't had in the minds of voters. Seeing her stop a kid in the park and talk about sneakers"—which the first lady had done before inviting us for coffee—"and sitting down for coffee with the enemy, where she was buying, and passing the cream and asking if you needed sugar and playing hostess in a restaurant, was at some level bizarre in the context of the campaign. But she was also being totally personal. And she used little tidbits of our lives to appear to be more personal. . . . I totally understand why you were talking about the potty-training of your child. Could a male candidate have done that? If it was Chuck Schumer, he probably would have found some other level of common ground—not hearth and home and family. Maybe something about Brooklyn or 'Hey, I was out in Prospect Park the other day playing Frisbee with my kids' as opposed to this. It wouldn't have been a woman-to-woman issue. It would have been a safer issue."

And in a way, it seemed only right that Hillary should hear about my kids, since they ended up hearing so much about her. One day when I went to pick up Nathaniel from day care, the director informed me that he'd walked into her office that morning and announced, "My mommy went to work."

"Yes?" she'd responded.

"And Hillary—" he began, then paused as if trying to gather the vocabulary to say what he wanted to say.

"Yes?"

"Hillary . . . Hillary . . ." This was turning out to be a big effort for a little boy, but finally he got the words out: "Hillary's running for Senate!"

A few weeks later my older son was sick at school and the teacher asked him whom she should call to come get him, his mommy or his daddy.

"Better call my daddy, he's a lawyer," Danny replied.

"Why? What does your mom do?" the teacher said.

"She's covering Hillary."

"Hillary who?"

Here Danny looked at the teacher as if she were from Mars. *"You know. Hillary!* The president's wife!"

"But what do you mean, she's covering Hillary?"

He shrugged. "I don't know. That's just what she does. She's covering Hillary."

Around the same time, Danny's Hebrew school teacher had asked the kids to make Rosh Hashanah cards for their parents for the Jewish New Year. I was amused but also slightly horrified to see the message Danny wrote inside: "Dear mom I hope you have a Happy time covering Hillry ok? Danny." When I showed the card to Liz Moore, she one-upped me, pulling a note out of her purse that her daugher had written to the tooth fairy after Liz—preoccupied as I was with covering Hillary—had forgotten to leave money under the pillow.

Both of my kids also pointed out Hil's picture in the newspaper without any prompting from me, and the little one had become so accustomed to my bringing campaign ads home with me on videotape that sometimes when I went to put a regular tape in the VCR, he'd say, "Is that gonna be Hillary?" There were evenings when I wrote my stories on the subway after leaving the office and then dictated them by cell phone while pushing Nathaniel's stroller on the way to get Danny from his after-school center. One evening I poured through campaign finance filings while sitting on the bench in a playground where they were soaking up the last bit of daylight before sundown. And many times I bribed them with candy and quarters to *please, please* be quiet while I just took one important phone call at home.

Not only did my children know all about Hillary, but when I flew up to Corning to take part in the big sit-down interview, I found out that Hillary knew about my children. It was in early July, nearly a year to the day since Hillary had launched her Listening Tour. She was giving a speech that day to a local Rotary Club, a squarely Republican group of middle-aged and older folks. Afterward, many of them told me they were extremely impressed by the first lady's knowledge of all kinds of arcane local issues—everything from the lack of a decent highway system in this part of the state to the tendency of young residents to leave upstate hometowns because there weren't enough jobs. "I'm volunteering for her campaign today," one Republican woman told me. "I think she's brilliant."

Since I hardly ever traveled outside New York City and the suburbs with her, a few of the other reporters started wondering why I'd suddenly shown up at this event, and one finally whispered, "Does AP have an interview?" I nodded. The campaign so rarely doled out these private sit-downs—it was only our second time—that if other news organizations didn't get their turn soon after ours, other reporters would have complaining rights with Howard.

When Hillary was done with the Rotarians, Howard hustled me, an AP photographer, and the AP reporter who usually covered her upstate into a small conference room at the hotel where the Rotarians had been meeting. A few minutes later, Hillary came in.

Someone had apparently told her that I didn't like staffing the campaign road trips because of my reluctance to leave my children overnight. I was surprised to hear her ask me about my kids right after we said hello.

"They know all about you," I said, smiling.

"Well, I bet they do, because I'm always taking you away from them," she replied sweetly. Then she asked me their names, said she had "something for them," pulled out a book and a pen, and began writing on the flyleaf.

"Dear Danny and Nathaniel," she wrote in a flowing cursive. "Best wishes, Hillary Clinton." Then she handed it to me. It was a copy of *Dear Socks, Dear Buddy*.

I was completely taken aback. Journalists are not supposed to accept gifts from the people they cover. If you go out to eat with someone you're writing about, you're supposed to pick up the tab. If a public relations firm sends you some type of merchandise, you either give it away, return it, or throw it out.

I briefly considered handing the book back to Hillary with an explanation of how I wasn't permitted to accept gifts, but that just seemed too rude, especially since she'd already written my kids' names in it. Besides, our time with Hillary was strictly limited. We had a half hour or so for our interview; I couldn't really justify taking up another five minutes with an argument over whether it was okay for me to take the book. I also needed to make sure I had time near the end of our interview to ask the favorites questions for the feature story Frank and I were planning.

Besides, in one way, the book was a nice gesture on her part. Hillary often talked about the challenges of making society and the workplace more accommodating to working parents, and this was a direct acknowledgment on her part of the juggling I was doing.

But I also felt angry that she'd put me in this awkward position. Didn't Hillary or her staff know better than to go around giving presents to journalists? I started worrying that I'd be in trouble at work for not having self-righteously handed it back to her while announcing, "You can't buy *me* off with a present, Mrs. Clinton." Of course, then I'd be putting her in an uncomfortable position, and she or her staff might take it out on me by giving us even less access than we already had. It was just all too complicated, and I wished that she'd never given me anything. In the end I just thanked her in a small voice, put the book in my bag, and we turned on our tape recorders and went ahead with the interview.

The book felt as if it weighed about fifty pounds as I carried it home through the airports. I couldn't wait to tell my editors and let them decide whether I needed to return it. But their reactions were so nonchalant that I felt ridiculous all over again. "That book has about a two-dollar value," the news editor said to me dismissively when I guiltily presented the book for a verdict. "She probably gets cartons of them to give away." My bureau chief, Sam Boyle, agreed, explaining that a book given by the author fell under the category of a "token" and therefore didn't need to be returned.

I hadn't yet shown the book to my kids, but now that I'd gotten clearance, I could let them see it without feeling guilty. "Look," I told them, "Hillary sent you a present. It's a book about the pets who live in the White House with her and the president."

My older son wasn't much interested, but the little one looked at the pictures and then at me. "Hillary have a puppy and a pussycat?" he asked hopefully. I nodded.

A month later Hillary spoke at Metropolitan AME Church in Harlem, an all-black congregation. She always seemed at home in places of worship (although she pronounced the word like a Midwesterner, so that it sounded as if she were saying "warship," which drove me crazy); she knew her Bible and could easily quote chapter and verse, expounding on the reading of the day with an unpretentious ease. Being a preacher was one of the many alternative careers I'd imagined for Hillary, along with elementary school teacher and hairspray saleswoman. She'd talked and written about growing up in a devout Methodist family with a father who prayed kneeling by the side of the bed each night, and she traced her political activism to a church youth group, the one that she frequently mentioned as having brought her to hear Martin Luther King Jr. speak and organized teenagers to baby-sit for migrant workers. On this particular Sunday at Metropolitan, the reading for the day was about Joshua being chosen to lead the Jews after Moses died. Hillary told the congregation that they, too, had a choice—a political choice. They could get involved, or they could do nothing. It wasn't enough, she said, to pray that God would "help me, lead me out of this dangerous place. . . . We also have to move our feet and hands."

The congregation loved her; she was immensely popular among black voters and knew it. Her challenge here was not to win them over but to motivate a good turnout on election day, and her interpretation of the day's reading was a pointed call to political action. When she sat down, the pastor, Robert Bailey, got up again and told his flock that God had given them a second chance to elect another Clinton. Hillary, he said, was their Joshua.

"Did you hear this lady?" he intoned. "We need Hillary Clinton in the White House!"

Behind him, Harlem congressman Charlie Rangel started calling out "The Senate!" every time Bailey said "the White House." But the pastor couldn't hear him and just kept repeating "the White House."

Hillary, seated behind the pastor, facing the congregation (and the press), appeared totally stone-faced. Her eyes were downcast and unblinking and she sat completely still. For months her enemies had been saying that what she really wanted was not to serve in the Senate but to run for president, and that she would use the Senate as a stepping-stone to try for the White House later. If there had been a spy in the audience videotaping the event for the Republicans, it would have made a perfect Hillary hate-ad: her sitting silently in a church while a black pastor says over and over again, "We need Hillary Clinton in the White House!" and the congregation cheering in response.

Her torture ended after a few moments when a deacon ran up to the lectern and whispered something in the pastor's ear. Bailey paused for a minute, then called out, "We want her in the Senate!" A relieved smile came over her face.

That night at home I was telling my husband the story over dinner and had just gotten to the part where the preacher keeps repeating "the

White House," when my two-year-old stood up on his chair. "You know what, Daddy?" he started saying. "You know what?"

"Just a minute," I said. "Let me finish telling this story—"

"You know what?" Now he was jumping up and down in his chair. "Hillary have a puppy dog and a pussycat! You know that, Daddy?"

At that moment I realized my life had truly been taken over by Hillary. Not only was I telling my husband Hillary stories over dinner, but my two-year-old was interrupting me to tell his own Hillary stories.

Only much later did I find out that Hillary had given small gifts to many of my other colleagues, too. After Hillary had visited all sixty-two counties, she presented Gregg Birnbaum and Eileen Murphy with "Longevity Awards" for making it to more of the countries than any of the other reporters. At the same time, during this little presentation to the press corps in the lobby of a Holiday Inn in Plattsburgh, the rest of the reporters on the trail that day got caps that said "Hillary 2000—62 counties." Of course, no reporter would be caught dead wearing a hat— or a pin or a T-shirt, for that matter—with a candidate's name on it. Gregg later determined that the caps were made in the Dominican Republic and tried to figure out which factory they had come from in case it turned out to be a sweatshop or an operation using child labor. But he was never able to pin it down.

Eileen had also given Howard a cartoon from the *New Yorker* about the human genome and got it handed back to her in a frame, signed, "Genetically yours, Hillary Clinton." Hillary loved to talk about the human genome; she'd mention it in nearly every speech, no matter what the ostensible subject was. One of the points she loved to make was that researchers had discovered that 99 percent of genetic material was the same in all human beings, regardless of race or other physical characteristics. (Of course we also share nearly that much genetic material with chimpanzees, but she never pointed that out.) This *New Yorker* cartoon showed a man saying to a woman, "What will we talk about now that they've mapped the human genome?"

Eventually it occurred to me that maybe Hillary had been dispensing little pieces of herself—her picture, her signature, her books, her mere name printed on some little something—to grateful fans for years in Arkansas and Washington. I couldn't decide whether her continuing that practice with the press corps in a Senate campaign was a nervy assumption on her part that we would care, or a thoughtful gesture on her part that *she* cared, or just some innocent but slightly misguided effort to generate goodwill by distributing favors from her little party. Maybe all these Hillary tchotchkes were like yarmulkes that you get at bar mitzvahs with the thirteen-year-old boy's name on them. You'd never wear them anywhere else, but they were a permanent reminder that you'd been to the type of bar mitzvah where the guests get keepsake yarmulkes. Certainly none of the press at City Hall was getting mementos from the Giuliani campaign, nor were the Lazio regulars getting framed pictures signed "Little Ricky." Lazio and Giuliani were giving bar mitzvahs with a serve-yourself buffet in the backyard; Hillary was giving a sit-down dinner in a nice catering hall. And once you had that party favor with her name on it, you could never forget it.

As for me, I'd never have gone out and bought *Dear Socks, Dear Buddy* in a million years. But now that it had been bestowed upon me, signed by Hillary and personally inscribed to my family, it was indeed proof that I'd once had an audience with Her Majesty.

My older son, Danny, meanwhile, had been lobbying for a long time to accompany me on assignment to a Hillary event. I felt a little funny about doing it for several reasons. One, I had a serious job to do at these events, and I couldn't take the chance that he might somehow disrupt the proceedings or take my attention away from what she was saying or doing. Two, I thought he might get very bored very fast, and most of these events were part of a long day of campaigning. There was no easy way to bring him to one small program and then somehow get him back home without taking me away from my need to either go back to the office and write the story up, or go on to the next event.

And three, it seemed a slightly gray area for me to use my privilege as a journalist to bring a relative in to a campaign event that would otherwise not be open to the public. After all, I didn't take Danny's grandma into that Listening Tour event; how could I now justify bringing him to a press conference or a fund-raiser?

On the other hand, if I was going to disrupt their young lives as much as I had by devoting myself to covering this campaign, in some ways it seemed only fair to let them experience the cause of the disruption firsthand. Even what I made for dinner each night depended on Hillary. My meal plan for the week included some dinners that required prep time for cutting up vegetables or lighting the oven, some that involved nothing more than throwing a package of frozen pasta in a pot of boiling water, and one night set aside for getting take-out food delivered to my door. If I had an early day with Hillary and actually got home by six o'clock, I'd plan on a prep-time dinner; if I had a late day, it was a frozen-pasta night. The takeout was my emergency crutch, to be saved for the nights when I was not only late coming home, but everything else went wrong, too—the train got stuck in the tunnel, Nathaniel was crying, Danny had a ton of homework, the kids needed baths, the garbage and the laundry baskets were both overflowing, and the VCR wasn't working. "Is the deliveryman coming tonight?" Nathaniel would ask hopefully if we were caught in the rain without an umbrella or the phone started ringing the minute we walked in the door. On those nights, instead of rushing through the door to get dinner going, I'd just collapse on the sofa, wallet in hand, and wait for the doorbell to herald the arrival of chicken sate from our local Thai restaurant. Sure, Hillary had been a working mother, resuming her law practice in Arkansas after just a few months of maternity leave for Chelsea, and I'd heard her tell stories about being stuck in a late-afternoon meeting the day of an important school play, but I wondered if she'd ever had to pull a juggling act like this in the governor's mansion.

One day in the fall when the quarterly Federal Elections Commission reports were due, both campaigns had scheduled to release their campaign finance documents late in the afternoon. I should have known it wasn't going to happen that way, that it would be delayed, and I'd have to get my husband to pick the kids up. But for some reason I stupidly thought I'd actually be on the subway in time to get the boys. By the time I found out that the Clinton reports were delayed by a Xerox machine breaking down at Kinko's and that the staffer who'd been sent to fetch the Lazio documents was taking longer than expected to return, I couldn't reach my husband. I phoned a neighbor to pick Danny up, then began a frantic back-and-forth with the long-suffering director of Nathaniel's day-care center. Eventually I got on the subway carrying a huge carton of documents, and at the point where the D train from Manhattan to Brooklyn emerges from the tunnel onto the bridge, I pulled out my cell phone and called the day-care center for the umpteenth time to see if my husband had come to the rescue yet. He hadn't. It was already by then 6:45 P.M.—not all that late in the life of a normal person, but I felt terrible that the day-care director was sitting there forty-five minutes after she was supposed to have left just because I couldn't get there in time to pick my child up.

By the time we all got home around seven-thirty, I had to lock myself in a bedroom and start combing through the documents, then pull out my laptop and try to write a coherent story while Danny banged on the door to ask if I could come help him with just one little thing in his homework.

If I'd had any illusions that I was leading a glamorous Brenda Starr–type of existence, they crashed right then and there with the reality that my life was a lot more like Erma Bombeck's. I wasn't chasing deadlines; I was chasing third-grade homework, bubble baths, and dinner that could be made in fifteen minutes or less while a screaming toddler grabbed on to my leg.

I have to pause here and give a small thank-you to several members of the Clinton campaign who did what they could to support my juggling efforts. One day when I was desperately trying to leave the office, I got word that the Clinton campaign was about to release a new ad. This necessitated my picking up a videotape at their headquarters and my writing an analysis of the ad. I e-mailed Howard asking when the ad would be ready.

"Please keep it under your hat for a bit," he wrote back.

"I'm not pressing for it," I responded. "On the other hand, I'm probably walking out the door at four-thirty, so if I need to plan a stop at your office on my way home, I need to know. Sorry, but it's the old conflicting-values dilemma. Hillary on the one hand. Seven-year-old Danny and two-year-old Nathaniel on the other . . ."

Two minutes later, another message from Howard. "Release is going out now—ads should be available at the office presently. I vote for the kids, by the way."

On a few other occasions when Hillary had an event that wasn't important enough for me to staff myself and was so late or in such a remote location that it wasn't even worth getting someone else from my office to fill in for me, Hillary's staff was nice enough to call me at home, by cell phone, just before she began speaking so that I could monitor her speech from home. I only did it two or three times, early on in the campaign, but each time it was a lifesaver, enabling me to keep tabs on the candidate while spending the evening with my kids.

Of course, I wasn't required to cover the campaign. I could have declined the assignment and stuck to the kinds of stories where I'd be able to leave work every day promptly after putting in my eight hours. But I'm hoping that my children, in the long run, benefit from having a mother who had an interesting career. Nobody ever wonders whether fathers with demanding jobs are doing their children a disservice. Both George W. Bush and Al Gore have happy families and successful careers even though their fathers both had time-consuming responsibilities that kept them away from home a lot. So I pray every day that rather than being scarred for life by the fact that I covered Hillary, my kids will look back on it as a fascinating little piece of history that they actually saw close-up.

That's part of the reason why, when Danny asked if he could tag along with me to see Hillary sometime, I agreed to try to find a way to do it. Only one other person, Dean Murphy of the *New York Times*, had brought a child along on the campaign trail, his six-year-old son, Christian, who spent a day in October going with us to black churches, riding around in the van, and even attending a press conference. Dean's family had recently moved back to the States from South Africa, where Dean had been a correspondent for the *Los Angeles Times*, and Christian was still getting used to the changes in his father's work routine. "Christian never asked to meet Mrs. Clinton, he just wanted to see what Daddy did every day," Dean later told me. Still, he shared my concerns about whether it was appropriate to let your kid tag along with somebody famous just because you're assigned to cover the person. Dean even sought (and received) his editor's approval to do it. A couple of the photographers in the press corps snapped a picture of little Christian shaking Hillary's hand when she noticed him standing in front of the pack at the news conference, but Dean decided not to ask her to autograph it. "I just didn't feel right making that request while covering the race," he said. "My wife has her copy of *It Takes a Village* and would have liked an autograph as well, but I didn't bring that along either."

Christian was better-behaved than some of the journalists that day; he never showed any restlessness during those long church sermons. He also displayed an impressive instinctual understanding of the photo-op concept, turning his face directly to the cameras as his picture was taken. But I think the funniest part of Christian's day with us was that, when it was over, he asked Dean, "Daddy, why does she say the same thing every place she goes?"

Eventually, the appropriate venue presented itself for me to bring Danny along. My husband is on the board of directors of a housing organization called Good Old Lower East Side. Before becoming a lawyer, he'd worked there as a tenant organizer, and he'd remained involved in the dozen years since he'd left. In late October, he got a telephone message from GOLES inviting him to attend a forum Hillary was holding in a church on the Lower East Side for tenant leaders and housing activists. It was scheduled to take place mid-evening, a few hours after her third and final televised debate with Lazio. I had to cover the debate and also planned to attend the housing forum even though I was fairly certain it would generate no news. Our coverage that day would by necessity have to focus on the debate.

So this seemed, at last, like the perfect opportunity for Danny and Nathaniel to see the woman who had been dominating their home lives for so many months. Their father would be there to deal with the kids if they misbehaved; I wasn't likely to be writing a story about the event anyway; and because their dad's invitation had nothing to do with me, they had a legitimate reason to attend.

We met up outside the church, and when we got in, I realized that most of the press was seated upstairs. "Oh, Mommy, I wanna go up there with you!" Danny whined. "Please!"

Their father stayed downstairs with the invitees and Nathaniel, while Danny and I headed up to the balcony. A Secret Service agent was posted on the steps to search everyone's bag. The photographer ahead of me was firing test flashes in her camera for him and unscrewing her lenses, and I took out my tape recorder and cell phone and turned them on to prove that they were regular electronic devices and not explosives. It had all become routine by now, but of course Danny watched intently with his eyes wide open. "Why do you have to do this, Mommy? What's going on?"

I explained that Hillary is a very important person and this gentleman who was looking in everyone's bags was supposed to protect her and make sure nobody was bringing in anything dangerous. Danny nodded and then started shoving his hands into each of his pockets. A moment later he produced a blue rubber ball from the cargo pocket of his jeans and with a smile proudly held it out to the agent to be inspected.

"Good job, Dan! You're right in the swing of things," I said.

I introduced him to some of the other reporters, and Edward Lewine of the *Daily News* was nice enough to let him play with his tape recorder. They interviewed each other and then we played Hangman on my notepad. Every now and then, I'd hear Nathaniel cry out, *"Mommy!"* and look up to try to find me in the balcony. It was going to be a long night.

Finally Hillary arrived. I saw her eyes rove up to the balcony to where we were all seated; she often took a quick glance at the press corps before starting. I couldn't be sure, but it looked to me as if she were looking at Danny, trying to figure out who he was. I put my arm around him and pointed to his head and then to me. She smiled and Danny waved at her.

She began speaking and within two minutes Danny was bored. "When is it going to be over?" he whispered.

I groaned. I should have known this was going to happen. "Danny, be quiet, you just have to sit through it. I really have to pay attention now. It'll be over in a little while."

He started moving around the balcony and accidentally poked my elbow. I'd had my notepad and a bunch of papers resting on the ledge of the balcony, and his hitting my arm caused me to push the whole thing over the ledge. I watched in horror as the notebook landed with a thud amid the seats below us and the papers fluttered down, one by one. A couple of the other reporters started laughing. I leaned over the balcony at the people who were seated below as they looked up to see what the hell was going on. The commotion put the Secret Service agent on high alert, too; I saw him looking at me intently, trying to figure out if he should take me out then and there or give me a second chance. "I'm sorry! I'm sorry! It was an accident! I'm so sorry!" I kept whispering as loudly as I could as the people downstairs glared up at me.

There was no point in getting mad at Danny. I should have known

A few days after joining the race, Rick Lazio gleefully wrapped his tongue around an ice-cream cone for the cameras at the Byrne Dairy in Syracuse, May 31, 2000. *Richard Drew, AP/Wide World Photos*

Hillary didn't like being photographed while eating, but by September 2, 2000, she finally realized the value of a food photo-op. Here, she and Bill wolf down sausage sandwiches at the Syracuse Fair. Lazio had earlier turned down the sausage sandwich, a local tradition. *Beth Keiser, AP/Wide World Photos*

When Hillary kissed Yasir Arafat's wife, Suha, during a visit to the West Bank on November 11, 1999, the photo made front-page news, and Hillary spent the rest of the campaign explaining the kiss as a "social grace" required of a first lady. *AP/Wide World Photos*

Lazio condemned her for it, but was called a hypocrite when a photo later turned up of him enthusiastically greeting Yasir Arafat in 1998 on an official visit to the Middle East. *AP/Wide World Photos*

Photographers asked for, but never received, behind-the-scenes access to Hillary, yet AP photographer Richard Drew was allowed to photograph the Lazios on the candidate's bus. Here Daddy Rick decorates the fingernails of daughter Molly with a pen, while his other daughter, Kelsey, watches. *Richard Drew, AP/Wide World Photos*

Chelsea Clinton took a semester off from Stanford University in the fall of 2000 to campaign with her mother. But while she was available for photo-ops, the first daughter was strictly off-limits to interviews by the press. Here, the Clinton women chat at a campaign stop in Long Beach, Long Island, November 3, 2000. *Kathy Willens, AP/Wide World Photos*

Hillary behind tinted glass, Secret Service agent at her side, as she leaves a campaign stop in Buffalo on October 13, 2000. No one from the press corps was ever allowed to ride with her. *David Duprey, AP/Wide World Photos*

Hillary was dogged by protesters of all types at parades, campaign stops, and outside her Manhattan campaign headquarters, where this man from the group Friends of Juanita Broaddrick showed up on August 19, 2000. (Juanita Broaddrick alleged that she was raped by Bill Clinton in 1978.) *Ed Bailey, AP/Wide World Photos*

DESPITE THE RANTINGS OF TRENT LOTT AND THE G.O.P., HILLARY'S AIR TRAVEL TO AND FROM NEW YORK ACTUALLY COSTS THE TAXPAYER VERY LITTLE

Sean Delonas's cartoons in *The New York Post* captured a certain brand of anti-Hillary sentiment by portraying the first lady on a broomstick. This cartoon refers to a controversy over her travel. As required by law, her campaign reimbursed the federal government for the cost of one first-class airfare for every campaign trip she made. But the actual cost of operating government jets was estimated to be thousands of dollars per hour. *New York Post*

Hillary often seemed more at home in black churches than on any other type of campaign stop. Here on October 15, 2000, she prays with Darlene McGuire, co-pastor of Emmanuel Baptist Church in the Bronx. McGuire led her congregation in singing a hymn in which the words were changed from "I told Satan, get thee behind" to "I told Lazio, get thee behind." *Stephen Chernin, AP/Wide World Photos*

The state Democratic Party sent a college student, Eric Shultz, to track Lazio's campaign events with a video camera, and Lazio's supporters did whatever they could to thwart him. Here, a Lazio aide blocks Shultz's view of the candidate with a campaign sign in Owego on August 17, 2000. *David Duprey, AP/Wide World Photos*

Standing in her Chappaqua garden on July 16, 2000, Hillary denied allegations that she used an anti-Semitic term during an argument in Arkansas in 1974. The first lady became increasingly emotional and appeared at one point to be on the verge of tears. But the photo was proof that she'd kept it together. "No tear?" went the conversation in the newsroom. "No tear," came the response. *Suzanne Plunkett, AP/Wide World Photos*

Hillary's campaign spokesman, Howard Wolfson, was generally calm no matter how big the crisis. Here he is forging ahead with a press conference on campaign finances in City Hall Park on March 30, 2000, despite the presence of a homeless man inserting himself in the photo-op. *Bebeto Matthews, AP/Wide World Photos*

Lazio was widely criticized for confronting Hillary with a pledge to ban soft money during their first debate in Buffalo, September 13, 2000. This photo, which made front-page news, captured the tension, with Hillary appearing to shrink away from Lazio as he strides toward her podium, pointing his finger. *Richard Drew, AP/Wide World Photos*

something like this would happen. I ordered him to sit far away from the edge of the balcony and moved myself back, too. I had an extra notebook in my bag and took it out, but there was no need. A minute later, someone from the audience appeared next to me holding the papers I'd dropped over the edge. I thanked her profusely, and she looked at Danny and smiled. They'd figured out what had happened and were being nice about it.

Then it was over. Hillary stayed around to shake hands, and Danny and I headed downstairs. The boys wanted to meet her. Again, I felt the conflict. Was this okay, or was it over the line? "The line" was such a vague, tricky thing. You didn't want to be in a position of seeking or receiving personal favors. But when you'd spent as much time covering someone as I had Hillary, and the person becomes, in some way, a part of your life, the way my children had become intrigued with her, some amount of personal interaction seemed only natural. I hooked up with my husband, put Nathaniel on my shoulders, took Danny's hand, and waded into the mob of people waiting to shake Hillary's hand. "Hillary! Hillary!" I could hear the little one calling her name when she neared us. She looked up and waved at him, then reached over and shook Danny's hand. One of her press aides, Cathie Levine, spotted us and motioned us through the line to a vestibule where I introduced them a few minutes later and guiltily snapped a quick picture. A few days later, I read in *USA Today* that the reporters covering George W. Bush frequently asked him to autograph a card, photo, or poster, and that he willingly posed for photos with reporters' relatives at various stops around the country. That made me feel better. If it was okay in the presidential corps, then it was probably okay to do what I had done.

But there was a funny ending to that evening in the church with my kids. My son Nathaniel, who had famously just completed potty-training a month or so earlier, told his dad he had to pee. So they went to the bathroom after the boys were done saying hi to Hillary, only to find a Secret Service agent posted outside the bathroom door. "Sorry," the guy said. "You'll have to wait fifteen minutes." Apparently the bathroom was in lockdown mode in case Her Majesty needed to use it.

"But my son needs to pee! He can't wait fifteen minutes!" my husband said.

The guy shrugged. "Sorry."

This section of the Lower East Side is relatively deserted. It's not as if there were a restaurant next store, or even in the next block, that we could have run into to use. So we did what any parents would do in the interest of avoiding wet pants: we took Nathaniel outside and let him pee in a vacant lot.

But in a lot of venues like fancy hotels or small upstate restaurants, the Secret Service did not put the bathroom in lockdown, and a number of stories actually involved press corps encounters with Hillary in the ladies' room. Anna Quindlen once wrote a column for the *New York Times* in which she noted that as a female reporter in the largely male press corps covering City Hall, she'd had "years of worrying that the best stories were coming out of conversations in the men's room" between the mayor, his male staff, and the male reporters. But other than an encounter by Gail Sheehy, who began one of the chapters of *Hillary's Choice* with the words "I ran into her in the ladies' room," I don't think any of the interactions anybody on the campaign ever had with Hillary in a bathroom ever made it into our coverage. Yet these run-ins were noteworthy, if only because there was something forbidden about them. We couldn't ride on her van or take her picture on her plane; we couldn't get her on the phone like a normal candidate; but, hey, if she had to pee and one of us had to pee at the same time, you could very well find yourself in the privacy of a bathroom with the very private first lady.

Lara Jakes of the *Albany Times Union*, who turned twenty-six shortly after she was assigned to cover Hillary's campaign, actually followed the first lady into a rest room on the very first leg of the Listening Tour. "I kind of got goaded into doing it," she recalled. "The guys on the bus were like, 'Jakes, go in there! Ya gotta see what's going on in there."

So Lara followed Hillary in at a rest stop on Route 88 between Binghamton and Pindars Corners. Hillary's personal assistant Kelly Craighead, a funny, lively woman with long blond hair who could also be as tough and protective of Hillary as any of the Secret Service agents, was standing by the sink as the first lady emerged from a stall.

"They're both giving me the hairy eyeball, looking at my tape recorder," Lara recalled. "I said something like, 'I'm not gonna ambush you in the bathroom. I'm just gonna make sure no news happens.' While she's washing her hands, this middle-age woman with two daughters comes rushing in to the back stall. Hillary and Kelly leave. The woman finishes helping her daughters and I say, 'Did you realize that was Hillary Clinton in there?' The woman goes, 'Oh my God, that was the first lady.' One of her daughter's names happens to be Hillary, and they go running out to find her."

Meanwhile when Lara got back on the press bus, she wasn't sure if she'd let down her colleagues or not. "I mean, this was my first real big political race," she said. "They send me in here to the bathroom and I don't know if I'm supposed to ask her about Whitewater or what. I'm thinking, 'What if I blow this?' We've got a year and a half to go in this race, and I just don't really feel comfortable asking her questions in the ladies' room. I kept thinking, 'What would a guy do?' "

Liz Moore also had a ladies' room encounter one day when we were at the Waldorf. She walked into the bathroom, saw Kelly at the sink, and realized that Hillary was in a stall. "I couldn't deal with it," she confessed when she came back to the press area. "I turned around and walked out."

"You did the nice thing," I told her. "You were just being human."

Eileen Murphy, who can do a wickedly funny imitation of Hillary saying just about anything, had a bathroom story, too. She was in a ladies' room somewhere upstate one day, mocking one of Hillary's anti-Rudy phrases—"I reject the politics of derision and divisiveness!"—and at the same time trying on a pair of Gucci sunglasses she'd just found. Kelly Craighead and Karen Finney were in the bathroom with her, telling her the sunglasses looked good. "I'm practicing the politics of destruction on myself!" she said, then noticed that the door to one of the stalls was opening.

All of a sudden, Hillary emerged, smiling.

Chapter 11

Keep Going!

October 1, 2000. It's a Sunday morning and I'm with Hillary. And that means I'm in a black church, because that's where Hillary goes every Sunday between Labor Day and election day. Some days we start with the 7 A.M. service and hit our sixth or seventh church around mid-afternoon, but today the schedule is light: just three churches before noon, and then I can go back to the office and write yet another story about the lovefest between Hillary and the black community.

We begin this morning at Memorial Baptist Church in Harlem. It's not one of the powerhouse churches Democratic politicians usually visit; but then, Hillary, overachiever that she is, isn't content to hit a half dozen churches like a normal candidate. Instead, in the two months leading up to November 7, she'll hit twenty-seven—count 'em, twenty-seven—black churches, from storefront tabernacles where the paint is peeling in neighborhoods where few white politicians venture, to better-known places like Abyssinian Baptist, run by the Reverend Calvin Butts, a prominent activist and power broker who once made headlines by calling Giuliani a "racist."

As always, the row of seats taken up by the press corps is just about the only part of the church occupied by white faces. Occasionally a black photographer or reporter is part of the mix, but today we are not only mostly white, we are also largely Jewish. And because it's the Sunday after Rosh Hashanah, we greet each other by saying "Happy New Year!"

Most of the worshipers are on their feet, clapping, singing, and rocking to an electric guitar, piano, and drum ensemble driven by the steady, happy jangle of a tambourine. "Lift Him up!" the several hundred voices sing as one, and within minutes, I and most of the other reporters stand up, too, clapping and swaying along with them; the music is irresistible. Still, we are interlopers, journalists in a place of worship and mostly white people in a place filled with black faces, and no matter what we do, we feel self-conscious.

Soon the booming sounds die away and we sit down. The Reverend Preston Washington gets up and shouts, "Let's give them all the news!" and the congregation—the men in dark jackets and ties and dress shoes and the ladies in satiny, jewel-toned skirtsuits with matching hats—lets out a cheer in response.

The reporter sitting next to me gives me a look of mock bewilderment. "Did he just say, 'Let's welcome all the Jews'?"

I stifle a laugh. He's joking, but it's clear that he feels, like I do, how conspicuous we are, a buncha white people talking about Rosh Hashanah in a black church, dancing like robots. "No," I reply, "he said, 'Let's give them all the *news*.' All the *news*, as in the Gospel, not all the *Jews*."

Now Hillary appears at the podium, a small, familiar blond figure in her going-to-church navy-blue suit with the skirt hem falling just below her kneecap. It's the Sunday version of her black pantsuit, her uniform for the job she's assigned herself today. A tumultuous cheer goes up, and a warm, wide, toothy, lipsticked smile blooms across her face.

"She's gonna win," declares the pastor. "And we are going to come out in droves for her."

It's a point that needs to be made. Nobody is doubting that black voters prefer Hillary over Lazio. But black turnout is unreliable in New York City. David Dinkins, the city's only black mayor, beat Giuliani when black voters made up 28 percent of the electorate. But Dinkins lost four years later when black voters made up just 21 percent of those who showed up at the polls. So the get-out-the-vote message is why we're here, and the pastor knows it.

"*Whoooo!*" Hillary hoots as the applause dies down and she looks around, feeling the love. "Thank you for the day the Lord has made!"

It's her standard opening line, a riff on the psalm that begins "This is the day the Lord has made; let us rejoice and be glad in it," and it goes over as big here as it does in every other church she's ever said it in.

"My Baptist husband says 'Good morning!' " she continues. (Hillary, as anyone in the press corps and most of the people in this church could tell you, is Methodist.) The reference to Bill—whose popularity in the black community is legendary—unleashes another ovation.

She throws out a few thank-yous to local politicians in the audience, most of them introduced as "my good friend" so-and-so, then lowers her voice and eyes, taking on a solemn aspect that is immediately sensed by the congregation, which becomes completely silent and respectful and still.

"I want to thank you," she says in a small, humble, grateful voice, "for the prayers and support and good wishes you have given me and my husband and my daughter over the last eight years. Those prayers have uplifted, sustained, and, I believe, protected us."

A smattering of applause and a murmur of acknowledgment ripples through the congregation. They are flattered and impressed. The first lady of the United States, the most famous woman in the world, has not only found her way to their small church on 115th Street this morning, but now *she* is thanking *them*. Now that's worth coming to church for.

Of course, the first few times I heard Hillary thank her black supporters for their prayers, I wasn't entirely sure what she was referring to. Then one day, when I was standing outside a restaurant where she was

holding a private meeting, a black lady who was part of the crowd outside waiting to greet her came up to me and, unprompted, explained it.

"Everybody loves her husband," she told me. "There were so many
churches that fasted and prayed for him during the impeachment.
Because they believed he was a good president. He's human. But he's for
the people. And I think she's a very good wife to stick with him. People
say she did it for the power. But she did it because marriage is for better
or for worse."

Now I understood. I thanked the woman and made a mental note to
spend more time talking to ladies on street corners in Queens and less
time talking to political analysts on the phone in Washington.

I tune back in to Hillary's speech at Memorial Baptist. Now she's
reciting some statistics from the Clinton administration's economic
miracle: the lowest child-poverty level on record. The lowest level of
African-American unemployment on record. More applause, then the
self-congratulations give way to a humble message in keeping with the
spirit of a religious service.

"But I don't believe that America is called upon to be the richest
nation," she says, pausing as a few voices call back "That's right!" and
"You tell it!"

"I believe it is called upon to be the best," she continues. "And I
believe our best days are ahead of us. That's why I'm running for the
Senate. I want to be part of making that future."

Now we are about to hear the press corps' favorite part of Hillary's
Standard Sunday Morning Sermon. She starts by noting that she's been
to all sixty-two counties in New York State, and that one of the many
places she visited along the way was Auburn, to see the house that Harriet Tubman had lived in after escaping slavery.

Harriet Tubman, Hillary adds, "is one of my favorite heroines in
American history. Because when she got to freedom, she didn't say,
'Well, I'm free. I'm just gonna sit back and live the good life,' did she?"

"No, she didn't," several voices respond.

"She decided to go back to the South and bring more escaped slaves to freedom," Hillary continues.

"Mm-hmmm!" the worshipers call back.

Now Hillary's voice drops to a stage whisper and she looks conspiratorially around the room, as if we are all on the Underground Railroad with Hillary and Harriet. Everyone becomes still again.

"She'd tell people to meet her at night in a swamp or a grove of willow trees. And she'd say, 'If you hear the dogs, keep going!' " Hillary says, her voice slowly rising.

"Yes! Yes!" the audience calls back.

I don't need to take notes anymore. I just write "Keep going!" in my notebook, put my pen down, and listen for the words that I and every other reporter here know by heart.

"If you hear the gunfire, keep going! If you hear the men shouting, keep going! If you hear the footsteps, keep going!"

She gets louder and louder to be heard over the growing din, but her cadence is as perfect as a real preacher's, every pause timed just right to allow for a response from the audience. We may feel that we don't belong here, we white reporters sitting in the back row, but that white lady in the front of the church, she's perfectly at home. She knows how to reach this audience, and even though when you come down to it, this is simply a sophisticated plea for votes, they sense that she respects them. It doesn't hurt her comfort level that she's spent years going around to churches in Arkansas with Bill. And it doesn't hurt that she's been on the campaign trail for over a year. In the early days of covering Hillary, we talked a lot about her tin ear. She'd drone on too long, she'd say the wrong thing, her message was clunky or vague. But in politics as in school, there is a learning curve, and we are seeing the result of it right now. Today, the first lady has perfect pitch, and her routine is going over big-time with the fans.

"We all have to keep going until we are a just nation," she says, practically shouting now as people begin to stand, cheering and clapping and loving every word out of her mouth. "But I need your help. And if you will help me, I will be there for you!"

Now she quiets down again in preparation for the grand finale.

"Because there is one thing you know about me," she says softly, then roars: "When I tell you I'll stick with you, *I'll stick with you!*"

As it always does, this line brings the house down. The first time I heard her say it, in a church in Brooklyn, I almost didn't believe what I was hearing. What exactly did that mean, "When I tell you I'll stick with you, I'll stick with you"? It appeared to be a veiled reference to her marriage. But that seemed absurd. Why would a woman who has gone out of her way to avoid explaining why she stayed with Bill suddenly be boasting about it? I asked a couple of the other reporters sitting near me that day for their interpretation and found them about evenly divided between those who thought it was about her marriage and those who thought it wasn't. So I went outside and started asking people as they left church. What was she talking about when she said, "When I tell you I'll stick with you, I'll stick with you"?

They looked at me as if I were an idiot from Mars, as if they were explaining two plus two to a little child.

"The average person took that to mean, 'I stood behind my husband,'" said one man.

"She had a right to stick with him," a lady told me. "And that means no matter how hard the situation is, she will hang in there for us."

I thought back to that day two years ago, the first day I ever covered Hillary, when everyone in America was gossiping about Monica and Bill, and she held court at a conference on global economics and pretended that the world outside didn't exist. Let everyone else discuss impeachment and infidelity; Hillary was going to quote de Tocqueville, and the rest of us be damned! But now I was covering her running for office, and she was using her marriage as a metaphor for political loyalty. She'd figured out how to take that doormat thing and turn it into a virtue. She was either shameless, or a genius, or both.

Back at Memorial, the church is exploding with applause now as she delivers her final exhortation: "Let's keep going! Let's have a great big turnout in the election! If you fight for me in the next five weeks, I will go to the Senate and fight for you for the next six years! Thank you, everybody! Thank you *so-o-o-o-o much!*"

The band starts up again and the applause turns into rhythmic clapping in time to the beat. The first lady and her entourage swoop out of the church, with us Jews and the rest of the press corps scrambling to follow and pile into the van before it pulls away from the curb behind the Speedwagon, en route to the next church. The very back seat in these vans is always the last to fill up, not only because it's hard to get to, climbing over everybody's legs and shoulders and knapsacks and cameras and cords, but because it's also the seat most likely to induce nausea as our drivers—usually campaign volunteers—struggle to maneuver our wide-bodied vehicles through city traffic and not lose the first lady's motorcade.

I'm sitting next to Tish Durkin, who writes for the *New York Observer*. She catches my eye and gestures for me to come closer to hear something. She opens her blue eyes wide, and the hint of a smile plays on her lips.

"I'm going to meet you in the swamp tonight at six P.M.," she murmurs.

I admit it, I'm kinda slow when it comes to catching on to these antics in the van, so I honestly don't see the next line coming.

"And if you hear the guns," Tish says, "keep going."

My colleagues are way ahead of me. From the seat in front of us, someone calls out, "What if we hear the men?"

Tish calls back, "Keep going!"

Now I get it. *Duh!* From the seat behind us, another voice says, "What if we hear the dogs?"

Everyone joins in on the refrain this time: "Keep going!"

I think of my biggest obstacles to perseverance on the Hillary trail and call out, "What if we have to go to the bathroom? What if we haven't had lunch?"

"Keep going!" the other reporters shout back. "Keep going!"

By this time we are all cracking up, pumped up and giddy at our cleverness. This doesn't feel like work anymore, it feels like I'm back in high school, giggling with my girlfriends in the stairwell.

We settle down in time for the next stop, a somber Episcopal church where a bishop tells the worshipers they are about to experience a "visitation" from Hillary Rodham Clinton. The atmosphere here is subdued, and Hillary is smart enough to save the "Keep going!" routine for someplace else. Instead, she trots out another one of my favorite Hillary church-shticks, which goes something like this: "Someone asked me the other day if I prayed. I said, yes, I do pray. I was fortunate enough to be brought up in a home where the power of prayer was understood. But I have to tell you, if I hadn't prayed before I got to the White House, I would have started after I arrived."

It's a funny line, and even in this buttoned-up place, people laugh. Part of what makes it funny is the surprise of hearing stalwart Hillary admit that times at the White House were rough enough to send her looking heavenward for help. Of course, none of us could ever get her to admit that. I remember when she was interviewed by Charlie Rose in front of a live audience at the 92nd Street Y, she had made one of her usual Pollyanna declarations about how she'd managed to find something good in every single day she spent at the White House.

"What was good about the impeachment?" Rose had asked.

"What was good about it was that we protected and saved the Constitution," she had said without a moment's hesitation, conjuring up a vision in my mind's eye of Hillary, like Dolley Madison saving George

Washington's portrait from the fire set by the British, throwing herself in front of the document signed by our first president as Trent Lott approached.

Now we are on to our third church of the day, St. Luke AME, where the preacher tells his congregation, "I'm glad we have a first lady of this country who has held her head high, and who is a scholar, and a lawyer, and a teacher, and a mother, and who is more than capable of being the senator from the state of New York!"

It's Hillary's turn now. She starts with "What a day the Lord has made," thanks everybody for their prayers over the last eight years, and launches into the "Keep going!" routine. But this time, just when I think it's over, she adds a piece I've never heard before and I have to pick my pen up.

"We have to keep going to freedom and opportunity," she says, her voice slowly getting louder. "And I will go to the Senate to continue that fight. I will go to the floor of the Senate every day and work my heart out for you. And I will *not* turn back! No matter *who's* behind me! Or *what* they're saying, or *what* they're doing!"

By the time she's done with that little speech, she's shouting, the audience is cheering like crazy, and I'm scribbling in my notebook: "VRWC after HRC again." (That's shorthand for "vast right-wing conspiracy.")

Then she segues back to familiar territory: "Because there is one thing you know about me. When I tell you I'll stick with you . . ."

I start gathering up my things in preparation to leave, and an older lady sitting behind me taps me on the shoulder. "She's going to be the first woman president," she informs me. "You know that, don't you? Maybe not in my lifetime, but you mark my words, it's gonna happen someday."

I'm tempted to say, "There are a lot of Republicans who agree with you," but I hold my tongue and thank her for sharing her thoughts.

The week before, a preacher had made the same prediction. "We're sorry we're losing the president," the Reverend Charles W. Mixon had told his congregation at Maranatha Baptist Church in Queens when the first lady arrived. "I think he'll go down in history as the best president we ever had. I'm not saying this because she's here. I'm saying this because of reality."

He added, "Mrs. Clinton has stood in his corner, and now she's here in our state running for senator. I'm telling you, I think she'll be the first woman president in the United States of America, with the help of me and my God." There was sustained applause, and I was so intrigued by the reverend's endorsement that I called him on the phone the next day. I really wasn't sure I understood what all this adulation for the Clintons from the black community was based on. It's not like Bill passed some great civil rights law; if anything, I would have thought welfare reform might have hurt his support among black voters.

Mixon had an interesting take on it. "Clinton has a black secretary," he said, referring to Betty Currie. "That means a lot. No other American president has had a black secretary. Plus the fact you had many people in his cabinet who are people of color. When he had trouble, he called Jesse Jackson. He called Vernon Jordan. He realized he needed people of color to help him through this thing. If I am not loyal to a man like that, who am I loyal to?"

Bill Clinton continued to generate goodwill among black voters even after he left the White House, by renting the penthouse of a Harlem building for his post-presidential office after Republicans complained that a midtown suite he'd originally picked out was too expensive. The decision to locate the office in Harlem instead was a brilliant political stroke; after all, he would always be assured of a warm welcome in the neighborhood, as his maiden stroll around the area, followed by hundreds of ardent supporters, showed. And, of course, the move would help ensure Hillary's popularity among black voters as well.

A few weeks before the election, the *New Yorker* published an article by Joe Klein about Bill Clinton, which was mostly fascinating, but which contained one assertion that made me wish Klein could have come with me to see Hillary in all these black churches, then heard Mixon try to explain why she and her husband are so beloved by black voters. In his article, Klein criticized the president for spending so much time after he was elected in '92 "working out a cabinet that looked like America, perfectly balanced—at least according to traditional liberal perceptions—along racial, ethnic, and gender lines. This was silly on several grounds. In the modern presidency, the real power resides in the White House staff; all but a few cabinet members are peripheral. Clinton seemed more preoccupied with the need for a second Hispanic . . . than with working out a coherent management structure for the West Wing."

It might have been silly on those grounds, but now that Hillary was trolling for votes in a place like New York, the diversity of her husband's administration helped cement the loyalty of millions of voters. No matter what ethnic group she was meeting with, there was someone close to her husband whom she could mention. I had never realized that the president's physician, Dr. Connie Mariano, was Filipino, but when Hillary marched in a Filipino parade in Manhattan, she made sure to bring it up, and it was clear that every cheering member of the crowd had duly taken note.

But it was also amazing to me how many of these black pastors actually seemed to know Bill Clinton personally. I had never been to most of the churches Hillary visited, despite years of following candidates around on their vote-getting treks, and I had never even heard of a lot of them, despite having lived in New York my entire life. But it seemed as if in every other church we went to, the pastor got up and talked about meeting the president, or speaking to him, or writing to him, or visiting him in the White House. Black voters often complain about being taken for granted by the Democratic Party, but the Clintons were obviously not guilty of this. One Sunday at Grace Baptist, a church in Mount Vernon in Westchester, not far from Chappaqua, the pastor, W. Franklyn Richardson, something of a bigwig in black Baptist circles, introduced Hillary by recalling a phone conversation he'd recently had with the president.

"I said, 'You're my new neighbor,'" Richardson recalled, "and Bill said, 'Yeah, and your old friend.'"

A few Sundays earlier, Hillary had been presented with a wedding anniversary present for herself and the president at an old-fashioned wood-frame church in the Bronx called Emmanuel Baptist.

"Our president, who we love dearly, and the first lady, just celebrated twenty-five years of marriage," copastor Darlene Thomas McGuire told her flock. "We want her to have a token of our love." Hillary was then handed a big box wrapped in shiny paper, which we later learned contained a silver ice bucket.

Then McGuire, like a lot of pastors, made a show of separating her tax-exempt church from a political endorsement. "I'm not speaking for the church today," she announced. "But as for me and my house, she's the next senator of the United States." Her lyrical phrasing was right out of the Old Testament: "Choose this day whom ye will serve . . . but as for me and my house, we will serve the Lord," Joshua 24:15.

Hillary, for her part, responded with a nice turn of phrase of her own, one I hadn't heard her use before that day, but one that became a standard part of her church spiel: "You know, I believe it takes a village to raise a child. And at the center of that village there must be a church, and people of good faith!" Naturally, this line went over big.

We were then treated to the Harriet Tubman tale, followed by prayers and hymns sung by the entire congregation, with Hillary joining in and McGuire leading.

I told Satan, get thee behind
I told Satan, get thee behind
Get thee behind

Get thee behind

Victory today is mine!

But on the second go-round the words changed. McGuire raised her voice above the rest and loudly led with new lyrics until the congregation heard the change and carried on without her. Hillary, I noticed, wasn't singing this version.

I told Lazio, get thee behind!

I told Lazio, get thee behind!

Get thee behind!

Get thee behind!

Victory today is mine!

Of course, for the rest of the day in the van, we sang nothing else—not because we disliked Lazio or thought he was equivalent to Satan, but just because it was so funny. At the Q-and-A later I asked Hillary what she thought of the new lyrics. She paused for a second, then smiled and replied, "I love hymns."

All of these forays in the black community seemed so effortless for Hillary. They loved her; she had a great stump speech. What could be bad? But sometimes, when Hil was in her glory, high on her own "Keep going!" riff or singing along to some hymn amid a sea of black faces in a Baptist church in East New York, I couldn't help but think back to one of her first public meetings with another powerful black minister in New York, the Reverend Al Sharpton. Sharpton, the city's most prominent black activist, is better known for creating a ruckus than for his sermons. But while he's a rabble-rouser to some, he's a solitary voice of truth to others. Either way, as one of my colleagues likes to say, at least he always returns our phone calls. If you need a comment on a racial incident or someone who's willing to challenge the prevailing political sentiment, you can always count on Al—with his James Brown hairdo and his Santa Claus physique—to have a sound bite at the ready.

On the other hand, while he's an important player in racial politics, he's extremely controversial. He began preaching the Gospel as a child, and as a young man, he'd been an FBI informant. He first got a lot of attention leading angry protests in connection with the Howard Beach case, in which a gang of white kids had chased a black teenager to his death. But he next showed up as a player in a far less credible case, as an adviser to Tawana Brawley, a black teenager who claimed that she'd been sexually assaulted by a group of white men upstate, including a prosecutor and a cop. The incident was strange from the start; she was dazed and bruised but there was virtually no evidence to substantiate her claims. A grand jury eventually concluded she'd made it up, and the accused men were all cleared. But Sharpton insisted, long after everyone else had ceased to believe Tawana, that she had been telling the truth.

More recently he'd taken on a more legitimate role of speaking out in response to the Diallo and Dorismond cases. He held press conferences, organized demonstrations, held vigils with the victims' families, and generally provided a counterpoint to whatever the official explanation from the police or mayor's office was. If you wanted to mobilize black voters in New York, as Hillary needed to, you had to reckon with Al at some point—if only so that he couldn't accuse you behind your back of being afraid of him. On the other hand, you couldn't cozy up to him, either; he had way too much baggage.

So it was with all of this in the background that Hillary's entourage had driven up to Sharpton's offices in a dilapidated building on 125th Street in Harlem on a bitter cold Martin Luther King Day in January. About three hundred people were seated inside; the reporters were squeezed between the last row of chairs and a wall. With no place to put our heavy winter coats and the heat in the room on full blast, we were all sweating like pigs within minutes. We were escorted into the room long before Hillary appeared and waited impatiently while

Sharpton, some of his associates, and a couple of other politicians like former mayors Ed Koch and David Dinkins who'd come to pay their respects were introduced. I was only half-paying attention when I suddenly heard the speaker at the podium say the words "A Jew!" as if he were spitting out poison. I immediately turned my tape recorder on and started scribbling notes. Everyone else in the press corps had also suddenly jerked awake; I was standing next to Gregg Birnbaum of the *New York Post* and heard him mutter, "This is like a movie!"

The speaker, the Reverend Charles Norris, was explaining why, as a young man, he had missed one of King's demonstrations. He'd had to work, he said, for a father-and-son operation that wouldn't have looked kindly on his taking the day off to go to a civil rights protest. Referring to his former employers, he said, "Miller number one was a Jew. Miller number two was a Jew. I was then employed by yet another Jew by the name of Jesus . . . and will not be fired until He thinks it's necessary."

It was shaping up to be Hillary's worst nightmare, and she didn't even know it. A few minutes later, she entered the room. Someone passed her a note about what had happened, and she quickly inserted a statement condemning anti-Semitism into her formal remarks on racial tolerance. When she was done, we were told to wait outside on the street for a brief avail. Five minutes turned into ten, and ten stretched into twenty; we were all shivering in the January weather by the time she came out to talk to us. My fingers were so cold I could no longer write; I just held out my tape recorder and hoped I'd pick up whatever I needed. She knew what she had to do, and before anyone could even ask her the question, she said, "I heard that one of the speakers made some divisive comments, which I soundly reject." And that was really all she needed to say. There would be no more fallout from that particular incident, other than a brief mention in some of the stories—including mine—the next day about Norris's comments and her response.

Unfortunately she'd made a different type of error at the same forum, and that did come back to haunt her. Among the people in the audience were the parents of Amadou Diallo, the unarmed African immigrant who was shot at forty-one times by four cops who mistakenly thought his wallet was a gun. In publicly giving her condolences to the grieving mother and father, Hillary referred to Diallo's death as a "murder." The officers had not yet been tried for the killing, and ultimately they were acquitted by a jury that accepted their explanations of the shooting, so Hillary took a lot of heat from cops and other critics over her use of the word *murder*. It was a slip of the tongue, she said in defense, and apologized for it for months afterward.

But she managed to capitalize on another police shooting of an unarmed black man after Giuliani bungled his handling of it. The victim, Patrick Dorismond, was working as a security guard in Manhattan when he got into a fatal fight with undercover cops who asked him if he knew where to buy drugs. First the police department released Dorismond's sealed juvenile record, which showed a robbery arrest at age thirteen, then Giuliani said Dorismond was a man with a "propensity to violence" and refused to offer condolences to the man's parents.

Hillary made headlines with a speech in Harlem criticizing the mayor's response. "You can look across this great nation and see city after city that has found the way to bring down crime rates *and* racial tensions," she said. ". . . But instead of learning from these examples, the mayor has hunkered down, taken sides, and further divided this city. . . . At just the moment when a real leader would have reached out and tried to heal the wounds, he has chosen divisiveness. At just the moment when a real leader would wait for the results of a full and fair investigation, he has led the rush to judgment. This is not leadership."

She added two of her favorite anti-Giuliani lines: "I want to engage in the politics of reconciliation, not revenge and retribution. I want to be known by who I lift up, not who I push down."

I have to admit I kind of missed those lines after they disappeared a month later, when Giuliani dropped out of the race. I don't think she ever came up with such a pithy putdown of Lazio.

In October, on a three-day upstate tour, Hillary's motorcade got to Auburn, where, as she'd pointed out in all her church speeches, Harriet Tubman's house is located. Finney told everybody on the press bus that Hillary, safely ensconced in her own van, had something to say to them. She hooked her cell phone up to a microphone and Hillary's familiar voice came through.

"I thought we would all like to see the Harriet Tubman house," she told them. "But we're running short on time to the next event. So we're gonna have to . . . *keep going!*"

The press corps collapsed with laughter. They also got a nifty little memento of the joke: a laminated press credential bearing a picture of a bus, the words "On the Road with Hillary" on the top, and a tiny "Keep Going!" written across the bottom.

Where's Lonzo?

A lot of politicians write long, single-spaced letters when they're asking for money. But Rick Lazio's most famous fund-raising appeal was just three sentences long:

> It won't take me six pages to convince you to send me an urgently needed contribution for my United States Senate campaign in New York. It will only take six words.
> I'm running against Hillary Rodham Clinton.

That letter helped Lazio raise $40 million in just seven months from Clinton-haters all over the country. "She has inherited most of my enemies," the president told a group of Hillary's supporters one night. "Maybe she's made one or two of her own."

But that letter was more than just a way to mobilize Hillary's foes. Its message in some ways summed up Lazio's candidacy. To most voters, he was never able to define himself as substantially more than the anti-Hillary, and Hillary had fun pointing that out.

"My opponent says you only need to know six words about him: 'I'm running against Hillary Rodham Clinton,' " she'd gleefully say.

"Well, I think you need to know seven words in order to vote for me. How about *jobs, education, environment, choice, health,* and *Social Security?*"

Of course, it wasn't just that Lazio failed to offer a substantial vision for what he wanted to accomplish as senator. It was also that, right out of the gate, she was famous, and he wasn't. One of the best stories about his obscurity came from Joel Siegel at the *Daily News.* Joel was walking next to Lazio in a July 4th parade in Ticonderoga when he heard somebody repeatedly asking, "Where's Lonzo?"

Joel turned around and saw a woman standing on the curb, watching the parade go by. "Where's Lonzo?" she kept saying.

"Lonzo—er, Lazio—was marching right in front of her," Joel recalled. He included the anecdote in a piece he wrote for the *Daily News* Web site. "From there it gained currency, and we later started calling him Dick Lonzo as an inside joke about his anonymity," Joel said. From then on, the question "Where's Lonzo?" was frequently heard on Hillary's press van, although Frank Eltman and I also had a soft spot for an earlier nickname we'd been using, Little Ricky, a moniker that had first turned up in one of Maureen Dowd's columns in the *New York Times.*

When Lazio first entered the race, those of us accustomed to Hillary's personal reserve and lack of accessibility, not to mention Giuliani's penchant for insulting any reporter who asked him a question he didn't like, were initially thrilled by Lazio's gregarious, accessible manner. He was about the same age as a lot of us, while both Giuliani and Hillary were a decade or so older than most of the press corps. Lazio, like Frank Eltman, was a big Allman Brothers fan, and his two little girls were about the same age as my oldest son. Liz Moore of *Newsday,* who lived in the same town as Lazio, had seen him shopping for the kids at Toys "R" Us. He was never mobbed in a public place the way Hillary was at Grand Union. When you went to a street fair with Lazio, he had to stride over to people to introduce himself.

In fact, that's how he fell on his face ten days after entering the race. He was zigzagging from side to side to shake hands with people while marching in a Memorial Day parade in Babylon, Long Island, when he lost his footing, fell, and cut his lip so badly that he needed stitches. "For the rest of the campaign, he was frequently seen tying his shoes," recalled Frank. When you went somewhere with Hillary, she didn't have to move a muscle. Hundreds of people would immediately surround her.

Lazio also had a regular-guy quality about him. We could relate to that, and initially, I thought the voters might respond to it, too. He'd lived on Long Island his whole life (or, as we often said on the van, quoting one of the many Lazio TV ads that showed him walking on a beach with his family, "He clammed on these Long Island shores!"), married a friend's sister who was a nurse, and worked as a prosecutor in Suffolk County and as a member of the county legislature before running for Congress. About the only choice he'd ever made that seemed out of character was enrolling in Vassar College just seven years after it went coed, when the student body was still mostly female. "Here's a trick well known to human-resources departments," wrote Michael Wolff in *New York* magazine. "Always hire the Wellesley girls (like Hillary); they're precise and indefatigable. Here's another trick. Stay away from Vassar boys, like Rick. They're precious and need quite a bit of pampering."

Lazio wore his middle-class lifestyle like a badge of honor. Early on, when ethical questions arose about some stock-option trading that had yielded him a 600 percent profit (the Lazio version of Hillary's cattle-futures trading), he told reporters he'd talked to his wife about it, then quoted her as saying, "You know what, we're honest, decent people. I clean my own house. We work hard. We have nothing to be ashamed of."

It was the equivalent of Richard Nixon talking about Pat Nixon's cloth coat. For months after that, the reporters covering Lazio made jokes "about getting a photo-op of Pat with the vacuum cleaner," recalled Frank. They'd ask Patrick McCarthy, one of the campaign press aides, "Hey, does Pat Lazio use a Sears or a Hoover?"

But I couldn't help but wonder how many women might actually have thought a little *less* of Rick Lazio after hearing that his wife was washing windows instead of paying someone else to do it. Pat Lazio only worked part-time as a breast cancer advocate, but I know a lot of working mothers—myself included—who look upon the cleaning lady as one of the most important people in their life. I only got one after I started covering Hillary, when I decided it was both a worthy use of my overtime pay and a way to get another couple of hours a week with my kids. Since I pay my cleaning lady about the same hourly wage that I get, I figure I don't have anything to feel guilty about. I certainly don't think it means I'm not a decent person. (P.S. Lazio was quickly cleared of any questionable activity in connection with the stock-option trade.)

One of Lazio's funniest TV ads featured the question "Can you name three things Hillary Clinton has done for New York?" and voters coming up blank in response. But I'm not sure most people could name three things any politician ever did for his constituents. One day I sat at my desk asking myself questions like "Can you name three things Ed Koch has done for New York? Pat Moynihan? Rudy Giuliani?" Actually, I bet most New Yorkers could name three things Rudy had done— maybe even more than three—but I'm not sure they'd all be things most people approved of.

From Hillary's point of view, of course, her résumé was loaded compared to Lazio's; he was an average guy, not a star, whereas she'd been making headlines ever since she was at Wellesley. She was a student leader during an era when the all-girl campus went from afternoon teas to women's lib, and she was the first student at Wellesley ever to speak at commencement. Her remarks—which included a brash comeback to a Republican senator who'd spoken before she did—made headlines in the *Boston Globe* and got her picture in *Life* magazine. At

Yale Law School she met Bill Clinton and cultivated Marian Wright Edelman, the head of the Children's Defense Fund, as a mentor. From there she went to Washington to help research the constitutional grounds for impeaching Nixon—"the real impeachment," as she likes to call it. Bill talked her into moving to Arkansas with him, and as his political career blossomed with her help, she worked as a law professor and then joined Little Rock's most prominent law firm. She was named to *American Lawyer* magazine's list of the country's one hundred most influential attorneys, was chosen by President Carter to head the Legal Services Corporation, and was always involved in some commission or other, whether it was chairing a committee on women in the legal profession for the American Bar Association or reforming the Arkansas educational system when she was the governor's wife. In the White House, she simultaneously became one of the most reviled and one of the most admired first ladies ever. Her health-care reform effort was a complete debacle, yet for her Senate run she managed to transform that failure into a symbol of perseverance. Her very first speech to New Yorkers on the subject back in the spring of '99 was the "I come from the school of smaller steps now" approach. But by the end of the campaign, she was no longer talking about her health-care ideas in a small, humble voice. She was instead roaring sound bites like this: "I believe health care is a right, not a privilege!" and getting ovations from her audience in response.

And if Lazio was Patty Duke, who'd only seen the sights a girl can see from Brooklyn Heights, Hillary was Patty's identical cousin, Cathy, who'd been most everywhere, from Zanzibar to Berkeley Square. The first lady liked to point out that she'd visited every continent except Antarctica. Reporters from foreign news agencies were always shouting out questions like "What is your message for the women of Italy?" when we were trying to pin her down on what she thought of the latest Giuliani edict or whether Bill was going to host a fund-raiser for her. And once in a while an event in New York would be related to her work on international affairs, and we'd be thrust into this odd world where Hillary was no longer the candidate struggling to win over undecided suburban ladies or the subject of some scandal involving Bill's old girl-friends, but was instead a revered international icon, famed as a feminist from Kampala to Berlin.

One of the first lady's pet projects was the expansion of microloan programs to women around the world. One night she received an award from the queen of Jordan, Rania Al-Abdullah, for championing the microcredit program. The speakers included a woman from Uganda who had used her microloan to open a restaurant and a tailoring business. A widowed mother of four, she had put the income from those businesses toward sending her children to school, buying a house and some land, and employing some of her neighbors. She told the audience that the loans had "transformed my life" and said that when Hillary had traveled to her country to support the program, the first lady's presence there had helped convince other Ugandans—including the country's president—who'd been skeptical of the idea that it was indeed worthy. Hillary had also arranged for a woman from India who was involved in a microcredit program there to attend an economic conference at the White House with the president, Bill Gates, and Alan Greenspan. It was the kind of networking that only Hillary could have pulled off: a woman from a third-world village sitting down to tell the president and America's most powerful businessmen what for.

One of the finest moments in Hillary's career had been a 1995 speech at a conference on women's rights in Beijing. It was a tough, passionate critique of abuses of women around the world delivered at a time when the United States was muting its criticism of China's human rights policies.

"It is a violation of human rights when babies are denied food, or drowned or suffocated, or their spines broken, simply because they are born girls. . . . It is a violation of human rights when women are doused with gasoline, set on fire, and burned to death because their marriage dowries are deemed too small," Hillary had declared, adding: "Human rights are women's rights and women's rights are human rights, once and for all." The Chinese government only underscored how threatened they were by her speech when they blocked transmission of it via radio and TV.

A reference to the speech eventually turned up in one of the TV ads for Hillary's Senate campaign. With various pictures of Hillary shown on the screen, a deep-voiced male announcer invoked an anonymous "they" and read the following text:

They tried to get her to back down on teacher testing. She wouldn't.

They tried to make her give up after health-care reform failed. She kept working.

They tried to silence her in China. But she spoke out for women's rights as human rights.

They criticized her book about children. She took the proceeds, nearly a million dollars, and gave it to children.

All her life, Hillary has stood up for what she believes in. For better schools, better health care. Now, she'll stand up for us.

I doubt that many New Yorkers knew or cared that when Hillary had led a commission to reform schools in Arkansas, the teachers union had opposed a proposal for teacher competency testing. And I don't think a lot of voters understood the "they tried to silence her in China" reference to the blacked-out Beijing speech. But you didn't have to get every detail to pick up on the big picture in this ad. "They" were after Hillary again! And if they're after her, that must mean that pretty soon they'll be after *you*, the voter-viewer. That means it's you and Hillary against the world, and what a team you'll be! Because despite this conspiracy—dare I say vast right-wing?—by the unnamed, ominous "they," Hillary, brave victim that she was, would always, like Harriet Tubman, *keep going!*

Why would Hillary's campaign resort to this bizarre drama? Well, her poll numbers were sky-high during the impeachment scandal; and somehow the combination of pity and admiration was magic for Hillary. This ad, and a lot of her campaign rhetoric, sought to re-create that dynamic between her and the voters.

In the middle of the Senate campaign, the United Nations held a follow-up conference to assess progress on women's rights in the five years since the meeting in China. Covering Hillary at this Beijing Plus Five conference in New York gave her Senate correspondents a small window on her international celebrity. I was astounded when women from Malaysia and Benin came up to me and started reciting the details of Hillary's life, saying they couldn't understand why New Yorkers wouldn't want her to be senator when it was perfectly obvious to them that she should be president.

But the most notable moment of that event came after Hillary described how, on a visit to India, women in colorful saris who had walked miles to see her began serenading her with a version of "We Shall Overcome."

Suddenly I noticed a woman in the audience stand up near the front of the room. In the time it took me to wonder if she was about to make trouble, it became clear that she wasn't. Instead, in a loud, clear voice, she began to sing the opening words to "We Shall Overcome," and within seconds, she was joined by hundreds of other women standing up around the room, adding their voices to the growing chorus of sopranos. Hillary seemed, at first, a little taken aback, as if she was unsure what was going on. But as the singing proceeded, she appeared grateful and moved. It became clear that this was a tribute to her, and a tribute to the solidarity of women around the world working to overcome the very real obstacles in their lives, a goal they believe Hillary shares.

I had to admit there was something wonderful about this moment, something thrilling and surreally perfect. I even felt a little teary-eyed as the singing died away. Then all of a sudden the cynical animal inside me took over. What if it had all been staged? I started to ask myself. I tried to remember exactly how it had happened, whether this woman who had first stood up could have prearranged this all with Hillary and the others. I got that panicky feeling that I get sometimes when I'm not sure I'll be able to figure out what's really going on and I know I'll have to take the chance of reporting something that I can't be 100 percent sure of. I canvassed the reporters sitting next to me. "Do you think that was spontaneous?" I asked. They all believed it was. And ultimately that's how I described it in my story. But I was always nagged by the feeling that I should have found that first woman who stood up, just to make sure.

I'd grown so accustomed to feeling that every little detail in the Clinton campaign was always planned out way ahead of time that it was hard to accept anything as truly spontaneous. I was still obsessing about it the next day and even tried tracking down the women in the Indian delegation by making calls to India's U.N. mission and searching the Web for e-mail addresses for them. I was fairly certain the first woman who had stood up had been wearing a sari, but I wasn't even sure of that. One of my editors said he didn't understand what the big deal was. I started to explain that I had this funny feeling that I had somehow been duped into thinking these women simply burst into song at the sight of Hillary when maybe, just maybe, it was the result of some top-secret plan . . .

Suddenly, of course, as I tried to put into words what I was think-ing, it all seemed ridiculous. Why, after all, did it matter? And why couldn't I just take it at face value? In the end I sent a few e-mails, but never heard back. And in the months that followed, I heard Hillary recount the story several times, and in each retelling, when she got to the part where the singing began, she said, "And all of a sudden . . ."

I watched her carefully each time, trying to detect her level of sincerity, and each time, I had to admit, she looked pretty darn sincere.

Maggie Haberman, who with Bob Hardt and Gregg Birnbaum covered both Lazio and Hillary for the *New York Post*, pointed out that the prevailing conversation on the Hillary van was often a deconstruction of Hillary, her motives and her plans, while the talk on the Lazio bus was also about sports, the presidential election, or the reporters themselves. One reason for this, she said, was that on the Lazio side, "we were getting so many avails that we always had a chance to ask him if something came up. There was a less speculative tone with Lazio, whereas with Hillary, there was all this talking about 'Well, what does she think about this and what's she going to do?' Her avail would be limited to two minutes and then she'd walk away, and that fostered more of a guessing game with her than there ever was with him."

Of course, the U.N. event also pointed to another big difference between the two, and that was what her advisers came to refer to as the "stature gap," the notion that Hillary Rodham Clinton was simply more senatorial than Dick Lonzo. Lazio wasn't being invited to give speeches at the United Nations, and Hillary was. Sure, she could say silly things about the Yankees or pander to Jewish voters with the best of 'em. And in the early days of her campaign, she stepped on every ethnic land mine in the city of New York, made stupid mistakes at Listening Tour events, and couldn't generate a sound bite if her life depended on it. But if Hillary started out all substance and no sound bites, by the time election day rolled around, she'd figured out how to deliver both. Lazio, in contrast, was too often all sound bites and *no* substance.

Hillary, for example, never gave us a Q-and-A without first making us sit through a message for the day or some kind of event themed around an issue like housing or health care or abortion. That's part of why her campaign hated the avails, because questions about whatever was on our minds detracted from whatever issue she was pushing that day. In contrast, as *Newsday* columnist Marie Cocco once observed to me, Lazio had to be accessible to reporters because he rarely offered anything else for them to write about *except* the answers to their questions. He had no message beyond the daily tit for tat of either defending himself against Hillary's latest charge or attacking Hillary for whatever she was doing.

The day Hillary addressed the Council on Foreign Relations was a case in point. She delivered a major speech to the council, a private, nonpartisan think tank in Manhattan, covering everything from the Balkans to missile-defense technology to human rights to Israel. Then she took questions from the foreign policy wonks in the audience as the cameras rolled. Lazio, in contrast, had scheduled a speech at the council and later canceled it. Days after Hillary had laid out her foreign policy vision, Lazio finally shared his in a small lecture hall at Syracuse University, in front of just a few dozen people and far from the media maelstrom. In reading his remarks—primarily a Bush-like critique of Bill Clinton's foreign policy—from a prepared text, he referred to the president of North Korea as "Kim Jong the Second" instead of "Kim Jong Il." It was a human error, and totally understandable. *Il* looks like the Roman numeral II in some typefaces, and Kim Jong is the son of the previous leader. It was a mistake any one of us might have made, any mere mortal. But it was also an error nobody could imagine Hillary making.

"Sometimes the contrast would be lost on you, but if you spent a few days with Lazio and then you saw her again, it was startling," Marcia Kramer recalled. "The day she gave that speech at the Council on Foreign Relations, Lazio went to a senior citizens center on Long Island. Whether or not you agreed with her positions, here she was talking about a huge breadth of world events with knowledge and insight and passion, while he was dancing the two-step with a nice little old lady from Long Island. Not to demean that little old lady, but it was a good juxtaposition of the two—the pictures of her being so senatorial, and him dancing."

Another time Hillary delivered a routine speech to an auditorium filled with students at Brooklyn Law School. It started out autobiographical, talking about how opportunities for women had changed since her days as one of the few female students at Yale Law School. She continued with a description of a legal-aid clinic she had run when she first moved to Arkansas with Bill and worked at a law school there. She kept butting heads with a judge whom she described as having been on the bench "at least since the Civil War" and who kept denying poor people the right to free legal assistance because of an old statute that barred free counsel to anyone with assets over $10. The judge used the statute to disqualify anybody who owned a car. "He told me, 'Professor Rodham, don't bring people in here who don't meet the statute,' " Hillary recalled.

Then came the kicker. "So," she added matter-of-factly, "I had to go and change the statute."

Everybody laughed. It was such a Hillary way to tell the story, as if that's how everyone who hits a brick wall at their job proceeds—by figuring out how to rewrite the law.

The speech ended with an extremely well-articulated argument for why the makeup of the Supreme Court matters—not just because of abortion rights, the issue she most frequently trotted out for voters to consider, but because of George W. Bush's views on constitutional constructionism, which in essence could lead the court to more strictly interpret the Constitution not in light of modern concerns but as it was originally written in the eighteenth century. This, Hillary argued, could lead to a dismantling of many of the federal protections we now take for granted.

Whether or not you bought the first lady's argument, you had to be impressed by how seamlessly she wove together her life with politics and legal procedure, how simply she'd rendered her points, and how interesting and pertinent she'd managed to make these arcane issues seem. I remembered, early on in the campaign, sitting in a room of people from the biotech industry as Hillary droned on and on about obscure economic-development proposals. When I got back to the office, Suzanne Plunkett showed me photographs she'd taken of a half dozen people in the audience who were fast asleep. But today it was obvious that Hillary had learned how to give a good speech. Every one of these law students was wide-eyed and on the edge of his seat. They'd obviously never been to a lecture in law school as stimulating as this one. They were, quite simply, blown away. One young woman told me she'd thought of herself as a Lazio voter until that moment. "I don't think Rick Lazio could top that," she said. "I don't think he could express what she expressed today. She's just completely articulate. And right now, I'm shaking."

Even the press—for all our complaints about Hillary—had to acknowledge that she was smart and frequently impressive. On a night in early October, Frank Eltman and I switched beats, as we occasionally did. My night was a comedy of errors. Lazio was doing a tour of Orthodox Jewish events in Brooklyn, and they'd hired a driver for the press van who had apparently never been to Brooklyn before. We got so lost between the first and second events that by the time we arrived, Lazio had been and gone. When we got to the third event, a celebration of the harvest festival Sukkoth, it turned out that women were not allowed inside. This was not an uncommon practice in the Orthodox Jewish community, which I'd covered for the AP for years. But in my experience, whoever was handling the press coverage always made arrangements beforehand to ensure access for female reporters, whether that meant cordoning off a small area where we could observe the proceedings without sitting among the men, or recruiting an Orthodox woman to explain to us what was going on so that we wouldn't miss anything, or even just having someone take our tape recorders inside and turn them on at the right time. None of that happened here. The women in the press corps with Lazio that night were simply left standing outside on the sidewalk while the men in the press corps and Lazio's all-male staff followed their candidate inside. At the next event, the same thing happened. A female camerawoman for NY1, the local all-news cable station, handed her video camera to a male producer for a different station and asked him to take it inside so she could at least have a little bit of footage.

I was furious by the time it was all over and we got back into the van. I asked Gregg if he had a cell phone number for Jonathan Greenspun, Lazio's adviser on Jewish affairs, so I could call to complain. But when I tried the number, I couldn't get through.

"What's the big deal?" Gregg said to me. "There was no news at any of these events."

What's the big deal? I couldn't believe he'd said that! I was momentarily speechless, just sputtering with anger. My fury boiled up to the point where I simply reached over the back of the seat in front of me to where Gregg was sitting and started punching him in the shoulder. Eventually I found my voice, but I was so mad that I'm not even sure what I said, and Gregg says he can't remember either—all he knows is that I totally lost it. I know I was thinking, "How would you feel if you showed up at an event and were told the *Times* and the AP can come in but not the *Post*? . . . This would never happen on Hillary's campaign! . . . How dare they do this! . . . And they didn't even say they were sorry. . . . I went to the Lubavitcher rebbe's gravesite with Benjamin Netanyahu and I got a front-row seat, but when I go with Lazio to Borough Park, I can't even get in the door!" and so on. At some point in the middle of my tantrum, as a perfect ending to the evening, I realized the driver was heading the wrong way—toward Staten Island instead of Manhattan—and I had to stop my little outburst to persuade the guy to turn the hell around while everybody else started frantically trying to pinpoint our location on a street map in the dark. The next day, I e-mailed Gregg my apologies, and I think—at least I hope—he's more or less forgiven me for assaulting him when I should have just done what I always tell my kids to do when they're fighting: *Use your words!* (I believe Gregg's ultimate revenge was reminding me of this episode—which I had sort of blocked out of my mind—and getting me to record it here for posterity.)

The next night, one of Hillary's Jewish advisers, Matthew Hiltzik, went back to the very same neighborhood to meet with leaders from the Bobovs, one of the Hasidic groups whose Sukkoth celebration Lazio had visited (and I had been kept out of). Ironically, it turned out that the route to a political endorsement from this group was not by dropping in on an all-male gathering as Lazio had done, but through a meeting with the chief rabbi's *wife*, known as the rebbitsin. "She's the classic example of a bold, strong woman behind the man," Matthew said. He was given the honor of being part of a group escorting the rebbitsin to synagogue that night, and on the Saturday night before the election, Hillary was invited to come to Borough Park herself, for a ninety-minute meeting with a group of Bobover men and women. Republicans with contacts in the community had pressured the rabbi's wife not to meet with Hillary, but the rebbitsin had done what she thought was right and gone ahead with the first lady meeting anyway. Lazio, in his contact with the group, had stressed his support for vouchers, which Hillary opposes. But she was able to talk about other issues that were equally compelling—housing, health care, and jobs—and in the end, Hillary got the Bobov endorsement.

The same night that I had gone to Borough Park, Frank had gone to some routine Long Island event where nobody expected Hillary to make news. The next day when I talked to him, he said, "You know, it's good to go see the other side sometimes. She gave a pretty amazing speech." It was shortly after the USS *Cole* had been attacked, and Hillary had attended the funerals that morning. Her remarks that night noted that the *Cole* was a symbol of democracy, and she added that, in a way, the sailors stationed there had died representing America's freedoms, including the right to vote. One way to honor them, she concluded, was to make sure we exercised that right in November, no matter whom we voted for.

Frank couldn't imagine Lazio giving a speech like that at a throwaway event; all his speeches were stump formulas. And I couldn't imagine Hillary's people dragging me way the hell out to some Orthodox Jewish neighborhood in Brooklyn and then leaving me standing in the cold because no one had thought to make accommodations for women. When Hillary went to an Orthodox Jewish event, her staff even recommended on the schedule advisory that women in the press corps wear long skirts so as not to break the prevailing dress code.

But my thrilling night in Borough Park with the Lazio campaign actually underscored another difference between the two campaigns. Lazio was surrounded by a bunch of white guys who were just like him. Only two women were on the staff, Eileen Long and Mollie Conkey Fullington, and by the end of the campaign, both of them had been relegated to handling the public schedule for Lazio's wife, Pat, and traveling with her. Besides, Eileen hadn't been just a random hire—she was the daughter of the head of the Conservative Party, Mike Long, who'd endorsed Lazio.

On Hillary's side, not only was the candidate a woman, but the staff was largely female. Sure, Harold Ickes, Bill deBlasio, and Howard Wolfson were important players, but there was also Ann Lewis, the senior campaign adviser; Mandy Grunwald, the campaign's media consultant, who created the ads; Neera Tanden, a brilliant young lawyer, the daughter of Indian immigrants, who was Hillary's main policy adviser on the issues and also the deputy campaign manager; Katrina Hagajos, Hillary's personal photographer; Kelly Craighead and Allison Stein, the two blond personal assistants who were never more than a few feet away from the first lady's side; June Shih, a young Chinese-American speechwriter; and the two Karens and Cathie Levine, who worked with Howard in the press office.

And finally, there was a difference in the makeup of the press corps. On Lazio's side, the number of women covering him ranged from zero to three. On Hillary's side, men were the minority. With the exception of writers for the three big dailies, the *Times*, the *Post*, and the *News*, the first lady's press corps was largely female. *Newsday*, the AP, the *White Plains Journal News*, Reuters, ABC, NBC, CBS, WNYC-AM, the *Forward*, *USA Today*, and various other news organizations that covered her periodically all had women assigned to Hillary's campaign. In most cases, the assignment was not consciously made on the basis of the reporter's gender, but on the campaign van a sorority atmosphere resulted. I went to an all-girl high school, and many a day on the campaign trail that's what it felt like.

One day when I was covering Lazio, I got my period on the way to catch the press bus, and let's just say I needed a change of clothes before I could go anywhere. Had it been the Clinton van instead of the Lazio bus, I could have marched right up and told everybody what had happened and they would gladly have waited for me. But I didn't have the nerve to describe my little problem to the men on the Lazio bus. I wasn't sure what I was going to do, but when I got there, someone informed me that the bus was running an hour late. That gave me enough time to scoot into a nearby Strawberry's, buy a $14 skirt with an elastic waistband that didn't need to be tried on, and head to the ladies' room at Grand Central to change clothes and clean up. Had I been returning to the Clinton campaign, I am certain one of the girls in the van would have noticed that I had changed out of pants and into a skirt, but the boys on the Lazio bus were completely oblivious.

And while kvetching about everything from the lack of food to the lack of access was one of the main activities on the Clinton van, on the Lazio side, Frank told me, "there was this whole macho, bravado thing about who could go on longer without a day off." Gregg was the winner of that particular contest, counting Yom Kippur as just about his only day off in the five months leading up to election day. Lazio ended the campaign with twenty-one straight days on the road, and most of the regular reporters covering him never spent more than a few hours at home during that entire three-week period. "We were really suffering from cabin fever on that bus, having been cruising around upstate for days, twelve, fourteen, sixteen hours a day," Gregg recalled, "and we were all a little bit out of our minds." When other reporters got dropped in for a day or two here and there, Frank told me the regulars would just say, "Those guys are such wimps!"

There was also a frat party sensibility on the Lazio bus, which occasionally manifested itself in high jinks worthy of *Animal House,* that all of the Clinton press corps' silly songs and vaudeville riffs on Hillary's speeches just couldn't measure up to. The most notorious prank played by the Lazio crew on one of their own came when one of the regular crew decided to take a Sunday off to see the Mets play the Cardinals in the National League championship series at Shea Stadium. Like the others assigned to cover the campaign full-time, this person was supposed to be present for every single public appearance Lazio had, just in case of an incident like the lip-splitting fall at the parade, or worse. "It's a reporter's worst nightmare to be caught where the story is *not*," Gregg later pointed out. But this individual decided to take a chance and skip a couple of minor Lazio events upstate to see the game. The events were unlikely to make it into anybody's stories, and he figured if any news did happen, his buddies would cover his butt and fill him in.

The other guys spent the day razzing their absent colleague: "What a dog!" "He really sucks!" "Wouldn't it be cool if something happened to Lazio while he was at the Met game?"

It wasn't much of a leap from that line of thinking to actually orchestrating the prank. As the Lazio reporters watched the Met game on satellite TV aboard the bus at around 9 P.M., Joel Siegel of the *Daily*

News placed a call to their unsuspecting colleague as he sat in the stadium. Siegel used the bus's satellite phone system, but because he knew the phone number would be recognizable when it appeared on the recipient's cell phone caller ID, he had the call placed through a third-party switchboard to mask its origin. He then disguised his voice, identified himself as someone from the victim's place of employment, and said, in a frantic, pleading tone, "Where are you? We've been trying to get hold of you for a half hour! There's an AP report that Lazio's bus ran off the road upstate and crashed. There's injuries! Hello? Are you there? This is really big!"

Within seconds, Gregg's cell phone rang. The boys on the bus looked at each other and smiled. They knew it was the panicked victim calling for help.

Gregg answered, "but I was already laughing so hard that all I could manage to say was 'They're coming out of the emergency room! Talk to Frank!' I tossed my cell phone to Frank because I was about to lose it."

Frank immediately continued the story, providing details of the phony crash on Route 81 in Syracuse and adding, "It was unbelievable! We crashed into the bus in front of us! We almost died!"

The poor guy on the other end of the line was by now completely freaked out—so freaked out that Frank could barely get his attention when he was ready to fess up. Frank had to call the guy's name a few times before he stopped ranting and raving and settled down long enough to hear Frank say, "We're fucking with you! We're fucking with you!"

Realizing suddenly that he'd been duped, all the guy could muster in response was an angry *"That's not funny!"*

The victim spent the rest of the campaign getting revenge in various ways, like leaving phantom numbers on Frank's beeper so he would have to chase down calls that hadn't been made.

The following night, the same individual was going to Shea again, this time to actually cover Lazio as he attended one of the games. As they rode an elevator up to their stadium seats with some of Lazio's staff, the congressman all of a sudden filled the few minutes of elevator silence by muttering, "Glad everybody is okay from that bus crash." He'd been told about the prank by other reporters and a few of his aides.

In '98, Schumer and D'Amato each did a few fly-arounds upstate, with news conferences for local TV in the airports and the occasional drive into town for a rally at a factory or a handshaking event. But Hillary set a new standard with her Listening Tour, visiting big cities and small towns alike, stopping at schools, hospitals, downtown districts, and historic sites all over the state, and Lazio was forced to try to match her reach. While some criticized his upstate effort as lackluster, his bus, named the Mainstream Express by his campaign, allowed him to create an instant rally site wherever he went, complete with loudspeaker, sound system, Lazio's kids waving American flags out the bus windows, and "Lazio 2000" stickers on the side of the bus as his backdrop. Among the songs they'd often blare over the sound system were an old Ray Charles number, "What'd I Say," with a line that was tailor-made for Hillary-haters: "Tell your momma, tell your pa, I'm gonna move you back to Arkansas . . ."

The press bus that followed behind the Mainstream Express had its own claim to fame in the form of a Southern Baptist driver named George Turnipseed, who quietly informed any reporter who tried to board the vehicle with a beer or a cigarette that there would be no smokin', no drinkin', and no cussin' on his bus. "At first we didn't believe his name was Turnipseed," Frank recalled. "We said, 'Show us your license.'" Thereafter, anybody joining the pack for the first time who expressed incredulity was immediately informed that a license check had already been performed.

On the night before the election, as everyone bid their good-byes with the knowledge that Lazio was likely to go down the tubes within twenty-four hours, Turnipseed approached Frank and Steve Yesner, a producer for ABC News, and asked if he could pray with them. "I was sort of flabbergasted," Frank said. "Then I was like, 'If you want to, George.' We're standing on the tarmac of this airport hangar at Republic Airport in Farmingdale, Long Island. It's almost like a scene out of *Primary Colors*—all of the balloons have fallen, the music is still blaring, but everybody's leaving. . . . He put his arms around me and Steve for this little prayer and said something like, 'Guide them in their future careers, thank you for letting us become friends, watch over them as they continue, and help them make the right decisions in life.' "

The next day, of course, was the end of the line for the Mainstream Express and the Lazio campaign. In his final afternoon on the trail, Little Ricky walked into a school in Syracuse where a crowd of Hillary supporters started chanting her name; then, somewhere between the school and the airport, he managed to step in dog shit. When he got to the airport, he headed into the men's room and was seen holding on to the sink with one hand to keep his balance while using his other hand to scrape off the bottom of his shoe with a paper towel. It seemed, in some pathetic way, like an appropriate ending for a guy who had started out the race by falling on his face, but the dog-shit episode never made it into anyone's story—it was just seen as too crude and, in the scheme of Hil's big win and his big loss, unimportant. Still, there were a lot of giggles about it in the Lazio van and on the press plane that day, and by nightfall, the media grapevine had spread the dog-poop tale to everyone who'd ever covered any aspect of the campaign.

Hillary, meanwhile, on the day after her victory, headed back to Grand Central for her third and final lovefest. By the time she arrived, the buzz had already gotten around the terminal's waiting room that she was on her way, and hundreds of people were waiting for her. "Then she comes out and a cheer goes up, with people shoving each other to get near her," Liz Moore of *Newsday* recalled. "It was like a scene out of *Evita.*"

Now there was a contrast I could wrap my brain around. This race hadn't been Lazio versus Clinton. It had been Dick Lonzo versus Eva Perón.

You've Got Campaign Mail!

November 1, 2000. It's a week before the election, around 7 P.M., and I see that I have a new message as I check my e-mail for what I hope will be the last time today. The campaigns are sending up to a dozen e-mails each every day now, mostly overheated rhetoric attacking the other side, and I'm praying that's all this one is so I can go home. I've already been in the office for eleven hours and I really want to see my children tonight before they go to sleep. I've given up any pretense of trying to pick them up from school or make dinner. In the last few weeks my husband has basically become a single parent. But it would be nice to try the old quality-time thing, even if we are all in a bad mood because I'm working too hard.

This particular e-mail contains the text of a new radio ad from the Lazio campaign. Titled "Extreme," it's airing upstate, and it criticizes Hillary's support for "a radical environmental treaty that would wipe out thousands of manufacturing jobs in New York." The documentation accompanying the ad identifies the treaty as the Kyoto Protocol. This doesn't immediately strike me as a headline-generating controversy for New York voters, so I close the file and head home.

But as I ride the subway home, I realize there's something weird about this radio ad. I'm no expert on environmental issues, but I seemed to recall that the Kyoto Protocol was widely accepted in environmental circles as a tool to reduce global warming. Lazio always portrays himself as a big environmentalist; he'd worked in Congress to clean up Long Island Sound and against the strip-mining and coal-burning that results in acid-rain damage to forests in the Northeast. It strikes me as a little surprising that he'd oppose the Kyoto Protocol. Still, I figure, it can wait till the morning.

The next day as I'm sitting on the Clinton van en route to some Hillary event, I take out my cell phone and call Frank Eltman, who's with Lazio.

"Ask Lazio about his position on the Kyoto Protocol," I say.

"What?" I hear Frank say between the crackles and buzzes. "His position on what? How do you spell that?"

I spell it and explain why I thought it might be an interesting story. When I get off the phone, my colleagues on the van started complaining that I'd been talking way too loud. Later Frank calls me back and says the reporters on the Lazio campaign were teasing him for asking about something as arcane as the Kyoto Protocol. Adam Nagourney of the *New York Times* had turned around and looked at him as if to say, "Where did that come from?"—especially since they were at a Long Island yeshiva where the subject du jour was the Middle East. Great, I thought, now I've made both of us laughingstocks over this silly thing.

Nevertheless, Frank has gotten the question answered. Lazio said he supported "the goals" of the treaty, but not the treaty itself. The protocol calls for reductions in the use of fossil fuels, and Lazio said he felt too many countries around the world would not have to abide by it, while countries like the United States would get stuck with the lion's share of the burdens.

"Now that I asked it, you better use it," Frank said, only half-serious.

But it still didn't seem like a story to me. Lazio was saying he didn't support the treaty, and therefore, I figured, it was fair for his campaign to attack Hillary for her support.

Later in the day I was obsessing aloud, as I often did, about how lame Hillary's events that day had been—a rally at a college and a visit to a senior center.

"What's the lead?" I whined to no one in particular.

One of the other reporters gave me that look that told me I was about three steps behind everybody else. "Kyoto Protocol," he said simply. "It's the story of the day."

"*What?*" I said. Then I found out that while we were riding around on the van, the Clinton campaign had sent out an e-mail accusing Lazio of hypocrisy, asserting that he had, in fact, supported the Kyoto Protocol in the past, and that his claims of being an environmentalist were a complete sham if he couldn't endorse the treaty. Around the same time, Adam ran into Frank at a Lazio event in Westchester and told him the same thing.

Within an hour, officials of the Sierra Club and the New York League of Conservation Voters were holding a press conference claiming that Lazio had told them he *did* support the treaty when they'd interviewed him before deciding whom to endorse in the Senate race. In the end, Lazio had lost those endorsements to Hillary, but he might have won the New York League of Conservation Voters nod had he not turned down their invitation to attend a forum on environmental issues.

Hillary, of course, had accepted the invitation, and a number of the NYLCV's board members felt Lazio had sent the wrong message by skipping the event. He got a small consolation prize from the national League of Conservation Voters, which is a separate entity from the state LCV. The national LCV, which had worked with Lazio on some of the environmental legislation he'd been involved in, had issued a dual endorsement, saying either Hillary or Lazio would do a good job in the Senate on environmental matters.

But I wondered if the national LCV would still support Lazio in light of his attacking Hillary over the Kyoto Protocol. I called the group's political director and found out that the organization was furious about the ad and had asked Lazio's campaign to withdraw it.

Then I phoned Lazio's spokesman Dan McLagan, but he denied that the ad was being pulled. A few minutes later, he called me back. "You're right," he said. "We're taking the ad off the air out of respect for the LCV." And moments later, Lazio pulled his motorcade over into a gas station–rest stop on the Hutchinson River Parkway in the Bronx and climbed onto the press van (they rarely used their big press bus inside city limits) to confirm that the ad was being withdrawn and explain why.

"I knew it was all over for him right then and there," Adam later told me.

Gregg's response was even more visceral. *"Lights out!"* he announced to the other reporters that night.

"You've got to picture this rest stop," Frank explained. "It's one of these quick pull-off-the-road places, so as Lazio is talking to us, he's in the van and one of his aides, Patrick McCarthy, and I are leaning in to hear from outside, with the doors wide open and cars speeding by. I'm thinking to myself, 'I wonder if any of these other drivers have any idea that a press conference with their Republican Senate candidate is being held in the dark on the side of the highway.'"

This was a lot bigger than one stupid little radio ad about the Kyoto Protocol, which most New Yorkers had never heard of anyway. This was about a campaign in free fall. It was a stupid screwup that pointed to so many larger problems—the stature gap, the nasty tenor of so many of Lazio's anti-Hillary ads, the impossibility of pinning him down on any controversial issue. Most voters would probably never know that this ad existed or that it had had to be withdrawn, but Lazio knew, and the press knew, that when a candidate stops his motorcade on the side of the highway at the end of a long day to try to talk his way out of something, there's a crisis going on. A few days after the election, Adam and Gregg reported that Lazio had actually opposed airing the ad, precisely because he feared it would make him look like a hypocrite on environmental issues. But, Adam and Gregg wrote, his chief campaign strategist, Mike Murphy, had gone ahead with it anyway—underscoring a general cooling off between the two men as the campaign had progressed and floundered.

While Lazio's Kyoto Protocol meltdown was taking place, Hillary was going through her own preelection crisis. It started with an October 25 headline in the *Daily News*: "Israel Foes Gave Hil 50G." The paper reported that a $50,000 fund-raiser for Hillary's campaign held in June in Boston had been sponsored by a group called the American Muslim Alliance. The paper quoted the president of the group as saying that U.N. resolutions permit the Palestinians to "resist by armed force" if peaceful negotiations do not lead to a Palestinian state. Of course, that individual was not at the Boston fund-raiser, but that was just one of many details that got lost in the firestorm surrounding the story. The *News* also printed a photograph of Hillary holding a plaque from the American Muslim Alliance during the Boston event. The photograph was on a Web site sponsored by the AMA, a Web site that also asserted that the group's Boston chapter had sponsored the Clinton fund-raiser.

Hillary was ready when the questions started coming at her avail that afternoon. "All fifty thousand dollars, every penny of it that was raised at that fund-raiser, is going back," she said.

She added that as far as she knew, the Boston event had been sponsored by a Muslim businessman who lived in the area and *not* by the American Muslim Alliance. "I resent deeply this organization acting as though it hosted this event," she added. "It was not the case. I also want to be absolutely clear at this time of danger and peril in the Middle

East: We have to be very clear that we denounce terrorism. We denounce violence."

Any Jew you can woo, I can woo better... Then I heard someone ask about the plaque. If this organization, as she was claiming, hadn't sponsored this fund-raiser, how come they took a picture of her holding this plaque with the words "American Muslim Alliance" printed on it?

"I don't know if any of you have ever been in this position," she replied, "but I have literally been handed thousands of plaques. As I was about to leave, I was handed this plaque. I left. I handed it to an assistant. That is all I knew about it. I was not aware they were claiming credit for the event."

Before the Q-and-A was over, we were treated to another installment in the "they're all out to get me" drama.

"Fasten your seat belts," she said, mixing her metaphors one after the other. "You have no idea what's gonna be thrown at me, including the kitchen sink."

I headed back to the office and started making phone calls, but no matter what I found out, the story just never completely made sense. The businessman whom the Clinton campaign claimed had hosted the event told me that, indeed, he *had* hosted the event. In fact his name—not the American Muslim Alliance—was on the invitation. So why was the AMA taking credit for hosting the event on its Web site? The Muslim community in Boston is very small, he explained, and some of the people he had invited did belong to the AMA, but he insisted that they hadn't organized it. He also pointed out that most of the AMA members in Boston are Pakistani, not from the Middle East, as everyone's stories suggested.

Okay, I was willing to believe all that, but if it was true, why had Hillary given the money back so fast? Here's this woman who supposedly stands for tolerance and diversity, and she was caving in to this witch-hunt without a murmur of dissent. Hillary had won tremendous praise from American Muslims for hosting the White House's first-ever celebrations marking the end of Ramadan, but I didn't hear her say one word against the disturbing notion being perpetuated here that all Muslims are the same, all Muslims are terrorists, all Muslims love Hillary, and therefore, somehow, Hillary is a terrorist. By returning the money without even attempting to sort out the political views of any of the individuals who'd attended this event, she actually gave credence to the idea that she had done something wrong simply by being in a room with these people. Her advisers later told me that they felt the press coverage of the incident was so overblown that she simply couldn't risk defending any aspect of it.

Meanwhile, I learned that the American Muslim Alliance had given money to a number of other politicians around the country in districts with large Muslim populations, and that the organization was actually considered relatively mainstream by middle-of-the-road members of Congress. The group had even just endorsed George W. Bush for president. In fact, one of the individuals who had given money to Bush as well as to Hillary had his checks returned by both campaigns once the story in the *News* appeared.

But Hillary's capitulation to her critics was all the Republicans needed to go hog-wild with the story. Lazio called the campaign donations "blood money." And the state Republican Party began making thousands of phone calls to voters around the state asking whether they were aware that Hillary had taken money from this Muslim group, and suggesting that the group was linked to the "same kind of terrorism that killed our sailors on the USS *Cole.*"

I couldn't decide who I was more disgusted with—Hillary, for not just standing up and shouting "This is McCarthyism! Stop the madness!" or Lazio, for jumping on the bandwagon instead of being his own man for a change. My moral compass was spinning, and a day or two after the Kyoto ad had exploded in Lazio's face, I decided to see if Frank had any surer sense than I did of who was right and who was wrong in the Muslim controversy.

"Frank, it's just you and me talking now," I said. "This isn't for our story. I just want to know what you really think. Do you think Lazio's right?"

"To tell you the truth, it feels dirty," Frank said.

I was relieved to hear him say that. I was beginning to think I'd been looking at it all a little too closely from Hillary's point of view. Then I offered my take on how it looked from where I was sitting, how disappointed I was that Hillary had caved so fast and hadn't even attempted to stand up and say, "You know, all this dumping on Muslims is really disgusting."

"Thank you!" Frank said. He seemed just as relieved as I was. "She's really gutless."

We managed to put it all together for the wire that day—minus our personal observations that the attack was smutty and the defense was chickenshit—but the story was far from over. After the Republicans began their phone calls linking Hillary to the USS *Cole*, Hillary's side put out a TV ad with a murky picture of the *Cole*'s blasted hull, attacking the Republicans for the phone campaign. Then the Clinton people put out a radio ad they said was based on a real e-mail from someone with a son in the Navy who was appalled by the GOP phone calls. And of course, Hillary continued almost daily with the line she'd begun before the *Daily News* story appeared, the one where she exhorted her listeners to vote as a way of honoring the memory of the brave sailors who had died protecting democracy aboard the *Cole*. It was enough to make me want to go live in a dictatorship.

Then, just as the whole issue seemed to be receding, on the Friday before the election, as I was leaving a hotel where Hillary had just made a speech condemning Lazio and the Republicans for exploiting the *Cole* disaster, Finney told me to stick around. The first lady was about to hold a spur-of-the-moment press conference. I soon found out why when I was handed a copy of a letter, on White House stationery, addressed to the chairman of the Massachusetts chapter of the American Muslim Alliance, signed by Hillary.

"It was a pleasure to be a part of the Massachusetts Chapter meeting of the American Muslim Alliance," the letter gushed. "The plaque is a wonderful reminder of my visit."

But hadn't she said the meeting wasn't sponsored by the American Muslim Alliance? And didn't she say she'd never looked at the plaque? Would this story *ever* make sense?

Several news organizations had obtained the letter earlier that day, and Hillary's campaign had decided to take the crisis-mode approach to public relations and just lay it all on the table before anyone could draw their own conclusions. Hillary told us the note was a form letter signed with an auto-pen, the type of thank-you note that is routinely sent out anytime one of those thousands of plaques she receives is logged in by the White House office where all these gifts end up.

I read the letter again as she spoke. It still didn't add up. "But you told us you thought the meeting had nothing to do with the American Muslim Alliance," I said, practically sputtering. "The letter says right here, 'It was a pleasure to be a part of the Massachusetts Chapter meeting of the American Muslim Alliance.'"

I looked at Hillary as if to say, *"Please make it all make sense now!"* But she just gazed back at me placidly with those big blue eyes open wide as if she weren't sure what I was getting at. Her look said, "And your question is . . . ?"

Finally I asked, "Doesn't the right hand know what the left hand is doing?"

It was a stupid way to phrase the question. I'd given her the answer she needed for her out, and she simply responded by agreeing, that, no, in fact, sometimes the right hand doesn't know what the left hand is doing. Weeks after the election, I was told by several people in the campaign that the person who wrote the thank-you letter for the plaque had happened upon the group's Web site and assumed that the assertion that the AMA had sponsored the fund-raiser was true. Why hadn't Hillary hung that person out to dry, I asked. "She was just taking responsibility, saying it was wrong, and moving on," one aide said.

Meanwhile, the *New York Observer* was reporting that Lazio's campaign had sent a fund-raising appeal to one of the AMA members who had given money to Hillary. So what? was Lazio's response; thousands of people were receiving his direct mail solicitations. But the hypocrisy on both sides was clearly waist-deep.

In *The Boys on the Bus*, Brit Hume complains that his fellow campaign correspondents "claim that they're trying to be objective. They shouldn't try to be objective. They should try to be honest. And they're not being honest. Their so-called objectivity is just a guise for superficiality. They report what one candidate said, then they go and report what the other candidate said with equal credibility. They never get around to finding out if the guy is telling the truth. They just pass the speeches along without trying to confirm the substance of what the candidates were saying. What they pass off as objectivity is just a mindless kind of neutrality."

Crouse added, "A reporter was not allowed to make even the simplest judgments; nor was he expected to verify the candidates' claims. . . . Using the time-honored techniques of objective journalism, they gave equal weight to each man's charges."

If I had one big regret in my coverage of this election, it was the feeling that too often I was guilty of precisely those sins. On the other hand, there were days like this where I tried to make a simple judgment—in this case, to determine if Hillary and her staff had lied about the fund-raiser, or if Lazio and the Republicans were making unfair charges—and I just couldn't figure it out. The next time I was on the van, I started asking my colleagues what they thought. Was the fund-raiser sponsored by this Muslim group, or not? A few accepted her explanation, and a few did not. Maybe it was better not to make that judgment after all, but instead just supply what both sides were saying and let the readers decide for themselves.

Writing about the debates between Hillary and Lazio was another situation in which it was difficult for reporters to make a judgment beyond the back-and-forth. That's why many news organizations use focus groups of undecided voters to provide postdebate reaction, because journalists often have very different sensibilities from people who are hearing and seeing the candidates for the first time.

In the first debate, for example, I thought Lazio did a great job, that he'd finally distinguished himself as more than the anti-Hillary, and that he'd shown he could stand up to her. But it became clear almost immediately that the very qualities that had impressed me had offended a lot of voters.

Basically Lazio made three big mistakes in that first debate. He jumped on Hillary after she'd answered a sensitive question about her marriage; he was too aggressive in asking her to sign a contract banning unregulated campaign donations known as soft money; and he declared that the upstate economy had already "turned the corner. . . . There's been great progress." Hillary, meanwhile, had spent months traveling the state with a detailed plan to help bring jobs back to areas that were losing population. Lazio dismissed this approach as depicting "the upstate economy on its knees. It's not."

Hillary responded perfectly, saying that she had "spent countless hours talking to parents who tell me with tears in their eyes that their children had to leave upstate, leave their hometowns, because there weren't enough jobs for them. I want to help address that, not ignore it, not put happy talk on it."

One reporter described that exchange to me as the "Stealth bomber" of the campaign—an issue that was lost in the immediate brouhaha over the soft-money ban and the talk about Hillary's marriage, but that came back to haunt Lazio big-time in the weeks after as upstate voters repeatedly complained that he just didn't get it. If you wanted to pinpoint the moment at which any chance of a Lazio victory began to burn out, that had to be it.

The exchange about Hillary's marriage began when one of the questioners, Tim Russert of *Meet the Press*, showed a clip from the famous *Today* show interview in which Hillary blamed rumors of Bill's philandering on the old "vast right-wing conspiracy."

"Do you regret misleading the American people?" Russert asked her.

She looked pained for a minute, but I didn't feel too sorry for her. I had to assume that she'd expected the subject to come up one way or another, and I also knew that anytime Hillary could play the victim and get people to feel sorry for her, it reinforced the notion many voters had that she deserves respect for her poise and bravery in the face of all this humiliation. Her answer, delivered in a humble tone of voice, played to all of that.

"Obviously I didn't mislead anyone," she said. "I didn't know the truth. And there's a great deal of pain associated with that. And my husband has certainly acknowledged that and made it clear that he did mislead the country, as well as his family."

Now it was Lazio's turn. "Frankly," he said when she was done, "what's so troubling here with respect to what my opponent said is somehow that it only matters what you say when you get caught. And character and trust is about well more than that. And blaming others every time you have responsibility, unfortunately that's become a pattern, I think, for my opponent."

Whew! Ricky wasn't gonna let a little thing like sympathy get in the way of punching her when she was down, and vulture that I am, I kind of respected him for it. But it turned out that I was out of step. The consensus the next day seemed to be that a bunch of guys had beat up on Hil, and Lazio had joined in when he should have stepped aside.

Then, right before the debate ended, Lazio left his podium on one side of the stage and strode over to where Hillary was standing. He was holding a contract to ban unregulated campaign donations known as soft money. It was a big issue in the national fight over campaign finance reform, and something Senator McCain had championed. It also wasn't really a new issue even in the New York Senate race. Hillary had proposed banning soft money back when Giuliani was the candidate, and Lazio had called for the ban back in July. But this was their first direct confrontation over it.

"Why don't you sign it?" Lazio said as he thrust the piece of paper in Hillary's face. "I'm not asking you to admire it. I'm asking you to sign it. Right here, right here! Sign it right now."

I was sitting in a pressroom adjacent to the TV studio where the debate was taking place, watching this unfold on one of the screens set up for the dozens of reporters who'd flown to Buffalo for it. I'd be lying if I didn't admit that there was something vicariously thrilling about watching Lazio try to pin Hillary down. It was like he was living out my fantasy.

Of course, she didn't sign it. She kept on smiling and said she'd be happy to agree to the ban when and if Lazio could produce signed agreements from outside political organizations like the state Conservative Party and the National Republican Jewish Coalition that had been using soft money to pay for TV ads for Lazio.

A few minutes later I saw on a photo editor's computer screen the picture that AP photographer Richard Drew had shot of the exchange over soft money. It showed Lazio towering over Hillary, his finger in her face, as she physically shrank back from him. It was an unforgettable image, one that crystallized the sense many viewers had that Lazio had been too aggressive, and one that would end up on a lot of front pages the next day.

After everyone's stories were done that night, we retired to a bar and talked about the evening. I was a lot more impressed by Lazio's performance than I had anticipated being; I thought he'd shown more backbone than I gave him credit for having.

But my analysis turned out to be completely off-base, compared to what the voters were thinking. Gregg Birnbaum of the *Post* had already filed a story essentially saying Lazio had "won" the debate, but by the time we started deconstructing it all in the bar, he was already beginning to tune in to the notion that our reactions might be different from the average New Yorker's. "I think we in the media have a high tolerance level for harsh rhetoric and political stunts that the average voter might not have," he said. "We judge it from the perspective of the political theater that we think debates are, but average voters don't look at things the way the media does."

In the days that followed, focus groups and polls showed Lazio taking hits, especially from women. Even those who hadn't seen the debate had seen that photo of Lazio bearing down on this smaller, older woman. The next day, Marcia Kramer asked Hillary if she'd wanted to "punch his lights out" during the exchange. And Hillary had answered, "The thing that probably prepared me best in dealing with things like that was having two younger brothers." Lazio, in turn, said he knew what it was like to deal with Hillary because he has three older sisters. So now the New York Senate race had been reduced to a food fight between an annoying little brother and a bossy older sister.

A few days later, Frank called to dump some quotes from Lazio characterizing the criticism of him as "sexist." I actually agreed with Lazio on this one. I think if Hillary had been a man, Lazio wouldn't have seemed like such a cad. Still, as I turned the "sexist" quote into the lead of our Senate story, I knew he'd done a foolish thing by saying it. It just made him look like a whiny kid. In a lot of ways the coverage of Hillary *was* sexist—all the talk about her clothes and her hair and her marriage, the quotes from the Hillary-haters about her being a doormat, the constant credibility battle she fought to have us and the voters take anything she did as first lady seriously. But I never heard her complain that the coverage of her was "sexist."

By the end of that week, after enough bullshit on both sides to fill a latrine, the two campaigns had reached an agreement banning soft money. Lazio tried to take credit because he'd brought it up at the debate; Hillary tried to take credit because she'd first proposed the ban back when Rudy was the candidate. Regardless, it seemed like a big deal, and we all wrote a lot of stories about how important and historic it was. There was only one problem: the voters didn't care. It was too complicated to explain and understand, it had nothing to do with their lives, and with new stories coming out all the time about Hillary's donors sleeping in the White House and the Republican Party paying for yet another Lazio fund-raising letter, the fine points of exactly which pile of dirty money the ban applied to was nearly irrelevant. "I don't know what soft money is and neither does anybody else," an undecided voter told the AP's Westchester correspondent, Jim Fitzgerald. As far as I was concerned, those were words to live by. I put that quote in a story and tried, thereafter, to write as little about soft money as I possibly could.

The second debate had far fewer fireworks. About the only interesting exchange once again concerned Hillary's marriage. Marcia Kramer, who hosted the forum, asked Hillary, "Why, after all the revelations and pain of the last few years, and because you are such a role model, why [have] you stayed with your husband?"

"For my entire life, I've worked to make sure women had the choices they could make in their own lives that worked for them," Hillary replied. "I made my choices. I'm here with my daughter, of whom I'm very proud. We have a family that means a lot to us. . . . I can't talk about anybody else's choice. I can only say mine are rooted in my religious faith, in my strong sense of family, and in what I believe is right and important. I want to go to the Senate to stand up for women's choices and women's rights."

This time, Lazio was on his best behavior. "I think that was Mrs. Clinton's choice and I respect whatever choice she makes. The fact is, this race is about the issues, about who can be most effective for New

York." Dick Lonzo had learned an awful lot since the first debate, that much was clear.

But I couldn't help but think that one important element—love— was missing from the list of reasons Hillary had given for keeping her marriage together. How about just saying, "Hey, I love the guy!" and leave it at that, instead of going on about religion and family and Chelsea and choices? Maybe, I thought, she's too much of a WASP to talk about her feelings that way. But I noticed a few months later she had no trouble declaring her affection for her brother. The occasion was a press conference, in Washington, on February 23, 2001, follow- ing the news that her brother Hugh Rodham had accepted $400,000 to help secure the pardons of a businessman convicted of fraud and a cocaine dealer whose father was a wealthy political contributor. Hillary repeatedly expressed her "disappointment" in her brother's poor judg- ment; he eventually gave the money back. But when asked if her brother had been a frequent guest at the White House during the final days of President Clinton's administration, she said he had been, and added, "He's my brother! I love my brother!" Apparently the word *love* was not so hard for Hillary to say after all.

One other interesting moment was related to the debate, but it had nothing to do with the Senate race. Hillary, asked what it means to be a New Yorker, had quoted E. B. White, and Governor Pataki, who was in the audience, mocked her afterward. "Mrs. Clinton quoted some guy, Wyatt or somebody—I don't think he was from Brooklyn—with some definition of a New Yorker that she had read somewhere," the governor said. "I don't know who that guy was. I don't know what he wrote. I don't know where he was from. But it sure doesn't sound to me like that guy was a New Yorker or understood New York the way we do."

When told by a reporter that Hillary had been referring to E. B. White, who'd written for the *New Yorker* magazine (and who, P.S., was from Mount Vernon), Pataki said, "Maybe the average member of the media who lives in Manhattan, when they're quoting New York, would use E. B. White, or whatever his name is. I don't think people from Brooklyn or Peekskill would have quoted that person." Now *that* was a much better story than the average day on the campaign trail with Hil and Rick.

A few minutes later, Lazio wandered into the pressroom and the first question someone asked him was whether he knew who E. B. White was. "He wrote *Charlotte's Web*," he replied.

My husband, like the governor, is a Yale alumnus, so when I told him this story, I added, "I sure hope our kids don't go to your alma mater, because you obviously don't get a very good education there."

By the third and final debate on October 28, Hillary and Rick could no longer maintain a civil tone toward each other. All they could do was snipe. The nastiness was intensified by the intimacy of the setting: a living-room-style studio at WNBC-TV where they sat on either side of veteran political correspondent Gabe Pressman. "Mr. Lazio *does* go on," Hillary said at one point, her voice simply bloated with disdain, while Lazio piled on the scorn with lines like "Please, Mrs. Clinton, don't lie."

At one point, Pressman asked them to name three things they like about each other.

"It seems like he has a very nice family; he has, you know, worked very hard; and that, you know, he's an attractive young man," Hillary said.

Then it was Rick's turn. "You're an attractive woman, you have a very nice family, I'm sure you're a very good mother as well."

Never had so many compliments sounded so insulting. In the remaining days of the campaign, Lazio liked to say that while it was fine for the first lady to name three nice things about him, it was too bad she couldn't name three things she'd done for New York.

The debates also illustrated how silly most of the campaign e-mail-was. A minute or two after each debate began, both campaigns would start a mad rush to discredit what the other side was saying. The Clinton campaign e-mails about Lazio were called "Rick Lazio Reality Checks," while the Lazio e-mails about Hillary were called "Truth: Lazio Fact Versus Clinton Fiction." A typical Lazio missive about something said during the second debate went like this:

"At 10:31 A.M., Hillary Clinton claimed she wanted to change the Medicaid formula. Truth: In 1997, President Clinton line-item vetoed a law—supported by Senators Moynihan and D'Amato—that would have changed the Medicaid formula."

Now, exactly why President Clinton's 1997 veto precluded Hillary from pledging to do something different in 2001 was not clear to me, making this e-mail about as useless as all the others.

The Clinton campaign's "Reality Checks" tended to be much longer and more complicated than the Lazio campaign's "Truths." They usually consisted of long citations of Lazio's voting records, often done in such a way that you could barely tell how his votes related to what he'd just said. For example, after Lazio said, during one of the debates, that he had voted for the assault-weapons ban, the Clinton campaign sent out an e-mail noting that six years after the assault weapons ban had passed, Lazio had "hesitated" on whether to vote for an amendment that would have strengthened background checks for gun-show buyers. Well, that might be an appalling revelation if you are concerned about gun control, but it didn't mean Lazio was lying. The fact was he *had* voted for the assault-weapons ban.

It all made me wistful for the Schumer-D'Amato campaign, when we'd gotten zero e-mails from either side. It was so quaint, way back when in '98, that Schumer's press people would just call me at home every night to tell me the schedule for the next day. But there was no such thing as getting Hillary's or Rick's schedule by phone. You just had to keep logging on to your e-mail all night till it turned up.

I also remember going to press conferences every time D'Amato unveiled a new TV ad. Now we got the texts of the ads e-mailed to us and could just go pick up a copy of the videotape from the campaign headquarters. Some of these ads, such as the one in which the ominously unnamed "they" are after Hillary, were unintentionally funny. My favorite silly Lazio ads included one inexplicably titled "Peach" and another called "Banana." They were a little like *Saturday Night Live* skits about Hillary's credibility problems with women voters.

"Peach" featured two women on the steps of a lovely suburban home with a beautiful garden, a dog at their feet. The text, spoken by one of the women, went like this:

"You know, there's something about Hillary. She's smart. God knows she's aching to be senator. But I wonder what she'd do in Washington. The one time she got her hands on something was health care, and look what a disaster that would have been. Even wrecking our teaching hospitals. I pay enough taxes now. I don't need Hillary hitting me up for more. Lazio's actually done something for New York, not just talked about it. Sure he's a scrappy guy, but, hey, that's New York. I like that."

"Banana" featured a woman on the phone in her kitchen preparing food and reading a newspaper. The woman is telling the person on the other end of the line, "Okay, so Hillary's not a real New Yorker. I've got other concerns. Like my husband and I. We started at the bottom and worked our tushes off. No, but Hillary, she just wants to start at the top, you know, the senator from New York. I mean, why not town council from Chappaqua or something? How about Congress? Sure she's involved with children's issues, but so am I, I've got two kids. No, just because someone is first lady doesn't mean they get to be senator right away. Certainly not a New York senator."

By this stage of the campaign, I and all of my colleagues in the press corps were feeling completely burned-out. I kept invoking Karen Finney's strategy for getting through the last days: "Deny yourself nothing." Ice cream, doughnuts, candy, cookies, chocolate, coffee, piña coladas, more chocolate, more coffee . . . I had a countdown calendar behind my desk so that I could tell myself every day, "Just twenty-three more days," or whatever it was. I felt like a student during finals, high on sugar and caffeine but otherwise weary and completely disorganized. In those final weeks I lost my wallet, my keys, my camera, and my tape recorder, and as further proof of my temporary insanity, I eventually found all of them. My husband was doing saint's work at home, and my older son, Danny, kept asking, "When are you going to be a real mommy again?" Danny had brought home from our Maine vacation a little garter snake that he'd found in the yard, but it became harder and harder for me to dig up worms in our tiny backyard for the snake to eat. When I left the house in the morning it was dark, and when I came home at night, it was dark. One day the snake died, and I realized he was just another victim of the Senate campaign.

All this drama inspired me to write a TV ad about my own stupid life. I called it "Persimmon." The text went like this:

"For more than thirty years, this woman has been writing about Hillary's Senate campaign. Her three-year-old tried to stop her, but she kept on typing. Her seven-year-old tried to stop her, but she kept on typing. The kids' pet snake died because she forgot to feed it, but she kept on typing. She's been ordering pizza for dinner for the past fifteen months, but she just keeps on typing.

"Now she needs your help to keep child welfare from putting those kids in a home where someone will pay attention to them. Because there's one thing you know about Beth Harpaz. When she tells you she's on deadline, *she's on deadline.*"

The visuals, as I imagined them, would show me typing intently at a computer, cell phone wedged between my ear and my shoulder, tape recorder on my desk blaring something incomprehensible. A toddler would be crying inconsolably in the background, "Mommy! Mommy!" while an older boy sits catatonically in front of a TV screen. When he notices the camera on him, he looks at the screen and screams, *"I hate you! Shut up!"*

Finney once said something to me about how "campaigns are the kinds of experiences that change you in ways that you don't really appreciate at the beginning." If there was one thing I had learned about myself during this campaign, it was that I needed a job that allowed me to be home every night for supper. By the time the campaign was over, I couldn't wait to go back to my old schedule of 8 A.M. to 4 P.M. I didn't care if I ended up covering stakeouts with the new hires or telephoning the Port Authority to check on airport delays.

I e-mailed "Persimmon" to Eileen Murphy. Her response was worthy of something Hillary herself might say: *"I care deeply about those children!"*

Senator Clinton

November 7, 2000. It was 10:50 P.M. and a recording of Frank Sina-
tra singing "New York, New York" was playing in the Roosevelt Hotel
ballroom when Rick Lazio finally took the stage to state the obvious.
Standing in front of an American flag, surrounded by his wife, the
mayor, and the governor, he grinned that boyish smile that made him
seem so likable and came up with a nice made-in-New-York metaphor—
the Subway Series—to describe his defeat to a woman who claimed to
love the Yankees.

"I feel like the Mets," he said. "We came in second."

Then he mentioned that he'd just called Hillary to congratulate
her, and everybody started booing. So what if she won big-time? That
didn't mean these people had to like her.

Rarely does a candidate claim success before the other side con-
cedes defeat, so it was no surprise that Hillary didn't make her victory
speech until after Rick had formally given up. Maybe he'd been waiting
to see what happened in the presidential race, hoping his own defeat
would be overshadowed by bigger news, good or bad, but whether that
was the reason for his delayed concession or not, he'd waited nearly
two hours to admit what every news organization had declared within

minutes of the polls closing at 9 P.M. But now it seemed that Lazio's bad timing was once again working to Hillary's advantage. The last words of his concession speech were barely out of his mouth when every newscast in New York switched to Hillary headquarters, a few blocks away at the Grand Hyatt. It was 11 P.M. and there was no doubt what the lead story was going to be.

Columns of red, white, and blue balloons festooned the Hyatt ballroom, and a giant "Hillary" banner was draped on the stage; now more than ever, no last name was needed. Four hundred journalists—many of them staking out their vantage points on a three-story platform in the back of the room—were among the two thousand people waiting for her to arrive, along with a host of local Democratic pols such as Carl McCall, city public advocate Mark Green, state attorney general Eliot Spitzer, and even Floyd Flake, a black minister and former Democratic congressman from Queens who'd crossed party lines in the last Senate race to endorse D'Amato and apparently wanted to make it abundantly clear whose side he was on this time. Six weeks later, Flake turned down an overture from the Bush administration to serve as secretary of education. Chuck Schumer was making the rounds, too; by the end of the night it seemed as if he had personally informed every reporter in the room that he and Hil would make a great team. The masses drank from a cash bar and ate New York street food—pretzels and hot dogs—at hotel prices, three and four dollars a pop, while a band played jazzy background music. But oddly, there was no buzz about the Senate race here, no question that she'd done it; instead, in a sign of what was to come in the weeks ahead, people were already obsessing about the presidential race, watching the results on big-screen TVs and cheering or groaning with every development. Hillary monitored the returns thirty stories above the ballroom in a hotel suite with her family and a small group of aides and supporters.

Then, finally, Hillary appeared on the ballroom stage, the president and Chelsea by her side, with Moynihan and Schumer joining them.

Hillary had chosen, for this night, a turquoise pantsuit, the better to stand out among the dark suits in her entourage, and a brighter, snazzier look than her usual workaday black. As the crowd cheered and chanted "Hill-a-ry!" the president "guided Chelsea into buffer position between them," as my colleague Tom Hays, who covered the event for the AP while I spent the evening in the office analyzing exit polls, recalled. "It was not unlike the scene of the family heading off for vacation after Bill finally fessed up to the Monica thing, where the three were holding hands, Chelsea in the middle, walking across the White House lawn to a waiting helicopter."

Schumer delivered the "she did it the old-fashioned way—she earned it" line that he'd been using for the past week, and Moynihan mumbled a few words by way of introduction. But there would be no tribute from the president tonight; there could only be one Clinton in the spotlight this time.

"Wow!" said Hillary as she surveyed her adoring fans and paused to savor the moment she'd begun imagining back in January of '99 at the height of the impeachment scandal. "This is amazing!" And in some ways it was. A first lady had made history. And a carpetbagger with a suitcase full of scandals had outdone a squeaky-clean local boy. On the other hand, the only news coming out of New York on election night was not that she had won, but that she had won by so much. Even her staff had anticipated no more than a four- to five-point win, so a twelve-point win was a sweet rebuke indeed—not just to the Hillary-haters who'd paid so much money to see her lose, but to anyone who ever said she wouldn't succeed and shouldn't try. I thought back to the early months of the campaign—the jokes about the Listening Tour and her love for the Yankees, the house-hunting that ended in Chappaqua, the split between New Yorkers who shouted "Go back to Arkansas!" and those who swooned and squealed at the mere sight of a first lady in their midst.

I tried to remember why, back in early '99, I had been so reluctant to believe that she was going to go through with it. At the time it had seemed impossible that a woman who'd never held elective office and never lived in New York would attempt this audacious feat, especially with all the baggage of her marriage and the impeachment. But even though it had seemed ridiculous back then, now, looking back from election night, it seemed almost inevitable.

In fact, Hillary's win did feel strangely anticlimactic, as if it were a logical outcome to anyone who'd been paying even a little attention during the previous six months. Sure, Hillary started out the campaign by pissing off Jews, homosexuals, Puerto Ricans, and nearly everybody else in New York, but she ended up an expert on everything from treating asthma in the Bronx to getting high-speed Internet access in Buffalo. Lazio, in contrast, fell down and split his lip on his way into the race and stepped in dog shit on his way out. In between, he'd stuck his finger in Hillary's face, called the leader of North Korea "Kim Jong the Second," and earned not one but two insulting nicknames—Dick Lonzo and Little Ricky—from a press corps that had no particular reason to love Hillary, her Secret Service agents, and their German shepherds. There was only one learning curve in this campaign, and it was all hers. Besides, if the presidential candidates had been so sure that Gore was going to win big in New York that they didn't even bother to campaign or advertise here, was it really all that surprising that the other Democrat on the New York ballot did almost as well?

"We started this great effort on a sunny July morning in Pindars Corners on Pat and Liz Moynihan's beautiful farm," Hillary said as a lead-in to what would be the most-quoted line from her acceptance speech. "And sixty-two counties, sixteen months, three debates, two opponents, and six black pantsuits later, because of you, here we are."

To those who voted for her, she added a "thank you for opening up your minds and your hearts, for seeing the possibility of what we could do together for our children and for our future, here in this state and in this nation." And to those who voted against her, she pledged "to work in the Senate for you and all New Yorkers . . . to reach across party lines to bring progress for all of New York's families. Today we voted as Democrats and Republicans; tomorrow, we begin again as New Yorkers."

She was gracious in recognizing the man she was replacing, saying, "Senator Moynihan, on behalf of New York and America, thank you," but oddly subdued in acknowledging the man who had played a much bigger role in her transition from being a political spouse to taking the political spotlight, a man who, like Moynihan, was leaving public office after two decades—Bill Clinton. Only after thanking Chuck Schumer, Rudy Giuliani, Rick Lazio, every Democratic official in the state of New York, her mother, and her brothers, did she thank "my husband, and my daughter." Chelsea had that doll-like smile plastered on her face while Bill looked on like Pygmalion, smug yet proud. Beneath a shower of confetti, Hil kissed and hugged sundry and assorted Dems like Nita Lowey and Carl McCall. No public hug took place between Bill and Hil; it seemed odd that they didn't want the cameras to record one, but the moment when it would have made sense for them to embrace quickly passed and was swallowed up in the chaotic celebration going on around them.

Then, together, the Clintons stepped down from the stage and waded into the crowd to greet their fans, their arms extended to shake the outstretched hands. For a moment, the president's eyes teared up, and as he left the ballroom, he told reporters, "I'm so proud of her."

When I left the office that night a little after 3 A.M., Hillary had long since vanished as a topic of discussion on TV, and Bush had been declared the winner of the presidential race. But by the time a taxi delivered me at my door a half hour later, Bush was no longer the winner and the country had embarked on the strangest postelection season of my lifetime. All I kept thinking was "Thank God this didn't happen in the Senate race!" I was ready to go back to living a normal life; I had been counting on the Wednesday after the election as a day without Hillary for a long, long time, and I pitied my counterparts in Washington and Florida who would not be doing their laundry or going on vacation or sleeping late in the days after election day as so many of them had planned.

I went to bed around 4:30 A.M. Wednesday morning and woke up at 9 A.M. It was the most restful, dream-free, and longest period of uninterrupted sleep I'd had in days. When I finally got to the office, I spent the rest of the day taking down all the cartoons, clippings, and photographs of Rick and Hillary that had appeared on my desk, on the wall behind my chair, and on the office bulletin boards over the past two years, including life-size masks on sticks I'd made of each of their faces from photographs on the cover of the Sunday *Times Magazine*. Then I dragged six cartons of FEC reports out from under my desk and left them where we stack old newspapers to be thrown away. And last but not least, I filled up two more cardboard boxes with the dozens of videotapes of campaign ads that had been precariously stacked in a couple of tall columns next to my computer.

Later that day, Hillary held her victory news conference in Manhattan, thanking "the members of the press, particularly the hearty band who covered me from July of 1999 until last night." She was then asked if next time she'd run for president.

"No," she said without hesitation. "I'm going to serve my six years as junior senator from New York."

That "six years" clause didn't just accidentally find its way into that sentence. She could just as easily have said, "I have no interest in ever being president." She's been asked the question many times since and refuses to admit any desire to return to the White House, but it's hard to believe that the only first lady to ever run for office and the first woman to win statewide office in New York hasn't at least fantasized about breaking the ultimate barrier as the first female president.

Yet Hillary is no Ralph Nader. She's far too pragmatic to run on principal alone. A February 2002 Marist poll showed Americans were two to one against Hillary running for president, and there's no way she'd do it unless she had a decent chance of winning. That requires at least one term in the Senate both to shore up her credentials and to silence critics who predicted a run in 2004. But none of that rules out a run in 2008, or even 2012, when she would be sixty-four.

Although she introduced a record seventy bills as a freshman senator, she kept a relatively low profile during her first year in office. Perhaps she was heeding the words of Trent Lott, who said within a day of her winning, "When this Hillary gets to the Senate—if she does, maybe lightning will strike and she won't—she will be one of a hundred and we won't let her forget it.".

Ironically, by the time her swearing-in rolled around on January 3, with the president sitting with Chelsea in the spectators' gallery, Lott and another of the old-line Republicans, ninety-eight-year-old Strom Thurmond, appeared to have softened their public stances a little. Thurmond rose to greet her just after she'd taken the oath of office, asked, "Can I hug you?" and wrapped her in a bear hug. Lott later said, "Well, she certainly is going to get extra attention because she is, after all, the first lady, the first one ever to be in the Senate."

One aspect of Hillary's victory that got lost in the history and novelty of a first lady getting elected was that she is now the first woman ever to hold statewide office in New York in her own right.* Before Hillary was elected, New York had never had a woman in any of the four statewide elected offices—governor, state attorney general, state comptroller, or U.S. senator. Geraldine Ferraro, one of the most famous female politicians in the country for her historic 1984 vice-presidential run, hadn't even managed to win the state Democratic primary in the '98 Senate race. Her loss in that campaign to Schumer, who was much less well known, inspired Hillary-skeptics to draw comparisons. So

---

*There have been three female lieutenant governors in New York, but lieutenant governors do not get their own line on the ballot in the general election. They are part of the governor's ticket the way a vice president is part of the president's ticket.

what, she's a feminist icon. So what, she's a celebrity. So what, she has name recognition. If Gerry couldn't do it, an Italian Catholic from Queens, then Hillary the Midwestern WASP couldn't do it either.

But a friend and colleague of mine at the AP, Karen Matthews, observed that maybe it took a woman from out of state, a carpetbagger, to persuade both upstaters and downstaters that she was worthy of support. And who better to be all things to all people than Hillary, who could be sophisticated and Ivy League on the Upper East Side of Manhattan in her black pantsuit, but then go upstate, play up her Midwestern accent, and be introduced by a local politician—as she was on one of her early trips to Buffalo—as someone who "shares our values" because she grew up in a Great Lakes state.

"I did grow up on the Great Lakes!" she crowed in response, and it occurred to me that I'd never heard her use that line in the Bronx or Queens. But it sure went over big in a city dominated by Lake Erie to have the first lady remind everyone that she had grown up near Lake Michigan.

Although I only accompanied Hillary upstate a handful of times, each time I went I also couldn't help but be struck by how well she fit in there. I was used to seeing her as the only white lady in a black church, or the only WASP at a luncheon of Jewish and Italian ladies. I'll never forget watching her in that crowd in Buffalo where she used the Great Lakes line. I looked around at the swarm of people and realized that unlike any group she'd ever spoken to in New York City, this one looked just like her! All these women had hair the color of straw, big blue eyes, round noses, and cheeks like rosy pancakes.

"I got a beauty shop and I got a lot of ladies who want to work for her," the proprietor of Williamsville Hair Fashions told me as I canvassed the crowd for comments. "These ladies range from twenty-five to seventy-five. She's hitting all kinds of women in different stations of life, because she's for families and children."

Giuliani was still in the race at the time, and another lady grabbed my arm and started telling me why he didn't stand a chance in Buffalo. "He's from the city, and they think anything north of there is another country," she declared. "He thinks fighting crime and drugs and this and that is important, but it doesn't have anything to do with us. He's as much a foreigner as anyone else. If he's gonna go to the Senate and only represent New York City, I don't need him! She's here to represent the interests of New York State."

When the election results came in, it was clear that Hillary's twin strategies of trying to win over women and paying a lot of attention to the upstate economy had paid off even more than her staff had anticipated. She won the majority of women's votes upstate, in Westchester, and in the city, losing them only on Lazio's home turf, Long Island.

Months before the election, John Zogby, the Utica-based pollster, had told me Hillary was smart to spend so much time in upstate regions perceived as conservative.

"Upstaters have usually felt as if they were orphans," he said. "What's always been important to upstate voters is physical presence. This candidate actually came here, spent some time here. And not just at the end. We can go back to the beginning, to the Listening Tour. It was criticized by a lot of people for a lot of reasons. But she was there. She physically touched down in every one of sixty-two counties."

On the Friday after election day, Hillary went on a victory tour to thank her supporters upstate. After all the no-news days everyone had put in on the road with Hillary before the election, nobody expected to get a decent story out of this fly-around. Especially with the drama over the presidential vote just beginning to unfold, Hillary's victory suddenly seemed almost uneventful. But she managed to make news that day in a way we weren't used to—on purpose. Without any warning to her staff or the press, she got up in front of her supporters upstate in one city after another and called for the abolition of the electoral college. She'd been senator-elect for all of three days, and here she was already leading the charge to rewrite the Constitution! Her aides were both amused and amazed; as one of them later told me with a smile, calling for the end of the electoral college definitely hadn't been discussed beforehand in their daily conference call that morning. But if this was any indication of how Senator Clinton was going to operate for the next six years, it was clear we had a lot of interesting times ahead.

In fact, even in her remaining days as first lady, hardly a day went by without some sort of Hillary story in the news. First there was her new book about the history of the White House, then there was yet another trip to Ireland, not to mention the controversial $8 million book deal for her memoirs and the purchase of a fifty-five-hundred-square-foot Washington mansion for $2.7 million, a nice home away from the Chappaqua home. Even her committee assignments sparked interest: the Health, Education, Labor, and Pensions Committee, which gives her a platform to continue her advocacy for health-care reform and better schools; the Environment and Public Works Committee, which Moynihan had served on; and the Budget Committee, which drafts Congress's annual budget plan.

Hillary had also scheduled a first lady trip to Vietnam for right after the election, but somehow I hadn't realized that the president was going, too. When I saw a headline in the paper that read, "Clinton Visits Vietnam," I assumed it was about Hillary. I started reading the story only to discover that Hillary barely merited a mention; this article was about *Bill* visiting Vietnam. So why didn't the headline say "Clintons" visit Vietnam?

Then I remembered. When Hillary's alone, she's the news. When Hillary was with Bill, he was the news, and she's only the first lady. A first lady doesn't count for much, even after winning a Senate race. What really mattered was that the president of the United States was on a friendly mission to our former enemy.

In a photograph from Vietnam, Hillary was pictured walking behind Bill. In accounts of events where he spoke, she was reported to have said . . . nothing. It reminded me of something she had once said when asked why all this work she was claiming to have done as first lady, on issues ranging from cancer to child welfare, had gone unnoticed.

"When you come out of the White House, there really is one voice, and that's exactly as it should be," she'd said. "Everybody is there because of the president. He selects the vice president, he brings his team with him, everybody is there furthering the president's agenda, so that no matter how much you do to help create positive results for the people as part of that overall agenda, it's only appropriate that the American public doesn't know much about it, because that's not where the rightful attention is drawn."

Hillary's side trips in Vietnam without Bill did get some coverage of their own, I guess because at those events she was free to speak and be heard without worrying about whether she was turning his solo act into a duet. She took a field trip to see microcredit in action in a small village. She attended a conference on the exalted role of Vietnamese women in their culture. But the story in the *New York Times* quoted an expert saying, "For all the talk about the advanced status of women, the numbers just aren't there." The expert pointed out that while more than a quarter of Vietnam's National Assembly are women, "in the more influential Politburo, there is only one woman out of nineteen members," or just over 5 percent.

Those percentages sounded awfully familiar to me. I pulled out my *Almanac of American Politics* 2000 and started flipping through the pages, counting women's faces. Out of fifty governors, three were women; that's 6 percent. Out of a hundred senators, nine were women; once joined by Hillary and the new female senators from Washington State, Michigan, and Missouri, women comprised 13 percent of the Senate. The percentage of women in the House was only slightly larger. I guess that means that in America, as in Vietnam, for all the talk about the equality of women, our numbers aren't there either.

Then I started reading the biographies of the six women in New York's thirty-one-member congressional delegation. All but one is older than Hillary. Their life stories include Louise Slaughter, first elected to public office at age forty-seven, after her children were grown; Nita Lowey, whose résumé includes being a PTA mom in Queens before she was elected at age fifty-one; Sue Kelly, first elected at age fifty-eight after she had raised her family in the Hudson Valley district she now represents, an area where she'd been a volunteer and had her own business renovating buildings; and Carolyn McCarthy, a nurse who ran for Congress at age fifty-two to work for gun control after her husband was murdered and her son wounded by a gunman on the Long Island Rail Road.

In some respects, Hillary's life story is similar—she was first elected to office at age fifty-three, as her daughter prepared to graduate from college and her husband prepared to leave the White House. But what's really stark is the contrast between all these women with their late-in-life transitions into politics, and the many men who were elected as twenty-somethings and thirty-somethings. Chuck Schumer, fresh out of law school at the tender age of twenty-four when he took elective office for the first time, as a state assemblyman from Brooklyn. Anthony Weiner, who took over Schumer's congressional district in Brooklyn, just twenty-seven when he was first elected to the City Council, and thirty-four when he went to Congress. Rick Lazio, thirty-one when he entered the Suffolk County legislature, and thirty-four when he went to Washington.

"I think the rhythms of our lives are different from men's," Diane Chapman Walsh, the president of Wellesley College, told me back when rumors first surfaced that Hillary might run for office and I just didn't understand why she would embark on a new career like this so late in her life. "We can stop and take stock and wonder about something quite different after our children have grown up and our lives are changing in various ways. That isn't as true for men."

Even though women ended up voting heavily for Hillary, back when Giuliani was still in the race, the polls showed white women preferred him over Hillary. I wanted to do a story exploring why, and Frank Eltman suggested that I go interview some soccer moms, a demographic group that had gone big for Bill Clinton. So one Sunday in early spring, just as the soccer fields in Westchester were turning green, I headed up there and spent the day chatting with women in jogging suits as they cheered their daughters' teams.

It turned out to be all about credibility. The feeling was that Hillary just hadn't paid her dues.

"We have some very good Democratic politicians who could have been the candidate for Senate, but it was *given* to *her*," complained one woman.

"She's smart and very focused, but I don't think she's right for New York State," said another woman.

"She's the president's wife, but that doesn't give her a right to run," said a third.

Around that same time, I noticed a change in Hillary's exit routine. For months, when she was done speaking somewhere, she'd magically disappear behind a curtain or a stage and then zoom away in the Speedwagon. It was a good way to avoid us, in case we'd had any ridiculous notion of staking her out, and it probably made the Secret Service happy as a secure, fast way to move her from one controlled environment to another. But now, as spring wore on, Hillary began spending more and more time hanging out after events, shaking hands and taking a minute to chat with people. At restaurants and hotels, she'd meet everyone who wanted a word with her, then make sure she'd also said hello to the cooks and the waitresses. At outdoor events, she'd sign autographs and pose for pictures with her fans, then go around and thank every police officer on security detail. Once, as she walked down a street in Queens, I heard her call over to a sanitation worker who was emptying garbage cans into the back of a churning truck, "Thank you for the job you do every day!"

Hillary's meet-and-greet efforts were particularly intense at ladies' lunches, especially those where the invites included these suburban women with ambivalent feelings. A lot of these luncheons were themed around a good cause like cancer research or child abuse prevention, and the audiences tended to be politically diverse, as opposed to a union rally or Democratic fund-raiser filled with Hillary supporters. So that made the events interesting for the press corps, because we could get before-and-after quotes from these undecided voters. Did their opinion of Hillary change once they'd heard her speak or got to shake her hand?

You betcha. "I'm not undecided anymore," they'd almost always say as they saw me coming back to find out what they'd thought of her speech. Inevitably they made the same three observations. One, she's so much prettier in person than she is on TV. Two, she's so much nicer and warmer than they thought she would be. And three, she's so brilliant, how could you not vote for her? It seemed that only die-hard Republicans couldn't be convinced to support her after hearing a good rendition of her stump speech and seeing her willingness to hang around afterward to meet every lady who lined up for a hello.

I also started hearing rumors that her campaign was holding meetings for women who didn't like her. The meetings were hosted by women who knew her and could speak favorably about her. I even came across a couple of women who'd attended some of these meetings, but they'd all been asked not to speak to the press and they took that pledge seriously. Eventually, near the end of the campaign, when the polls finally began to show Hillary leading Lazio among white women, Ann Lewis, who had worked as a top adviser to the president before becoming one of Hillary's senior campaign strategists, told me what these meetings were all about.

"The idea of women getting together in their homes to talk about things that matter to them really is a tradition if you think about it," she said. "We called them advocates' meetings. They were led by women who really knew her, women who could say, 'I've known her, I've worked with her, she's somebody who rolls up her sleeves and works.'"

Ann also defined Hillary's problem with women and explained the campaign's line of attack in solving it: "Women responded to how hard she has worked over the last year and a half. Talking to women on the way in with her, there were questions about whether she was serious about this, whether she was going to work to earn it. I think her opponents had painted this as 'she thinks she's entitled.' . . . But she proved her credibility. She committed to it. She always expected she would have to work hard to get it."

About a month before the election I also interviewed a woman, Sheila Gordon, who'd hosted one of these advocates' meetings in her apartment. "I'd invited mostly people in my neighborhood who I knew had reservations about Hillary," she said. "But I think that virtually every woman I had invited, who came feeling on the fence and unhappy about Hillary, feels confident voting for her now."

What accounted for the change? "The length of the campaign has allowed people to examine their thoughts and feelings. They had to try and disengage themselves," she said. "It is so challenging to see ourselves out there. And we see a lot of ourselves in her—like the question of why we didn't do things more quickly" in terms of fulfilling long-held dreams or advancing careers.

I thought back to what Diane Chapman Walsh had said, about the rhythms of our lives being different from men's. Sheila was on the same wavelength.

Hillary, she added, is a "lightning rod for all kinds of things. We really haven't learned to evaluate a woman who's accomplished, and feminine, and also like us." She said she thought it took time for women voters to say, "If her marriage works out differently than mine, I still would like to have a good, strong, smart person as my senator. . . . Some people want her to show all her emotions and start crying every time someone brings up Monica. To a certain extent, people want to know that it hurt her a lot. But we are holding her to a higher moral standard."

One of the ladies I'd met at a Hillary event in September, a teacher who'd started out the afternoon describing herself as an undecided voter and ended up telling me she'd vote for Hillary, made a similar point. "A year ago I would say, 'I don't know why she stayed with him,'" meaning Bill. "But I'm not even thinking in that area anymore," she told me.

I also called some of the soccer moms back in the fall, five months after I'd interviewed them. "She earned my respect, she's earned my vote," one of them told me. "It's her understanding of the issues, her passion for the issues, her ability to listen."

"She really has proven herself," said another one. "I've changed my mind about her. I like a lot of her stands on the issues. I know she's an advocate for children, even if she doesn't have children in the local schools." In other words, it's okay to be a carpetbagger if you can prove you know what you're doing.

The Clinton campaign staff always felt the press corps underreported how much support for Hillary there was out there all along. "There could be two hundred people at an event cheering for her and one person with a 'Go Home' sign, and the 'Go Home' sign will always make it into everybody's story," campaign aides would commonly grouse. And I think it was true, as another reporter once put it to me, that a lot of us were "uncomfortable in conveying the positive reactions Hillary was getting."

But when you've heard a hundred gushy tributes to a woman who's been handed "thousands of plaques," you don't really feel that it's news, in the strictest sense. Tish Durkin of the *New York Observer* once pointed out the "Miss America quality" to much of Hillary's support. She was always being given bouquets and baskets and compliments about her appearance. It was hard to predict whether that type of adulation would translate into broad political support or not. And when someone who strives to be as perfect and scripted as Hillary does makes a mistake or gets heckled, that's the definition of news, and therefore worthy of a story.

Besides, the people who hate her are always more dramatic than the people who love her. One weekend in Ithaca, as Hillary and Chelsea arrived for a rally at Cornell University, a man began screaming, well within earshot of the first daughter, "Who's your father raping now?" A month after the election, a Syracuse man was arrested for threatening her life in a letter to the house in Chappaqua. On the Internet, there is a SlapHillary Web site, where you can interrupt an image of the first lady babbling with a click of your mouse and watch her get smacked into silence. You can also order a "Hillary Doormat" imprinted with her face and slogans like "I've always been a Yankees fan!"

And here's one of my favorite experiments. Just mention Hillary's name in a public place and see what happens. A few weeks after the election, I was sitting in a restaurant in midtown chatting with a friend about the campaign when the man sitting next to us started growling, "Hillary's a Communist!" Then, as the Florida recount wore on, I got sent to cover a demonstration by Bush supporters in Times Square, and a man there told me that he could never vote for Hillary because of her maiden name: "*Ham* is unkosher and *rod* is like the man standing with a rod, striking the people down." We covered Lazio at every public appearance in case he had another pratfall, but we all knew the *real* reason we had to stay in the room until Hillary left or wait outside until she was safely in her van. We almost never talked about it, but it was always there in the back of our minds: the possibility that, someday, someone might try to hurt her.

Still, I wonder: Did I pay too much attention to the Hillary-hater who ran down the street screaming "You're an enabler" and not enough to the ladies who told me how brilliant she was? Would the coverage have had a different tone had the preelection polls indicated more strongly how decisive her victory would be? All along, we depicted Hillary as someone who was attempting to scale a difficult mountain with Lazio nipping at her heels, instead of depicting her as someone who actually had a lot of built-in advantages—her celebrity, her marriage to a president New Yorkers strongly supported, the fact that Democrats outnumber Republicans five to three here, and her name appearing on the ballot beneath that of Gore, who was accurately predicted to win in New York by a landslide. If you looked at the campaign with those factors in mind, the race was hers to lose instead of a challenge for her to win. In the end, the percentage of New Yorkers who supported Lazio on election day was nearly identical to the percentage who had supported him the weekend he entered the race. The Republicans probably could have run Alfred E. Newman on that ballot and done nearly as well. Those people who screamed "Go back to Arkansas!" weren't part of a movement; they were a static minority.

On the other hand, while they could tell she was being received well upstate, even Hillary's staff never took victory for granted. "Everyone who says Lazio ran a terrible campaign, and everyone who says they knew he was going to lose all along, did not live the life we led," one of her top advisers told me wryly shortly after she was sworn in.

But the focus on scandal and screwups flared again shortly after the Clintons left the White House, reviving the dynamic we so often experienced during the campaign of the press corps running after bad news, while Hillary just kept plugging away on her favorite unglamorous issues. She followed through on her pledge to introduce legislation to help the upstate economy; she held a news conference to express her opposition to the new attorney general, John Ashcroft; she even schlepped back to a couple of black churches, pledging to make racial profiling illegal and expressing support for a new holiday honoring—guess who?—Harriet Tubman!

But all that boring good news about New York's junior senator was drowned in a flood of headlines over Bill Clinton's pardons and their connections to Hillary. The pardon recipients included Marc Rich, whose ex-wife Denise was a frequent White House guest and prominent supporter of Democratic Party causes, including Hillary's campaign and Bill's Arkansas library. Four Hasidic men whose sentences were commuted came from New Square, one of the only Hasidic communities to support Hillary for Senate. And of course, Hillary's brothers, Tony and Hugh, successfully sought pardons for several felons who'd made their acquaintance; Hugh even took—but was forced to return—a $400,000 fee for his pardon-getting services. (If I'd still been on the campaign van, a parody of the "Chattanooga Choo-Choo" would have been a natural: "Pardon me, Hil, I need a presidential pardon!" But after the election I didn't often see my colleagues from the campaign press corps, and singing the "Chappaqua Ka-chink, Ka-chink" alone at my desk was no fun at all.)

The uproar over the pardons even overshadowed the scandal over the thousands of dollars in gifts the Clintons received, as if they were newlyweds, when they permanently left the White House for Chappaqua—china, televisions, and furniture, including—oops!—a few items that were supposed to have been left in the White House and not removed for the Clintons' personal use. Of course, Clinton defenders pointed out that these gifts and even the pardons were not all that different from the patterns set by previous presidents. But as I always tell my kids, just because somebody else uses a bad word or acts up, doesn't mean it's okay for you to do it.

In the middle of the pardon furor, I called a few of the soccer moms again, and they told me they felt betrayed. They'd supported Hillary because she seemed so competent, but with all the new scandals, they were reminded of their initial reservations about her candidacy. A Marist poll taken near the end of February 2001 showed that about 60 percent of New Yorkers believed Hillary had done something unethical or illegal in connection with the pardons, but the survey—like other recent polls—also found a bedrock of support that roughly equaled the percentage of people who voted for her, with a little over half of those polled saying they still thought she'd be a good senator.

And that, it seemed to me, was the story of Hil's political life, just as it was for Bill's. She'd get dragged down again and again by scandals, some real, some exaggerated or imagined by her enemies, some that were really more her husband's fault than her own. And then eventually, simply because she'd show up to work each day and plug away on issues like the upstate economy, health care, education, and racial tolerance, she'd win everybody over again. If all it took to wipe Hillary out was a string of bad headlines, she'd have been finished off by the Suha kiss, the St. Pat's parade, the FALN flap, and every other controversy from the early days of her Senate race. Instead, just like her husband, she always managed to stage a comeback.

During the first few months of the Bush administration, it was hard to remember that the Clinton administration was over. After all, Bill and Hil were in the news every day; George and Laura were all but invisible. One reporter for a tabloid told me that with Republicans in the White House, the governor's mansion, and City Hall, the Clintons were the only available target. It reminded me of something Crouse had written in *The Boys on the Bus:* "Conservative Republican presidential candidates usually receive gentler treatment from the press than do liberal Democrats. Since most reporters are moderate or liberal Democrats themselves, they try to offset their natural biases by going out of their way to be fair to conservatives. . . . Reporters sense a social barrier between themselves and most conservative candidates; their relations are formal and meticulously polite. But reporters tend to loosen up around liberal candidates and campaign staffs; since they share the same ideology, they can joke with the staffers, even needle them, without being branded the 'enemy.' If a reporter has been trained in the traditional, 'objective' school of journalism, the ideological and social closeness to the candidate and staff makes him feel guilty; he begins to compensate personally, the harder he judges him professionally. . . . Most of the reporters who covered George McGovern in the fall campaign preferred him to Richard Nixon and ended up voting for him (if they voted at all)."

Were we somehow harder on Hillary because we were trying to

compensate for some built-in pro-liberal bias, or because we identified more closely with her than with Lazio? I can honestly say that I'm actually not sure whether the average reporter's politics were closer to Hillary's or Lazio's. A lot of reporters I know voted for third-party candidates in the last few elections—ranging from Perot to Nader. And the general public might be surprised to hear that we actually didn't talk much about our personal politics during the campaign. It's not like we ever sat around on the van debating the death penalty or partial-birth abortion or gun registration. We just tried to get the quotes right and complained about the lack of news—not to mention the lack of food.

Many of the reporters I know also have a self-imposed policy of not voting in elections they cover. Myself, I don't have a hard-and-fast rule on it, but I did fall victim to a different occupational disease: cynicism. In the end I couldn't bring myself to vote for anyone in the Senate race.

But regardless of whom they voted for or whether they voted at all, I'm not sure how many reporters could say of the Clinton campaign, the way Crouse did of the McGovern campaign, that they personally "preferred" Hillary to Lazio. Often, covering Hillary was like running through an obstacle course, only to find when you finally got to the candidate, there was no there there. And if what Crouse referred to as "social barriers" existed in the New York Senate race, they were not between the press and Dick Lonzo; they were between the press and the Democratic candidate, simply by virtue of her first lady trappings and her reserved personality. That's why it was such a big deal anytime she did drop the formalities and crack a joke with us, invite us for coffee, or hand out doughnuts.

The morning she turned fifty-three, for example, she greeted voters in Grand Central, then turned to us for a press conference. We sang her "Happy Birthday," and I handed her a little cupcake with a candle on it. We'd actually had a debate among ourselves about whether it was "over the line" to give Hillary a cupcake, but, hey, sometimes you just throw all caution to the wind. Then someone asked her, "Do you get to do anything fun today at all?"

A huge smile broke across her face as she spread out her arms as if to embrace the entire press corps.

"Well, here I am with all of you!" she said, her voice dripping with sarcasm as we started laughing nervously. "It's the way to start any day! And now I have to show my absolute affection and devotion to my hardworking press corps that has followed me through—how many counties? Sixty-two! And what is it that we have in common? . . . Thank you, Bob!" (Here she nodded to Bob Hardt, who had called out the answer she was seeking.) "The human genome! We are ninety-nine point nine percent the same. I find it absolutely thrilling that you and I are ninety-nine point nine percent the same!"

She then handed out doughnuts to each and every one of us. It was about a startling as the "C'mon, let's go have coffee!" day, or the day she sent a basket of candy back to the press van or handed out the cookies with her picture on them. On the other hand, as Maggie Haberman of the *Post* pointed out to me once, it was also a little unsettling that anytime Hillary had an informal interaction with us, she made it clear that she knew exactly what we were saying behind her back—thanks to the campaign staffers who reported back to her all the little things we made fun of in the van.

"It was funny, like, okay, she's mocking herself and that's kind of cool," Maggie said. "She was connecting with us and attempting to humanize herself. But she also knows what we're saying when we're not in her presence. On one level, 'Yes, I'm connecting,' but on another level, it's like, 'Don't think I don't know what's going on.' It's like your mother."

I'll never forget how, on Lazio's first weekend on the trail after launching his campaign, the baby-faced congressman from Long Island wrapped his tongue around the white ball of a vanilla ice cream cone at the Byrne Dairy in Syracuse while photographers snapped away. It was not a pretty picture, but it was actually an interesting picture, and for a guy as little known as he was at that point, running against a woman as famous as Hillary, it was a smart thing for him to do. The picture was widely used, it made his face a little more familiar to voters around the state, and it even made him look like a regular guy—the type of grown-up who licked a drippy cone with the enthusiasm of a little kid.

When Bill Bradley was still running for president, I'd covered his wife, Ernestine, one day in a similar situation. She had a photo op at Gray's Papaya, a fast-food joint on the Upper West Side with a big "Bradley for President" sign in the window. Ernestine is slim and elegant, with short hair and a German accent and hardly any makeup, and she was wearing a beautiful, artsy brooch pinned on her lapel instead of a button with her husband's name on it. She looked like a lady who works in a museum instead of a candidate's wife. After she thanked the proprietor for his support, she ate a hot dog. The cameras loved it as she opened her mouth wide, stuffed it in, chomped and chewed. She liked it so much that when she was done, she ordered another. I couldn't help thinking back to the day in June of 1999 when we weren't allowed back inside Tavern on the Green until Hillary had finished eating lunch.

But two months before the election, Hillary and Bill visited a state fair in Syracuse. Lazio had been there earlier and had passed up an offer to eat a sausage sandwich, which is something of a local culinary tradition. One of the Clintons' supporters, Terry McAuliffe, a Syracuse native and the same guy who'd gotten in a little trouble for fronting the Clintons the money to buy their Chappaqua house before they went for a traditional mortgage, had told the press in "mock horror that Lazio had had the effrontery to refuse a sausage sandwich and predicted that we wouldn't see Hillary make the same mistake," Liz Moore of *Newsday* recalled. With that, the scenery was set for Hillary to upstage the regular Joe in this race at his own game. As the cameras recorded the big moment, she tore into a messy sausage sandwich with gusto, her mouth wide open as the thing spewed stuffing out the sides. The president dabbed her mouth with a napkin.

"After the other Senate candidate refused to eat a sausage sandwich there, this one did not," the president proclaimed. "Let's get right down to the basic issues in this election."

When I saw that picture of Hillary eating that sandwich, I thought, boy, have we come a long way since Tavern on the Green. Maybe in her case it was less an evolution in her personal reserve than an evolution in her political savvy, but either way, that's how you break down the social barriers the voters perceive—by occasionally appearing human and enjoying something good to eat instead of acting like a robot who must never yawn when exhausted, cry when upset, or have a hair out of place on a windy day.

In fact, once she lost her first lady staff and started her new job as senator, even the pouffed, glued-down coiffure we'd seen nearly every day of the campaign occasionally gave way to a bad-hair day. The *Washington Post* described her hair in this new, less-than-flattering look as hanging "like rain-battered weeds." Asked about it at a press conference, Hillary simply said that some days she had time to fix it, and some days she didn't.

My mother, a lifelong Republican, worked, as a young woman, for Senator Margaret Chase Smith, the Maine Republican who was the first woman to serve in both houses of Congress and the first to serve four full terms in the Senate. Margaret Chase Smith was also the first woman—long before Elizabeth Dole—to try for the presidency on a major-party line. "Is a woman acceptable?" she wrote to my mother late in 1963 as she mulled over her decision. She eventually ran against Barry Goldwater in several primaries, and her name was submitted for the nomination at the 1964 Republican Convention. I grew up hearing the story of how, in 1950, Margaret Chase Smith became the first member of the Senate to stand up to Senator Joseph McCarthy. "I don't want to see the Republican Party ride to political victory on the four horsemen of calumny—fear, ignorance, bigotry, and smear," she'd said. Other families hung pictures of the pope or John F. Kennedy in the hallway, but in my house there hung a framed photograph of Margaret Chase Smith, not in homage to an early feminist, or to a great Republican, but just because she was a decent, courageous individual who stood for the right things, and who had some small connection to the life of our family. That she was a pioneering female politician really had nothing to do with it.

But I wonder sometimes what she would have thought of Hillary. I'm sure she would have disagreed with a lot of her politics, spoken out about the Clinton scandals, and been privately appalled by some of her personal choices, but I bet there might also have been some mutual admiration had she and Hillary been contemporaries. I certainly can't imagine Margaret Chase Smith using the phrase "maybe lightning will strike" in the same sentence as the first lady's name. And I suspect they could have had an interesting conversation on the subject raised in the letter to my mother: "Is a woman acceptable?"

Chapter 15

The Girls in the Van

Ellen Wulfhorst, Reuters

There was this New York Democratic women's luncheon at the Plaza in February [of '99]. This is when I decided she was absolutely running, even though maybe it was still subconscious to her. The reason I remember thinking she was going to run was because she showed up in a black pantsuit. And I thought, she's running because she figured out how to dress like a New Yorker. She gave this speech that was all about having an obligation to public service, a lot of Eleanor Roosevelt allusions, and a lot of stuff about women. It was very feminist. She's really good in front of women; she's best in front of women. I was sure she was going to run then.

She's not very likable. She's very, very distant. She's in one room, her emotions are in another. I understand why she would be so guarded. She was the most humiliated woman in the world. I often thought, I wish I liked her more. Then I'd think, maybe it's even sexist to even think that; would we ask that of a male candidate?

Geraldine Ferraro had been one of my heroes when I was younger; she was so inspiring. I look at my mother's generation and say, this is what you could have done if you weren't waylaid by your own self-doubts. I always thought Geraldine Ferraro is what my mother could have been. Then I had this one-on-one interview with her, and she was so chilly and chop-chop, and I wanted to say, "I am glad you're not my mother."

Remember the day after the election when Hillary thanked the "hearty little band of reporters" who had followed her around? I heard that and I just thought, "You don't like us." And Karen Dunn was like, "Yes, she does." But Hillary's very calculating, she has cold eyes just like her husband.

When we were on the last bus tour before she did the final fly-around, you could tell there was something up. The Secret Service was passing around a flyer with a person's picture on it. Clearly they were worried about it. I think some of the times she showed up with a lot more security than other times.

I think we tended to forget sometimes that it was feminist history in the making. Along with just a very famous person running, it is an amazing moment in women's history, even if you don't like all the details of how she did it or what her policies are or what color her jacket is.

I remember covering this "Women for Lazio" thing on Fifth Avenue and Seventy-second Street. It was all these Upper East Side women with facelifts and hair highlights and Gucci coats and little dogs carried under their arms, saying things like "Look how early everyone had gotten up" and "She has a job as first lady—she could be hosts to all these dinner parties and heads of state instead of running for Senate."

Stephanie Saul, *Newsday*

The Lazio campaign was controlled in a different way from the Hillary campaign. He would answer three or four or five questions, but we didn't get a substantive interview with him until the campaign was over. We had been requesting an interview with him ever since he got in the race, but he never actually gave us one—other than ten minutes on the bus here and there. Even though he was giving all these avails, I never really felt like I had access to him or that he let his guard down. And even though I spent all that time with him and even got to ride on the plane with him, I never felt like I ever had a real conversation with him. I'm not sure if that was his choice or his staff's. I really got the feeling that the people running his campaign thought he wasn't as articulate as Hillary was. When they started the Mainstream Express, everyone thought it would be like the McCain Straight Talk Express, but it wasn't. His campaign aides intimated that he wasn't as seasoned as McCain. I think they were underestimating him. He's not a dumb person. He's a bright man and he's definitely a cut above the average congressman. So I think he could have handled that kind of exposure, but they were just afraid of it.

Lauren Burke, Photographer

I've taken pictures of a lot of campaigns—McCain, Bush, Gore, etc.—and one of the things you find is that there are always a lot of male people running around with clipboards. I thought it was really impressive that Hillary Clinton had a lot of young female people running around doing the work. You find with a lot of these campaigns, there may be a lot of women there, but they don't have substantive roles. She put her money where her mouth was.

I expected this campaign to be a little bit more formal and arm's length, and it was to some degree. But she wasn't any more behind the curtain than McCain or Gore. In a way, I was a little surprised at how much I saw of her during the campaign—much more than I saw of her at the White House. At the White House, she comes out, does her thing, and goes back behind the curtain.

I remember the Salute to Israel parade. She was getting screamed at. As you would imagine with Bush and Gore, they don't get anywhere close to people. It doesn't happen. For somebody who's getting hate mail with the best of them, I was surprised at how out there she was.

I used to work with Cokie Roberts at ABC News, and one of the things I learned from Cokie is that you should assert yourself when you feel you're being passed over, but you have to pick your battles. You begin to notice in a really male environment—and photojournalism is extremely male—that if you're young and female, you're kind of discounted. You're not really taken seriously. It doesn't matter how big the organization is. We've had plenty of people—usually male people, Jon Corzine or somebody who has money and feels like running—who has no background. Geraldo Rivera, Jesse Ventura, can run and that doesn't matter, but somehow she's supposed to be John Foster Dulles. There were so many times when I said to myself, "If she was a man running for office, nobody would care."

Maggie Haberman, *New York Post*

A couple of times I was the only woman on the Lazio bus. The Hillary van tended to feature more men than the Lazio bus featured women. But in the beginning on the Lazio side it was an all-male bus, and I think that mentality never left. There were a lot of people playing practical jokes on each other, there was a certain camaraderie there that actually wasn't there on the Hillary van.

Part of it, I think, was actually physical. The Hillary van was kind of small and cramped, but the Lazio bus was set up like somebody's 1970s rec room. You had everyone lounging around on couches eating junk food, and staffers were up front. On the Hillary van, you had Cathie Levine and Karen Finney sitting right next to us.

To a certain extent I give credit to both campaigns because it was like having twelve children. We were always complaining about something—"This sucks!" "We need food!"

Marcia Kramer, WCBS-TV

Having the White House and the Secret Service surrounding her added a level that was different from covering other politicians. Other politicians are much more accessible, and when they don't want to deal with me or you, they can't retreat behind a cordon of Secret Service officers. Here's a person who understandably has reservations about the press, and this gave her the ability to retreat when she wanted. If Chuck Schumer or Ed Koch or Rudy Giuliani didn't want to answer a question, you could always get to them. But because she has Secret Service protection, she was able to get away with it. With anybody else you could stake out their car. We know which way the car is and which way they're gonna exit. They're either going to answer your question or not. With the Secret Service, there's even a question of whether you'll get close enough to her to ask.

Noreen O'Donnell, *The Journal News* (White Plains, N.Y.)

When I called Howard up to tell him I'd be covering Hillary for my paper, he was surprised. He asked me about other veteran political reporters he was more used to working with—at my paper and at Gannett News Service. I told him, no, Howard, me. Of course they also wrote stories about the race, especially the Gannett News Service reporters in Albany. We tried to split the work so that when she was upstate, they covered the events, though I often traveled. But for my paper, Howard mostly dealt with me.

We came in during the middle of this play. There had already been all these first acts and second acts in Washington, and people had already been writing about her clothes and how often she changed her hairstyle and who is the real Hillary if she can change her external appearance.

She's just a fascinating person. She's so polarizing and she elicits all these strong, passionate feelings. When I look at her, I don't see why. Why is she the lightning rod? She doesn't seem radical enough to me to be the lightning rod. Some of her positions aren't liberal at all, especially for New York—supporting the death penalty, for example, and opposing gay marriages. I do understand that people focused on her because she was the first lady and that lots of people across the country were upset about her health-care reform, and angry about the Clintons' fund-raising—having supporters stay in the Lincoln bedroom, etc. But I think she's often painted as more liberal than she appeared to me, especially on social issues. When she talked about wanting women to be able to make their own choices, to stay home with their children or continue working, the only part that got repeated was the "stay at home and bake cookies" comment.

Maybe it's because she isn't somebody who's so far at the extremes that people can dismiss her. She's talking about women's issues, yet she followed a sort of traditional woman's life—she got married, went to her husband's home state, worked her career around his. I don't think most women live either a perfect feminist life or a conventional life. It's a hodgepodge of different things. And sometimes it's not a perfect match.

Whenever I had to write about a state assembly race or state senate, I could just call the person who was running for office at home and say, "Hi, it's Noreen, it's election time, why are you running?" You couldn't do that with her.

Anytime she was in front of us, she was fair game, from what she was eating to how she was dressed to anything that was said. You get to a point where you say, "I don't want anyone staring at me anymore."

She seems pretty reserved. She's not a backslapping sort of person. She behaved how a reserved person would behave. I'm not really outgoing either, and I'd always try to picture, if she was doing something clumsily, what if I were in her position now? I would be doing it less skillfully.

That day she invited us for coffee, she had this pack of people following her all the time, but she genuinely was trying to reach out to people and have a relaxed time. But you know she's also thinking, even though I see these people every day, they are not my friends. I can buy these people coffee today and try to have a relaxed moment with them, and if I screw up tomorrow, they'll be all over me.

I remember the first time she went to Elmira. I think they published the menu of what she was eating for lunch. There was another article where they interviewed people whose house she stayed at. But by the end, just from sheer repetition, no one was doing those kinds of stories.

Tish Durkin, *New York Observer*

The thing that struck me about Mrs. Clinton as unusual for a politician is this incredible chemical aversion to self-revelation on any level. Which, given her history, is totally understandable. I completely sympathize with her not wanting to put herself personally on the line. She had been exposed in so many different ways—even forgetting the Monica stuff and the scandals.

Take the "I didn't stay home to bake cookies" remark. If you look at the whole comment she made, it wasn't such a bad comment. It wasn't a masterpiece of diplomacy, but if you read the three sentences, they're about women being able to make choices. Even the so-called gaffe itself wasn't a gaffe. Even if she hadn't tacked on the thing about making choices. Look at the pure hell that a thing like that caused her. In that sense I'm completely sympathetic. If you multiply that experience by a million, then you add the health-care debacle and the Ken Starr episode, you can understand her saying "I'm not saying anything except the sky is blue."

But I also think the candidate and the campaign never established that there is a difference between questions that are insulting and constitute garbage-picking through the soul of a human being, and questions which are either very material to one's fitness for office or kind of interesting on a human level and harmless.

There was one day she came on the bus that was meant as a way to sort of humanize her. It was a response to Rick Lazio doing the same thing, but what it really did was to make that wall all the more visible. You could sort of sense that people were not going to throw her a bunch of really tough questions. We wanted her on the bus. We wanted her to loosen up. So I asked her, "Mrs. Clinton, you're really famous. Tons of stuff is written about you all the time. When you're reading the coverage of yourself, what's the thing that you think, 'Oh my God, that's not really me'?"

She could have said some issue or I think I'm softer or I never thought my hairstyle would become so big. I mean, it's not a trick question. But she said something like, "I really can't speculate on other people's motives." If there was ever a time for someone to open up slightly, that was it. And I just felt sorry for her in a way.

But she also refused to reveal anything anytime push came to shove on a policy matter. And at the same time, when it was convenient to be part of the administration, she did seem to pop up at every meeting that went well and seemed to have taken a powder whenever it wasn't convenient. To the degree that she could avoid answering anything, she did.

Eileen Murphy, ABC News

One of my favorite things ever was when she was at the Salvation Army in Tonawanda, outside of Buffalo. She was in the back doing three-minute interviews with the TV affiliates and we walked in there to kind of force a Q-and-A on her. The place had a chapel, and all of us were in there, laughing and joking around, and she comes in, puts her hands up and says, "What a perfect setting. . . . Now let us pray that it will be about issues, not insults." Then the TV guy says to her, "Just now we saw a different side of you. Everyone says you're funny, but that's not a side of you we normally see." But all she could say in response was, "I may be new to your neighborhood but I'm not new to your concerns," a line from her campaign kickoff speech. It was like someone pushed the wrong button on the back of her head. I looked at one of the other reporters and one of her aides. We just shook our heads.

It was such a long and grueling campaign. I think I missed maybe four or five events in sixteen months. There was always this fear of God—what if something happens? I look back and it just seemed like it was built up to be this huge thing, but it was actually pretty normal. There seemed to be days and days where nothing happened.

There was that day at the North Shore Towers when Chelsea was asked to say a few words, and for a split second we actually thought Chelsea was going to come to the microphone and finally speak, and then she just says, "Hello." That was like a metaphor for the whole campaign. You get all worked up—and then she just says hello.

Beth J. Harpaz, Associated Press

I remember going to this rally for Hillary on Long Island three weeks before the election. The president was there and people kept shouting "Four more years!" and "Thank you, Mr. President!" "We love you, Mr. President!" Forget about Al Gore and never mind Hillary—all they wanted to do was tell Bill how much they loved him.

When the event was over, there was this sea of arms reaching up from the audience to touch him. He walked to the edge of the stage, leaned over at the waist, and stretched both of his arms down into the crowd. There was an agent on either side of him, grabbing him under each arm to keep him from falling in or from being pulled in, and his face was all red, but he seemed so into it. All of a sudden I understood why they called him Elvis. It was so different from all the ladies' lunches where Hillary was shaking hands politely on one side of a velvet rope.

A couple of weeks after the election, I got invited to a Christmas party at the White House. The party was just for journalists, and it was on a Sunday evening. At first I wasn't going to go. I just kept saying, "I'm not going to let Hillary mess up another one of my weekends! I'm not shlepping all the way down to Washington to spend another hour with her!" But then everybody told me I'd be crazy not to go, it's a once-in-a-lifetime opportunity, etc. So finally I called to RSVP, and of course they ask for my date of birth, my Social Security number, they tell me to bring photo ID—all the usual hassles of covering Hillary.

I was allowed to bring a guest, so my husband and I drove down to Maryland and dropped the kids off with friends there for the evening, and then one of our friends drove us over to the White House. It was like a lot of other Hillary events: show ID, walk through a metal detector, wait on line, get your bag checked for weapons. Only this was a party. Gee, what fun! Search your guests before you let them in.

There were hundreds of people there. Most of them were people who usually cover the White House. But I ran into a few of the Hillary regulars: Eileen from ABC, Tish from the *Observer*, Joel from the *News*, Dean from the *Times*, Gabe from WNBC, Andrea from WNYC. We were all trying to get to a long table laid out with shrimp and little quiches and sushi, but there was this huge crowd around it which never seemed to move, so you just had to jostle your way in. It was actually kind of humiliating; it was like trying to score the last doughnut in a box on the press van, only we were at the White House and we were pretending to be civilized. Then my husband went to use one of the bathrooms, and he was told by a Secret Service agent that the bathroom had been shut down because the president was in the building. It was so funny, because the same thing had happened the night he tried to take Nathaniel to the bathroom at the church where Hillary was speaking.

I was surprised at how beautiful the White House was and how awesome it felt to be there. The walls were covered with portraits of all the presidents and first ladies, and there were Christmas decorations everywhere—giant wreaths and a gingerbread house and a couple of big trees all twinkly and lit up. I walked into a small, peaceful room with a green carpet that was named for Ben Franklin, and for a while I just looked out the window at the white columns outside and thought to myself how strange it was to be on the inside looking out instead of on the outside looking in.

Finally we headed downstairs for the evening's grand finale—a photo and a handshake with Bill and Hillary. All these hundreds of people were funneling into a single-file line; it took more than an hour, but eventually it was our turn. Someone announced our names, and there we were with Bill and Hillary. Up until that moment, I'd always thought of Bill as the people person, the one who loved human contact, and I guess I'd thought that Hillary found the glad-handing part of her job sort of distasteful. But the funny thing about going to the White House was that they were exactly the opposite of what I'd expected. The president was acting like a robot, and Hillary turned out to be the charming one.

I guess Bill probably hates the press to begin with, and it must be awful to stand for three hours at a party shaking hands with all these people you don't know and don't like. But he just kept saying over and over in this monotone, "Thank you very much. Thank you very much. Thank you very much." If you said, "How are you?" he'd say, "Thank you very much," even though it didn't make any sense to respond that way. His face was completely expressionless and his eyes were narrowed down to these tiny little slits. Like an idiot, I actually tried to say something like, "Hi, I'm Beth Harpaz, I covered Mrs. Clinton's Senate campaign in New York," but all he said in response was, "Thank you very much, thank you very much."

Hillary was standing next to him, wearing this red plaid outfit that was very Christmas and very un-Manhattan. She put out her hand and said, "Hi, Beth!" in a big, warm tone of voice. I hadn't seen her since the election, so I congratulated her and said what I thought was appropriate for a journalist to say, something about how hard she'd worked, and how much she'd impressed us all with her energy.

Then I introduced my husband, assuming she'd never remember the brief moment in the church on the Lower East Side at the housing forum where he showed up with the kids.

As she shook his hand, a look of recognition flickered on her face. "I think we met before, didn't we?" she said.

I was amazed at her memory. She really had turned into the consummate politician. "Um, actually, that's right, you did," I mumbled.

My husband smiled. "Beth would never say this," he told her, "but we're thrilled that you won."

I shot him a look and nearly kicked him. I mean, what's with the "*we*"?

Hillary smoothed it over in an instant. "Well, now we've got to get to work on housing and all those other issues, right?" she said, raising her eyebrows meaningfully. We laughed and nodded, but I couldn't help being impressed with her ability to conjure up a small detail like that and make a personal connection. Then it hit me: I wasn't just a journalist anymore, I was a constituent! And she wasn't just someone whose every move was fodder for my stories; she was my senator!

I realized our little moment with the Clintons was over; it was time for us to move along and let the next couple have their turn. As we stepped away through a doorway and into an adjacent room, I suddenly noticed Howard Wolfson standing there waiting for us. I was just about to make a joke—had he been posted there to spin the Christmas party in a positive way, or did he just happen to be there as we walked by?—when I heard Hillary speaking again in my direction.

I turned back toward her to catch what she was saying.

"Say hi to the kids," she called after us, "will you?"

"I will," I called back. "I will."

Index

READING GROUP GUIDE

1. The author hopes that "rather than being scarred for life by the fact that I covered Hillary, my kids will look back on it as a fascinating little piece of history that they actually saw close up." Are children harmed when mothers work long hours or do they benefit from mothers with meaningful careers?

2. The president of Wellesley College explains Hillary's decision to run for office late in life by saying that "the rhythms of our lives are different from men's." Do you think women are more likely to change direction in midlife than men? Why?

3. After Hillary wins by 12 points, Harpaz wonders whether the media underreported her support. Was the media fair to Hillary? Should reporters change how they cover campaigns? Should politicians change the way they campaign?

4. The author describes various ethical dilemmas, such as whether she should help her mother-in-law get into a Listening Tour event, whether to accept a book from Hillary, and whether to lead with the mistake Hillary made at the gun control forum. What would you have done in each of these situations?

5. Why is Hillary such a polarizing figure, passionately admired by some and totally despised by others?

6. What do you make of Bill and Hillary's marriage?

7. Do you believe Hillary will run for president someday? Do you think she could win?

8. The author's husband tells Hillary that he and Beth are "thrilled" that Hillary won. What do you believe are the author's true feelings about Hillary?

**For more reading group suggestions, visit
www.stmartins.com**